High Adventure

HIGH ADVENTURE

Porter Harvey and the *Advertiser–Gleam*

By Sam Harvey

The Black Belt Press

P.O. Box 551

Montgomery, AL 36101

 Published in the United States by the Black Belt Press, a division of the Black Belt Communications Group, Inc., Montgomery, Alabama.

Library of Congress Cataloging-in-Publication Data

Harvey, Sam, 1930–

High adventure : Porter Harvey and the Advertiser-Gleam / by Sam Harvey.

p. cm.

Includes index.

ISBN 1-881320-98-7 (softcover)

ISBN 1-881320-96-0 (hardcover)

1. Harvey, Porter, 1903– . 2. Journalists—United States—20th century—Biography. 3. Advertiser-gleam. I. Title.

PN4874.H274H27 1997

070'.92—dc21

[B] 97-37310

CIP

Design by Randall Williams

Printed in the United States of America

97 98 99 5 4 3 2 1

The Black Belt, defined by its dark, rich soil, stretches across central Alabama. It was the heart of the cotton belt. It was and is a place of great beauty, of extreme wealth and grinding poverty, of pain and joy. Here we take our stand, listening to the past, looking to the future.

TO

Alice Wells Harvey

WHO ALLOWED IT ALL TO HAPPEN—
SOMETIMES IN SPITE OF HER BETTER JUDGMENT

CONTENTS

FOREWORD

By **JERRY ELIJAH BROWN**
Professor and Head, Journalism Department
Auburn University

In August of 1982, Sam and Val Harvey took a rare, week-long vacation, and Sam asked me to serve as "guest editor" of the *Advertiser-Gleam*. The title was, at best, a misnomer; at worst, a practical joke. I'd edited a weekly for three years and was starting my fourth year as a journalism professor, but my real assignment was to keep pace with Sam's father, Porter Harvey, then a mere 79. One afternoon, I was sitting across a desk from Porter, trying to unravel the details of a complicated story. As I recall, Guntersville policeman Mike Keller was pulling over a speeder when another car topped a rise from the other direction and sideswiped the patrol car. The officer ordered the stopped motorist to sit tight while he jumped in his vehicle, cut a 180, chased down the sideswiper, wrote that ticket and returned to finish the original job. Or so it appeared. I asked Porter to help, and I read to him aloud from the policeman's report, "I was *fixing* to pull him over . . ." Porter looked over his glasses and said in the softest voice, "Leave that in." With those three words, he completed a lecture on style. I cast aside the stilted prose of the academy and was liberated to write the way people talk.

The lessons Porter Harvey taught through example extend well beyond how to use the vernacular to set a newspaper's tone. When he died at 91, writing nearly to his dying day, he left a newspaper that should serve as a summons to publishers, editors and reporters too anxious or ambitious to appreciate taproot journalism. Porter demonstrated that a newspaper that went directly to the interests of its readers, that reported in a language readers understood and that was as fair as it was factual could succeed and even attract a following beyond its own community. At Porter's death, the *Advertiser-Gleam* had the highest circulation among Alabama's non-dailies and one of the highest advertising rates. Under the guidance of his son and son-in-law, it continues as a flourishing enterprise in northeast Alabama. Readers are fascinated by its success in an age characterized by garish graphics, tepid writing, shoddy reporting, chain ownership, and public journalism posturing.

The key to this newspaper's success is Porter Harvey—a man remarkable enough to deserve a biography, and fortunate enough to have this one. His son's detailed account, written in *Gleam*esque prose, shows how many forces figured in that success—talent, vision, luck, love, endurance, sacrifice, and a simple delight in, as Porter used to say, "finding the news and writing it up."

Though he started the paper in 1941 and was both its publisher and editor, Porter's primary role from first to last was that of reporter. He published what readers need and want—not only what the cops, courts, and councils of government were doing, but also how much rain was falling in different hamlets of Marshall County, where a column of ants in a bank parking lot was going, how the coin laundry was finally getting a restroom, and which hymn and stanza a man was singing when he dropped dead at a church service. Porter knew how to excite through understatement—a rare talent that involves skill both at writing and display. Who can flip past a two-inch story stuck at the bottom of page three under the headline "Hit with a Meat Cleaver"?

News was too important for Porter to divert much attention to such matters as editorial pages or showy photographs. Early editorial stands against racism and dry laws carried plenty of influence, but he lacked the correction compulsion of the editorialist. Mostly, he was happy trusting people to do what they would do, and then reporting it. As for photographs, the *Gleam* still runs little Polaroid shots, from cameras almost as old as the manual typewriters in the office.

Though Porter had been educated at Emory and Harvard, his paper never put on airs. He never went in for design changes, keeping his paper looking like an antique, with its vertical format and tiny 14-point headlines, yet never trading on retrograde quaintness. As times, trends and technologies have changed, the *Advertiser-Gleam* has remained a constant, and its readership, pages per issue, and ad rates have increased.

So distinctive has been the Harvey stamp that it is easy to focus on the personalities of the principals and overlook the more fundamental sources of the newspaper's strength. Porter Harvey apparently understood in his bones the looming paradoxes of newspapering: how to be both a part of the community and apart from it, how to serve the needs of both readers and advertisers, how to balance public and private responsibilities, how to distinguish between sentiment and sentimentality, and when to report and when to comment. He thrived within these tensions. I never expect to meet a person who loved newspapering more or who generated such copy between its polarities.

Even the young could sense his passion. A couple of years ago, I used the *Advertiser-Gleam* in my Newspaper Management course and on the final asked the students to comment on lessons the paper might teach publishers concerned about the loss of readers and advertisers. Here are two representative excerpts:

"Discover your readership. . . . Cover the community; give the people the news they can't get elsewhere. Change with the times but 'if it ain't broke, don't fix it.' And, finally, love what you do."

"Stories in the *Advertiser-Gleam* are filled with facts . . . in a prose style that is packed with drama, interpretive analysis, and dialogue. The newspaper makes you feel at home and like you were present when the event was taking place. This paper is for readers, not lookers."

Although the *Advertiser-Gleam* is still the lengthened shadow of one man, Porter Harvey was not William Allen White or William Randolph Hearst. He never aspired to national recognition or political power. An unassuming patriarch if ever there was one, he channeled his energies into the paper and the family. As a publisher with business responsibilities, he knew the value of the dollar, but he lived just as plainly as he wrote. Scary carnival rides, long river trips, and the famous bungee-jump-at-age-90 tell us much about a man who was comfortable with himself, his work, and the world around him.

Though Sam's biography is mostly about his father and the *Advertiser-Gleam*, it radiates in other interesting directions. Porter's own character and intelligence were met and matched by those of Alice Wells Harvey, whose letters back to Kansas reveal what a keen observer and adept writer she was. Porter was typically understating when he noted near his death that she was the best thing that ever happened to him. The whole family—in-laws and grandchildren included—is remarkably talented and, in an admirable and unusual way, selfless. Sam Harvey and Don Woodward, both former presidents of the Alabama Press Association, form an enviable team of news and advertising types, and they are ably supported by Val Harvey and Mary Harvey Woodward. Porter was as wise as he was generous in setting up a profit-sharing plan. Long-term staffers are a part of the newspaper family and a reason for the paper's continuing success.

The clearest indication of its impact may be seen in living rooms and on front porches and, beyond Marshall County, in newsrooms and classrooms. In these settings are the readers who look forward to the *Advertiser-Gleam*—and who marvel twice a week at stories about policemen and sideswiping speeders, or about Aunt Nanny, age 88, who died looking at the sunset, or about a highway line-painting crew that striped over a dead dog, or about folks with names like Big John, Dimple, Clelton, and Velpo.

True to the *Advertiser-Gleam* standard, this book will serve many readers. For relatives, it's an invaluable history, as carefully researched as it is affectionate. For those in the community who miss Porter Harvey, it's a eulogy, with the assurance that his style of reporting survives. But for all who care about sound journalism, it's even more. Now we get the full story of how this remarkable newspaper developed from one family's tireless teamwork into a guide.

You might say, from a *Gleam* into a beacon.

PREFACE

Porter Harvey rode into Guntersville, Alabama, on a Trailways bus, rented a one-room, second-floor office, set his typewriter on an apple crate, and started putting out a weekly newspaper, the *Guntersville Gleam*.

The odds against him were formidable. He had worked on daily papers, but never a weekly. He had never run a business or sold an ad. He was a stranger in a town that already had a newspaper with lineage stretching back 61 years. And still another newspaper had been launched just before his.

The first issue of the *Gleam* came out on his 38th birthday. He worked at the paper until two months before he died of cancer at age 91. By then his twice-weekly *Advertiser-Gleam* had attained the largest circulation of any non-daily in Alabama. And it was fondly known in journalistic circles for cheerfully ignoring many of the rules that are supposed to determine whether papers succeed or fail.

He had become something of a celebrity late in life, especially after a bungee jump at age 90 at Raccoon Mountain High Adventure in Chattanooga, Tennessee. That landed him in newspapers and on TV all over the U.S. and even overseas. But he never sought the attention that came his way. His byline never appeared in his paper although he probably wrote 100,000 stories, big and small. He almost never printed his own picture. For the last 25 years he insisted that his name not be listed in the paper's masthead; he said he wanted to show that the next generation had taken over.

When he first went into newspaper work, he had trouble holding a job. On the two daily papers where he managed to stick, he grew frustrated because he felt he wasn't getting anywhere. After he started his own paper, he reported only the events of his rural county in northeast

Alabama. He wrote no editorials on the national political or social issues that sometimes bring outside attention to small-town newsmen.But his death was reported in a lengthy article by the Associated Press. The *Huntsville Times* ran a front-page story with a color photo of him and his wife Alice. *The Birmingham News* put it on the front of their local section. Channel 31 of Huntsville sent a TV crew to cover his funeral.

An editorial in the *Arab Tribune* 12 miles away called him "a one-of-a-kind, legendary figure in Alabama newspapers." Columnist Bill Easterling wrote in the *Huntsville Times*, "Newspapering the way God intended it lost an icon when Porter Harvey died."

Three weeks before his death he sat at his typewriter at home for the last time and wrote a note for his family. He had a few requests for the funeral ("the coffin as inexpensive as it can be without seeming too cheap") and a couple of suggestions about his obituary. He wanted his final job to be listed as "part-time reporter."

"I'm ready to go," he wrote. "I've had a wonderful life, especially since I found Alice."

This is an attempt to tell the story of his life, his newspaper, and the woman he insisted was the real star of their 65 years together.

• • •

This book would have been impossible without the assistance of a great many people. I am especially indebted to my sister Mary Woodward and my brother Joe Harvey for their help in researching and remembering, to Jerry Brown for his wise and generous advice on the manuscript, and to my wife, Valerie Harvey, for her unfailing encouragement and support.

SAM HARVEY

High Adventure

CHAPTER 1

The Rome Years

His was a comfortable upbringing, and he sometimes joked about it.

"I grew up in the hill country of northwest Georgia, where the land was poor and the living was hard," he wrote in 1976.

"Sometimes it seemed that all I did was milk, churn, cut stove wood, work in the garden, tend to the hog and fix the pasture fence. We lived in a remote area, nearly a block from the Rome City Hall. We had only one car, and except for Sundays we children hardly ever got to ride in it except when Daddy took us along to deliver milk and butter that our family sold people to help eke out a meager living.

"We lived more than four blocks from the nearest theater and although the show changed three times a week, we frequently didn't get to go more than twice. We lived a mile or so from the country club our family belonged to, so we did most of our swimming in a muddy old river that ran near our home. Since there was no way out of this unhappy situation, we managed to convince ourselves that swimming in the river was actually more fun."

1903 was an uncommonly eventful year. Theodore Roosevelt was president. The *World Almanac* finds only one event worth reporting each year in 1901, 1904, and 1905, and none at all in 1902. But the book tells of 6 happenings in 1903, including the treaty to build the Panama Canal, the Wright Brothers' first flight and the first auto trip across the U.S.

Somehow, the *World Almanac* fails to note the birth on May 1,

Evan Porter Harvey Sr.

1903, of the first child of Evan Porter Harvey Sr. and Fanny Coley Harvey of Rome, in northwest Georgia. They named him Evan Porter Jr. and decided to call him Porter.

His father was the son of a Rome judge. Evan went into the real estate business as a young man and stayed in it all his life. Much of his work was managing rental property owned by other people. He also bought and rented property of his own, and he developed at least one residential subdivision, known as Oak Park. He helped start the National City Bank. In 1912, at the repeated urgings of a group of businessmen, he ran for mayor. He lost in a close three-way race, but he said he was proud of the fact that he got his votes without buying any like the other candidates. "My votes came from the best people in Rome and I am proud of them," he wrote in his journal.

Porter's mother was also born in Rome but only lived there briefly when she was young. Her father was an Episcopal minister. They were living in Demopolis, Alabama, when he suddenly died of a heart attack when Fanny was only two. Her mother moved back to Rome and there she met and married a Mr. Armstrong. They moved to Kansas City and Fanny grew up there. Mr. Armstrong also died, and Fanny and her mother and her older sister moved back south. For a time they lived in Sewanee, Tennessee, where an Episcopal college is located, and she operated a rooming and boarding house. Later they moved back to Rome, this time to stay. And there Fanny met Evan Harvey.

Actually they had met before, but it's doubtful either one remembered it. Their mothers were acquainted. When Fanny was six weeks old, Evan's mother carried him with her when she went to call on Fanny's mother.

Their second introduction led to their wedding on June 18, 1902. Evan was 30 years old. Fanny was 29.

He was a Methodist who took an active role in church affairs. She was an Episcopalian and remained one all her life. He carried the older children to church with him while she stayed home with the younger ones. All the children were to grow up Methodist, although Porter was baptized an Episcopalian.

Porter and his mother, Fanny Coley Harvey.

Porter's birth on May 1, 1903, was followed by the birth of a daughter, Mary, who died young. Another son, Coley, was born when Porter was five. Porter was seven when Ellen was born and 10 when Frances came along.

"It was a wonderful time to be brought up, and we were blessed to have the parents we had," Ellen said. "The freedom our parents gave us is hard to believe as I think back about it."

When Porter was three he came down with polio, or infantile paralysis as it was called then. It left him with almost no muscles in his left leg, so he grew up walking with a severe limp. His parents took him to New York to see a specialist, Dr. Virgil P. Gibney, surgeon-in-chief at the Hospital for Ruptured and Crippled. He told them there was a doctor in Atlanta who could do everything for Porter that he could do. After that Porter was treated in Atlanta by a Dr. Hoke, who was on the staff of Emory Hospital. Porter wore a brace for a time. He had two operations to fix the tendons in his ankle so his foot would stay parallel to the ground instead of dragging, since he had no muscles to hold it up. It was considered experimental surgery and Dr. Hoke had it filmed so it could be kept on file and referred to later. It isn't known how old Porter was when he had the first operation, but he had the second one when he was 14.

It's hard to know how much his lameness affected him while he was growing up. His parents evidently were determined that he learn to do as much as possible for himself and not get in the habit of relying on other people.

"They didn't pet him," Coley said. "If they had, it would have ruined him."

He joined the Boy Scouts. One requirement was that a boy go a mile in precisely 12 minutes, using what is known as Scout's Pace—running 50 paces and walking 50. Porter couldn't run in the normal sense, but he could limp at a pretty good rate. He spent hours circling his block in practice for his test till he passed it.

"His ailment didn't seem to make any difference at all in how he went about things," Ellen said. "He had the most normal family life anybody could have had. When we lived on West First Street, there were some steps coming up from the street and then a pretty long sidewalk leading to the house. Several times when Porter was coming home from school, he'd get to the top of the steps and walk on his hands from there to the house. He was real strong in the arms and shoulders."

When he was a teenager his best friend was Harry Powers. His brother Coley said Harry was just about the only person Porter would accept any help from.

"Sometimes he'd let Harry know when he was having a hard time physically and needed a hand, but he wouldn't ask help from anybody else," Coley said. "I had a stroke not long ago and one of my legs wouldn't work right. I told Porter I realized for the first time what he's been up against all his life."

Porter started to first grade when was seven, attending a school run by Miss Goetchius. He did so well in first grade that the next year he skipped the second. He quickly moved to the head of his class in arithmetic, but lost his papers one day "and had to go to the foot," his father wrote in his journal. "It was a hard pill for him." By February, his father wrote, "Porter is doing well at school. He has not only kept up with the third grade but has made the highest marks of anyone. He learns easily." He stayed in Miss Goetchius's school through the fourth grade, when he transferred to the public school. "Porter likes the public school," his father wrote that year. "He was on the honor roll both September and October."

His father started keeping the journal in 1911, when Porter was eight. He wrote almost every day. Much of what he wrote dealt with his vegetable garden, apparently so the results of one year could serve as a guide in the next. But he also wrote about his family and about the children's activities and ailments. The entries became less frequent as time went on, although he kept at it sporadically until 1925. The entries paint a picture of a happy, loving and close-knit family. Here's a sampling, primarily of those concerning Porter:

1911

June 28—Porter and myself went fishing in river from 5:30 to dark. Porter caught small turtle. I caught small mud cat.

June 30—Porter is keeping his turtle in a tub of water in yard. Planted about 12 hills of pole beans.

July 4—Porter, Coley and myself celebrated the 4th by going to the country to pick blackberries, shoot fireworks and swim in creek. Found a good wash hole in which we had good sport. Coley (three years old) had never been in before. He tried to swim and did well. Turned Porter's turtle in the river at pumping station.

July 21—Porter took four tomatoes and some okra down on Broad St. to sell for 10¢. He sold them to a Negro barber.

August 5—Porter and myself dug two hills of his sweet potatoes for dinner tomorrow. We got several rather small ones but enough for our dinner. Porter's first sweet potatoes were very good.

August 12—Porter has been peddling tomatoes and beans. Sold 50¢ worth today. We give him the money that he makes this way and he really likes to do it. Coley goes along and gets a little of what they make.

August 15—Porter and Coley traded some vegetables to a barber (Lewis Barrett) for a haircut for Coley.

August 16—Porter and myself spent the day fishing down at Mr. Parker's. Cooked four little perch for our dinner. Caught ten in all.

August 20—Porter, Coley and myself went down in pasture after dinner and threw rocks in the river.

August 22—Porter and myself got up at 4:30 to go fishing before breakfast. We fished for an hour but never got a bite. Then we took a boat ride up to the mouth of Reece's Creek. It was cool and fine on the river.

August 24—We all went down to the Van Dyke farm in an auto to see the Negro girl Willie who used to nurse Porter and Mary. She is very sick.

August 25—Willie died this morning at five o'clock.

August 28—I had Porter say all of his multiplication tables tonight after supper. He seems to know them very well.

September 1—Fanny, Mamma, Porter, Coley, Sister Georgia and myself went to see the motion pictures this afternoon.

September 9—Porter and myself went to Atlanta to see Dr. Hoke and have him direct the making of a new brace and raised shoe for Porter.

October 4—I sold my horse and bought a Hudson automobile, which cost me $1,600.

October 7—Fanny and Porter went to Atlanta to get Porter's new shoes with brace attached.

November 25—Porter, Coley and I went out to see a flying machine. Had a long wait and had several narrow escapes from horses and mules, but to see the man fly was worth all of the trouble.

December 25—We had a pleasant Christmas. The children were of course delighted and each of us received many good and useful presents.

December 28—Little Ellen attracts attention everywhere. She is pretty and friendly and rather smart for her age.

1912

January 7—Everything is covered with snow and it makes a beautiful winter scene. There is no wind at all. Porter, Coley and myself took some things to Mr. and Mrs. Jack for their dinner and walked back in the snow. We had a fine time playing snowball, etc.

January 16—The Committee of 70 (or Law and Order League) requested me by a unanimous vote to run for mayor of Rome. Coming from this body of men I consider it no small honor.

February 18—I am not enjoying my race for mayor but it is some satisfaction to find out who are real friends . . . I rather expect to be defeated.

February 21—I am working day and night on my mayor's race. So many good friends have come to my assistance that I have a good chance to win.

February 27, Election Day—The count tonight gave Yancey 540, Hankes 473 and myself 455. We spent no money for votes in any way while the other two spent money freely and really that is what beat me.

May 1—Porter's birthday. We gave him a ball and bat. Cost 10¢ each.

May 31—For the first time in my life I have a cow that gives as much milk as I want her to. I milk till my hands are tired.

June 17—Porter and myself got up at 4:15 this morning and worked sweet potatoes for two hours before breakfast and again this afternoon for an hour and half. Finished working out the patch.

June 18—We have been married 10 years today. They have been short happy years.

June 28—Porter and myself got up at 5:00 and worked sweet potatoes. Porter has ideas about making money far in advance of his age.

August 28—Porter and myself greased my auto this morning. He is a big help, gets under it so easily. He also mixes the cow's feed and helps in many ways. We brought a puppy with us from the Merediths, a nice white pointer about three months old. They gave her to Porter.

September 11—Coley is affectionate in disposition and therefore is a special joy to us.

September 29—The boys and I went to S. School. Porter and myself went to church.

November 7—We have decided to keep the new cow's calf. I have traded it to Porter for his sweet potato crop.

1913

September 5—State Mutual Life Insurance turned me down on a $5,000 policy. Dr. Funkhouser said there was a little murmur in one of my heart valves.

September 11—Porter started to the public school 5th grade Monday. He likes it.

October 18—Frances Burton Harvey was born at 8:30 this morning. Weight stripped 9 lbs. 2 oz.

1914

August 11—Mrs. Woodrow Wilson was buried at Rome today. Mama, Fanny and myself attended the services at the Presbyterian Church. Biggest crowd Rome ever had.

1916

November 20—The New York Life Insurance Co. has issued a $5,000 policy by charging $10.95 extra on account of my heart murmur. I was glad to get it.

1917

July 10—Took Porter to Atlanta and Dr. Hoke operated on his ankle.

1920

May 22—We are raising Beauty's calf Betty. Porter taught it to drink milk when about a month old.

Ellen and Frances remember Porter as being more attentive to his little sisters than most big brothers.

"He was always good to us, and we loved him," Ellen said. "Even when he was off in college we couldn't wait for him to come home."

Once he took Ellen and Frances on a long boat ride up the Oostanaula River, which ran right behind their house on West First Avenue. They carried a picnic and went to a place they called the Monkey Hole in an old flat-bottom bateau.

"It was quite late when we got there, so when we got through eating it was dark, and going down the steep bank to our boat was really something," Frances said. "Porter didn't paddle going home but just guided the boat and let the current take us. Ellen and I lay in the bottom of the boat and watched the stars all the way. When we got home about 10:00, Coley and his friends were under the street light in the alley, knocking at bats with long poles."

If their parents were alarmed at having three children out on the river late at night, neither Ellen nor Frances remembers it. They were given an uncommon amount of freedom to come and go, something that Porter was to do later in raising his own children.

Porter and Coley spent considerable time together despite the five-year difference in their ages.

"Once we found Daddy's and Mama's love letters in the attic," Coley said. "We really caught it over that."

The family boat got stolen, and somehow the boys heard that it was tied up some distance down the river. Porter and Coley and some friends went down and found it.

"It was locked with a chain," Coley said. "But we knew how to break a lock open by pouring in sand and hammering on it. We brought the boat home and whoever had stolen it didn't come after it again."

The children learned frugality primarily from their mother. Fanny had grown up having to pinch pennies. Her father died when she was two, and her stepfather died when she was still at home. So she spent a good many of her early years in what would be called today a single-parent household.

"I really don't know what they lived on," Ellen said. "They didn't have social security back then. I know our grandmother sewed things to sell. Her next-door neighbor ran a dry goods store, and on the third floor our grandmother had a sewing shop that she called Lana's Rags. Mama always dressed Frances and me out of Lana's Rags. We were embarrassed about our clothes. I'm sure they were pretty but they weren't ready-to-wear."

Fanny made some of the children's night clothes out of flour sacks. Once the family went on a vacation to Florida and took an overnight ride on a river boat. Porter embarrassed his sisters half to death by walking down the hall to the bathroom in a night shirt with "Omega Flour" printed across the back. Coley remembers Porter getting quite a kick out of it.

His happiest times as a boy were spent with Harry Powers. They were distant kin by marriage, and their families had always been close.

"I was about a year older than Porter so I started out a grade ahead of him," Harry said. "But we moved off to Rockmart for a year and the school there wasn't accredited, and when we moved back to Rome I had to drop back a grade. Porter and I were in the same grade after that. In high school he and I were the only boys in some of our classes, including French. We took most of the same subjects. We were both on the staff of

The Roman, which was the school newspaper. He and I generally saw alike and we tended to like the same things."

They spent a lot of time on the river, sometimes in the bateau, sometimes in a twenty-foot canoe they borrowed from another family.

"We'd get off in the afternoon from whatever we were doing and go up the river as far as we could go," Harry said. "We'd camp out at night and then go back the next day. When we'd come to a swimming hole we'd always stop and go for a swim. We decided one day to see how far we could swim. We went up to Whitmore Island and let the boat float down while we swam. We swam about three miles without ever touching bottom.

"Porter wanted to try all sorts of things. Once we climbed up on a bluff across from Whitmore Island to a little shelving rock that had some little caves running back from it. We decided that would be a good place to camp in case it rained. We built a fire and the smoke got back in the cave. There was a skunk back there, and he came tearing out. It smelled so bad in the cave that we decided to stay outside and take the rain."

There were rope swings here and there along the river that people had put up, and Porter found them especially appealing.

"He liked to swing out to the middle of the river and dive off just at the end of his swing," Harry said. "You had to do it just right or you'd hit flat and really knock all your breath out. Porter also liked to get up on high places along the river and dive off. Of course, he had that bad leg that would swing around because he had no control over it. But he believed in trying everything at least once."

Once Porter told Harry he'd like to get drunk, just to see what it was like.

"He said he didn't intend to be a drinker, but he wanted to get drunk once. I tried to talk him out of it. I told him he might do something he'd be sorry for. And finally he didn't do it."

It was just the two of them on nearly all their outings. Harry thinks Porter's lameness had something to do with that.

"He didn't want anybody to give him anything extra on account of that leg. Not everybody understood that like I did. They'd want to make allowances for him, and he didn't like that. One time we went tramping out in the woods near my granddaddy's place. We came to a rough field. His foot would get tender pretty easy. He said, 'I can't walk across that.' I said, 'Let me carry you.' He wouldn't allow it till I promised him that I wouldn't tell anybody. I draped him across my shoulders, holding a leg with one hand and arm with the other."

Harry played football, basketball and track in high school, and later coached in high school. Porter couldn't take part in those sports. But he liked to excel in the things he was able to do.

"There was this big beech tree up the river a ways," Harry said. "Beech trees don't have big long limbs, but they have a lot of short limbs at pretty regular intervals all the way up the trunk. Well, Porter and I came to this tree when it was about time to stop for the night and camp. It looked like everybody who had ever been there had cut his initials on that tree. Porter decided to see if he could put his initials higher than anybody else. He was good at climbing because he had so much shoulder and arm strength, and he was light in the legs. He got up above all the other marks. He hung on with one hand while he carved his initials with the other hand. His pocket knife wasn't too strong and it kept closing up on him. He came down with his hand all cut up, but he'd put his initials higher on that tree than anybody else."

Neither Porter nor Harry had a lot to do with girls while they were in their teens.

"I didn't care much about girls then, and I don't guess Porter did either," Harry said. "I suppose he saw girls he liked but he wasn't the sort to tell you about it. I didn't go with girls much even when I was in college and I don't reckon he did either. I wouldn't be surprised if Alice was the first sweetheart he ever had."

When Darlington Prep School was started, Porter's parents took him out of the public school and sent him there.

"During World War I they put in military training at Darlington, and Porter couldn't do that," Ellen said. "So after a year he went back to the public school and finished high school there."

Harry left school after the 11th grade to go to the University of

Georgia. He had been scheduled to be the editor of *The Roman* his senior year. It came out three times a year as a school newspaper, and its final publication was the yearbook. Harry and Porter had worked on it together, and when Harry left school early, Porter stepped up to editor.

Porter delivered the inspirational "Message to Garcia" in a declamation contest in the Rome City Auditorium in April 1920, when he was a high school junior. History fails to record how the judges scored him. As a senior he played the title role in the school play "Professor Peppe," a three-act farce. The program notes list the professor as "a nervous wreck."

After Porter finished high school a man asked him what he planned to do now that he had graduated.

"I'm going to college," Porter said.

"Your daddy's pretty smart to send you," the man said, "since you're crippled and can't work."

CHAPTER 2

INTO THE WORLD

It's not clear when Porter first began to entertain thoughts of newspaper work as a career. He had been the editor of his high school paper, *The Roman.* But when he graduated in 1921 and started to Emory University in Atlanta, it was with the idea of becoming a doctor. His father discouraged that ambition. He didn't think Porter was observant enough to succeed as a doctor. How his father felt later about a poor observer's chances in the newspaper business can only be guessed at.

Clearly Porter felt drawn to newspapers. At Emory he carried a paper route for a Hearst paper, the *Atlanta Georgian.* He worked part-time for a while in the mailing department of the *Atlanta Journal.*

Colleges didn't offer much in the way of journalism education in those days. But Emory had a course or two, and Porter took them. He worked his last two years on the student paper, *The Emory Wheel.* As a junior he was on the circulation staff, assistant exchange editor and "special reporter." As a senior he was assistant editor.

Harry Powers was about 65 miles away at the University of Georgia in Athens. When Georgia played a football game in Atlanta, Harry would sometimes go to the game and look Porter up. Sometimes he traveled by hitching rides on freight cars.

"One time Porter wanted to ride the train back to Athens with me," Harry said. "He'd never ridden a freight before. To get on you had to grab hold while it was moving and jump on. Well, where we were standing, the train was moving so fast I was afraid Porter would get hurt if he tried to catch it, because of his leg. I told him I'd see him later and I got on. After the train had gone a little ways I felt somebody slap me on the back and I nearly fell off. It was Porter. The train had started up a little grade right after I got on, and it had slowed down enough to where Porter felt he could grab hold. He got aboard several cars back. He went over the tops of the cars till he got to where I was crouched down. He went on to Athens with me and then he hoboed back to Atlanta. He wasn't scared of anything."

He was something of a joiner, at least in his senior year. His activities took 17 lines to list in the 1925 yearbook. He was vice-president of the Few Literary Society, vice-president of the Student Lecture Association, and a member of the Eagles Club, the Campus Social Club, Pi Delta Epsilon journalism honorary and the Peed Mathematics Club. He joined the debate team. As a senior he earned an athletic "E" by serving as manager of the tennis team.

He acquired the nickname "Cork," evidently because of the cork insert in the shoe of his game leg, but it didn't seem to follow him beyond college.

His literary endeavors weren't limited to journalism. He developed a feeling for rhyme and meter, and the following poem was given a full page in the school yearbook, *The Emory Campus*, his senior year:

ODE TO THE TEMPORARY CHAPEL

How dear to my heart is the temporary chapel,
When fond recollection recalls it to view:
The scriptures, the hymns, the daily announcements,
And the world-famous speakers that we listen to.
The iron-bound speakers,
The moss-covered speakers,
The world-famous speakers,
That we listen to.
They usually tell us we're picked individuals,

The fate of the world is depending on us;
We think, as we look at the specimens about us,
The world's future prospects are not worth a cuss.
Those inspiring speakers,
Those soul-stirring speakers,
Those heart-rending speakers,
That we listen to.
Most all of them warn us to steer clear of licker,
And night-life and necking, and other such things;
They say it's our duty to stick to our studies—
And so they rave on till the dinner bell rings.
Those long-winded speakers,
Those time-killing speakers,
Those world-famous speakers,
That we listen to.

—Porter Harvey

He worked the summer after his freshman year as a door-to-door salesman for Wearever aluminum cookware, going into homes and putting on demonstrations. He got his introduction to daily newspaper work in the summer between his junior and senior year. He worked as a reporter for the *Rome News-Tribune* in his home town.

"I think he did general reporting," his sister Ellen said, "One time Miss Isabel Gammon, the society editor, was out of town and Porter had to write up a tea. He was supposed to tell what everyone wore and who the hostesses were and who the guests were. Well, he got just so far and couldn't get any farther. He gave his copy to the printer with a note at the end, 'Ask Miss Gammon.' It came out that way in the paper, and I don't think they sent him to cover any more teas."

The managing editor at the *News-Tribune* was R. H. Claggett.

"Porter thought the world of Mr. Claggett, and I'm sure he had an influence on Porter wanting to be a newspaperman," Ellen said.

During his senior year at Emory, Porter worked for the *Atlanta Constitution* as their campus correspondent. So during his college career he managed to be employed by three Atlanta newspapers in one capacity or other.

He had given up any thoughts of majoring in medicine, but he was getting pretty far along in college without another major to take its place. Emory didn't offer a degree in journalism.

"It got down to the time I was about to graduate and I didn't really have a major," he said. Emory had just recently started offering degrees in electrical engineering, but they weren't having much luck attracting students. "I went to the counselor and we figured out that if I took a few more courses, I would have a degree in electrical engineering. So that's what I did. I have a degree in electrical engineering and I can't even screw in a light bulb without blowing a fuse."

Regardless of his degree, by the time he finished at Emory in 1925, he knew he wanted to be a newspaperman. His father felt he still needed some more schooling. He convinced Porter to spend a year in Boston at the most prestigious college in America, Harvard University.

"We had a good friend living next door, Henderson Lanham, who was later a congressman," Ellen said. "He had gone to Harvard. I guess Daddy thought Porter was too smart not to go there too."

At Harvard he ran into the same problem he'd faced at Emory: what to specialize in. His advisors looked over his records from Emory and shook their heads. They told Porter he probably ought not to go for an advanced degree but simply to enroll as a special student. That way he could take the courses he thought would do him the most good. He concentrated on English and writing and took a course in public speaking.

"He wrote home once a week, and Mama wrote to him once a week," Ellen said. "It was quite a ritual. He got on a rowing team at Harvard. That was a sport he could take part in, and he thought it was real exciting." It also helped satisfy the love of rivers that he had developed as a boy on the Oostanaula with Harry Powers, something he was never to get out of his system.

Frances remembers that the family couldn't afford to have Porter come home for Christmas.

"We didn't know Porter had any money for Christmas presents for us, and frankly we didn't think he knew how to spend money," she said. "So imagine our surprise when we got a very impressive box filled with marvelous presents. Among them were my first silk stockings, with double heels no less, a 'When We Were Very Young' book, and a darling wooden-jointed Felix the Cat." Ellen got a brown leather pocketbook and some unfinished bookends, the Lions of Lucerne, with the paint to finish them.

While he was at Harvard, Ellen and Frances wrote him some letters in rhyme. He replied with a poem that wound up being printed in the *Rome News-Tribune* after the family doctor saw it and slipped it to the editor. The paper noted in its introduction that Porter had worked there while he was in college. They said the poem was "purloined for publication." Here it is:

> Dear Ellen and Dear Frances: Your letters came last week
> and both your poems surprised me so that I could hardly speak.
> I knew a boy once in my life who wrote that kind of poem;
> His name was Coley Harvey. I thought you all might know him.
> There's only two things wrong about the poems you sent this time:
> and that is Ellen's spelling is as bad as Frances' rhyme.
> When poets are B-r-i-a-n and H-o-m-e-s,
> I think this country's poetry will be an awful mess.
> There's one big famous poet here, his name is E. J. Root.
> He's blacker than the ace of spades—he surely is a beaut.
> He really ain't a beaut at all, he is an awful sight.
> But beaut's the only word I knew to make the rhyme come right.
> A man that's here at Harvard for the first time like I am,
> must go to see the doctor for a physical exam.
> They never charge you anything, the doctor does it free.
> So I went around the other day to let him look at me.
> He started on me just as soon as I'd got in the door,
> and asked me more fool questions than I'd ever heard before.
> He asked me what year was I born; and how long were my legs,

and how I brushed my back jaw teeth, and how I liked my eggs;
and were my folks alive or dead; and did my father chew;
and was my great-grandmother a Spaniard or a Jew;
and did I drink or smoke or cuss; and did I say my prayers;
and who were my first cousins; and had I any heirs;
and had I ever had a job; and did we keep a cow;
and about a million others that I've forgotten now.
And then he got some ribbons in a little pasteboard box,
all different kinds of colors like fancy teahound socks.
And then he thought he'd get my goat, and have some fun with me;
so he picks him out a red one and "What color's this?" says he.
"It's green," says I, sarcastic like, to show I didn't mind;
and he wrote on my record card: "This man is color blind."
And then he said to tell him the diseases I had had.
I said I'd do the best I could, my memory being bad.
I scratched my head a minute and then I started off:
"Chicken pox, and toothache, and mumps and whooping cough;
and infantile paralysis, and dandruff and a cold;
and croup and teeth and colic when I was ten months old;
and cramp and cinders in my eye, and once a sty there too;
and heartburn and diphtheria, and tonsils and the flu;
and a touch of mild insanity, and blisters on my hands;
and a bad infected sinus, and swollen thyroid glands;
and a broken arm and sunburn, and running sores and itch;
and poison oak or ivy, I don't remember which;
and adenoids and measles when I was four or five—"
"Stop!" says he. "For the love of Mike! And are you still alive?"
I told him that I thought I was, and he said "Go in there;
sit down and take your clothes off, plumb to your underwear."
And so I took my clothes off, plumb to my B.V.D's ,
and stood there feeling like a fool, and just about to freeze.
And then he took his coat off, and began to do his stuff;
and never, only in a fight, have I been done so rough.
He punched me in the stomach and rapped me on the back,

and hit my kneecap with a stick to see if it would crack.
He weighed me on his doctor's scales, then looked at my tongue;
and got his long thin earphones out and listened to my lung.
He said for me to say, "One, two," and every time I'd speak,
he'd put his listener on my chest and hear my innards squeak.
And when at last he'd finished, and I was getting dressed,
he drew some blood out of my ear '"to make a Tallquist test."
He wiped it on a paper slip and put it on his shelf.
I didn't like the idea, and says I to myself;
"This Tallquist test may be all right, but it might happen so
that he'd find out out a lot of things he didn't oughta know."
He went to file my record and as soon as he was gone,
I found a slip of paper like the one my blood was on.
I grabbed his red ink bottle, and got a drop of ink,
and wiped it on the paper in a lovely smear of pink.
I changed it for the sample he had set aside to dry;
and when the doctor got back, I was straightening my tie.
About six hours later, I was crawling into bed;
I received a short night letter and this is what I read:
"Dear Sir, You may not know it, but you're in an awful fix.
Your stock of white corpuscles is absolutely nix;
All your red corpuscles are decomposing fast;
your blood is strongly acid—your hopes are nearly past.
Now don't delay an instant, but come straight back to me.
I'll save your life if possible. Signed, Foster Mott, M.D."
I haven't got a grudge against this Dr. Foster Mott,
but I'd hate to have him curing me of things I haven't got.
I guess he thinks that by this time my blood has ceased to flow;
perhaps it will be better if he keeps on thinking so.
This letter's taken longer than I had thought it would;'
at writing snappy poetry I ain't so awful good.
It's sure a lot of trouble to find words that will rhyme,
and still make any kind of sense; I've had a terrible time.
Now you all be good children, and help your mother too,

and study hard and don't flunk out, like I'm about to do.
And when you're not too busy, I hope you'll write to me.

With love and many kisses.
P. Harvey, R.F.D.

WHEN HIS year at Harvard was ending and it was time to find a job, his thoughts turned not to the South but to the newspaper capital of the country, New York. His father wrote him in May 1926 with advice.

"I think you should try to scrape up some pull in connection with your job hunting," his father wrote. "Surely some of your teachers know somebody who can turn the trick. You may feel that you do not want to get a job on someone's pull. If so, you are wrong. Use all the pull you can in securing a job and all the perseverance and ability that you can to hold it after you get it. Should you get to the man from whom you hope to get a job, make him understand that all you are after is a chance to show what you can do. Tell him that you do not know how your work will compare with others and that you do not ask for an agreement as to salary until you have shown what you can do.

"I am not expecting you to do much at first," his father continued. "I think you will have to get money from me for the first few months in order to keep going. That will not bother or disappoint me in the least. I know there are many small caliber reporters hanging around New York and I think it will take you a little while to rise above them. Of course, your education will soon tell, and I have no fear as to the final outcome.

"You may be correct to start work on a New York paper, but somehow I doubt if it can be done. When I was on the school board here, we much preferred to employ teachers who had experience. We would say to beginners, 'Get a job in a country school and see if you are any good. If you do, come to us after you have had a year's experience and we will give you a place.' If I were running a big paper, I would look at it the same way . . . I realize I have written much about something of which I know very little."

His father closed with a report that he currently had 44 young chickens, and they were doing fine.

Porter went to New York and managed to land a job as a night cub reporter, not on a New York paper, but on the *Brooklyn Times*. A month later he was hired as a reporter on the *New York Post*. At that time the *Post* was one of eight or nine dailies in New York. Today it is one of only three that still survive. In those days it was a conservative, somewhat staid paper, nothing like today's screaming tabloid.

Forty years later, when he was elected president of the Alabama Press Association and had to write about himself in the *Advertiser-Gleam*, Porter said of his time on the New York paper, "The *Post* had such a big staff that he was there three months before they discovered he didn't know anything."

One of his friends from Rome, Bob Shahan, was in New York one day and called Porter on the phone, disguising his voice. The *Post* ran daily lists of the ships that were arriving and leaving New York harbor. Bob asked Porter if he could check on when a certain ship was due.

"What ship is that?" Porter asked.

"The *Nina*."

Porter searched the lists and reported that the *Nina* wasn't expected.

"How about the *Pinta*?"

Porter couldn't find it either.

"Well, could you try the *Santa Maria*?"

With that the cub reporter finally realized that his leg was being pulled and that Columbus's three ships weren't headed for New York.

The *Post* reorganized its news staff three months after Porter started work there and fired six of its greenest reporters, including him. He was one of three who had been hired with no experience at all, as a sort of experiment, and he took some consolation in lasting longer than the other two. Before he left, his boss told him he thought he had the stuff to be a newsman, but he needed some time on a small-town paper before he would be ready for New York.

"What size town did you have in mind?" Porter asked.

"Let's see," the man said, "you're from Georgia. Maybe some place like Atlanta."

Porter didn't leave New York immediately but hung around to see if he could find something else. He wrote home once that he was putting water on his cornflakes to stretch his money. Then as later he sometimes found pleasure in squeezing by.

His father wrote him on September 26, "I have thought of you so much since receiving your Monday night letter. I doubt if you can ever realize how your mother and I feel toward you. And when you get disappointed, it makes us feel so keenly for you. . . . Be sure to keep us posted as to your movements."

Finally Porter decided to head back south. He wired his parents, "Kill the fatted calf, I'm coming home."

He held odd jobs while waiting for a newspaper job to turn up. Coley recalls that Porter helped build a cooling tower on top of a three-story building in downtown Atlanta, catching red-hot rivets in a bucket after they were thrown from the ground and then putting them in rivet holes.

"He probably got a kick out of that, like bungee jumping later," Coley said. "He'd do anything to make a nickel."

Porter wrote to R. H. Claggett, who had been his boss at the Rome paper and who was then on the *Evening Appeal* in Memphis. Mr. Claggett wrote back, "I have no employing authority or I would fire somebody to make a place for you . . . Meanwhile I would suggest that you stick around Atlanta. Get acquainted with the newspaper men there. Personal acquaintance down in this part of the country counts for a lot. That's the reason I have the job I am now engaged in."

In his letters to newspapers, Porter wrote, "I am a reliable reporter, a fairly good re-write man, a rather poor head writer, a fair police reporter, a good court reporter and a good sports writer. I am 23 years old, unmarried and willing to work hard for a small initial salary, provided there is a reasonable chance for advancement."

He didn't mention that he had gone to Harvard.

Finally, some five months after losing his job in New York, he found himself back on a newspaper—*The Nashville Tennessean.*

"I feel so good I can hardly keep from hollering out and waking the roomers here at the Nashville YMCA," he wrote to his mother and father on February 17, 1927. "I feel like grabbing everybody I meet on the streets and kissing them, it feels so good to be at work again. I didn't do much today except catch on to how things run, but did write a couple of stories. It's a great feeling to be in a newspaper office and feel that I'm part of it, instead of an outsider trying to get in."

Porter had gone to Nashville for an interview with the managing editor.

"He talked with me a while and then said, 'Well, when do you want to start?' 'Right now,' I told him, and he said 'Hop to it,' so I did. He and the editor are both friends of Mr. Claggett and had written to him when they got my letter. He must have told them I was all right. They kind of apologized for the salary being only $130 [a month]. I didn't let them see how big that sounds to me. With the training I've had in the past few months, I can live like a king and still save about half of it."

He was delighted to be on the staff of the afternoon paper, so he would be working days instead of nights. "The men I'm working under are the nicest I've been under since Mr. Claggett. They've done everything they can to make the starting easy for me, and to make me feel at home . . . Write me at YMCA, Nashville."

The Nashville job lasted till July. Then he was let go, in a reduction of the reporting staff. The city editor and managing editor promised to give him good recommendations, and he started writing to newspapers again.

No record exists of just which papers he wrote. But one letter survives, because the man who received it simply wrote on the bottom, "Sorry, but we do not need a reporter at present" and mailed it back, and Porter kept it. It was from the managing editor of the *Caldwell Messenger* in Caldwell, Kansas. How Porter came to seek a job way out in Kansas in a town whose population even in 1990 was only 1,351 is a mystery. He couldn't possibly have written papers in all the thousands of towns larger and closer by. But for some reason he wrote to that one. He said he hoped they'd have an opening in the future and would keep him in mind. This time he said he could write headlines fairly well, in addition to being able to function as a reporter. "Although I have had very little experience with political or police news," he wrote, "I am confident that my training as an all-around street man has been thorough and varied enough to qualify me for any kind of work that might be required."

He decided to go call on editors in person while waiting for answers to his letters. He headed north into Kentucky, Ohio, and Indiana. He kept a log of his travels on a single sheet of paper which he folded into quarters so it would fit in his pocket. It still survives. From July 17 through July 31 he listed 67 newspapers that he visited, averaging between four and five a day (even small towns in those days were likely to have two papers). A single day in Ohio saw him go to papers in Marion, Delaware, Marysville, Bellefontaine, Lima, Celina, and Van Wert. On the back of the page he listed the papers where there seemed to be any possibility of an opening. The *Richmond Palladium* might need a man in sports the last of August. The *Kokomo Dispatch* may need a man about August 15, and the *Findlay* (Ohio) *Courier* about September 1. And so on.

His trail led to Indianapolis, and there he took a job dishing up food in a cafeteria. There was a typewriter shop in the same block. On his own lunch hour he would go there and use one of their typewriters to write newspapers too far away to visit easily. Once again something turned his eyes toward Kansas. He wrote the *Daily Globe* in Dodge City, a town of about 10,000 people and more than a thousand miles away. And this time he got the answer he was hoping for: Yes, they had a job for a reporter, and he would do.

His father wired him money for a train ticket. He traveled to Dodge, found a place to live, and was told by another man on the *Globe* staff about Mrs. Reynolds's boarding house. Porter decided to take his meals there. At the boarding house he noticed a trim brunette school teacher who, like him, was new in town. She was getting ready to start her first job. And somebody introduced him to Alice Wells.

CHAPTER 3

THE GIRL FROM KANSAS

"All my life," Porter wrote, "I have benefited from things that happened just by pure luck; the luckiest breaks I have had were concerning Alice. It was a thousand-to-one shot that I found her. Alice and I would never have met if either of us hadn't taken just the turn we did at various times. Every time I got laid off from a job, or didn't get a job I was trying for, it seemed bad at the time but it was really the best thing that could have happened. If things had gone any different I wouldn't have gone to Dodge City in the fall of 1927 and started eating at Mrs. Reynolds' boarding house, and getting acquainted with Alice across the toaster at breakfast time."

Alice Alberta Wells was born to Thornton and Ada Daniels Wells during a snowstorm, in a hotel dining room, just down the street from the Garden of Eden, delivered by a doctor who may have been drunk. But that's getting ahead of the story.

Her grandparents on both sides had gone west while they were in their twenties. Central Kansas was still raw frontier Indian country. They arrived there a decade or so after the Civil War, around 15 years after Kansas became a state. The government offered land to people willing to help change the wild prairie into farmland. The settlers' lives were incredibly hard by today's standards. But the prospect of starting fresh and doing better was a powerful lure to the adventurous and the determined.

Thornton W. Wells

Ada Daniels Wells

Thornton's father, George Wells, had spent several winters in the 1850s hunting and trapping in Minnesota and Illinois. He fought in the Iowa Infantry in the Civil War. He then worked as a butcher in Chicago and was proud of his record of butchering a steer in 19 minutes. While there he met and married Elizabeth Jane Thornton. Soon after the war they moved to Missouri and took up farming. Elizabeth had vetoed the life of a trapper's wife in Iowa. For one thing, she couldn't stand the smell of the animal skins sitting out and curing. George prospered at farming but decided in 1879 to move still farther west to secure land for his six boys. They traveled by covered wagon to Russell County, near the middle of Kansas. George traded his team of horses for a 160-acre homestead relinquishment on Goose Creek. A two-room half-dug-out, stone house became their home. Buffalo bones were scattered over the prairie, although the animals were by then extinct there. Russell County was to gain a measure of fame a century later when a native son, Bob Dole, became the nation's most powerful senator and a presidential nominee.

When George and Elizabeth arrived in Kansas and started farming, one of their children was two-year-old Thornton Wells, who had been born in Missouri in 1877. There were to be 10 children in all. Thornton was the eighth. When he was only six, his father died of complications from a malady he contracted while serving in the Civil War. His death came the same day his youngest daughter was born, and in the same room of their home. The midwife held the baby up while George was still conscious so that he could kiss her.

After his death Elizabeth and the children moved to Great Bend in the next county. A teacher's college was located there, and Elizabeth took in boarders and roomers, mostly students. The older sons worked, and the family managed. Some years later Elizabeth married a Mr. Dodge, and she was known as "Grandma Dodge" to Alice and her other grandchildren.

In those days people frequently started teaching school as soon as they themselves finished high school. And high schools didn't always go through all 12 grades. Thornton was only 16 when he did his first teaching. It was Pilot Rock School, a one-room school he had attended as an elementary student. He taught there from January 1, 1894, until the term ended in early February. He taught at other schools and in 1900 he became the principal of the school in Luray, a small town in the southern edge of Russell County.

One of his students at Luray was Ada Daniels, whom he was later to marry. She had evidently gone back for another year of schooling so that she could teach. Her father, W. B. (William Billings) Daniels, was a member of the Luray School Board that had hired Thornton.

W. B.'s early life was the stuff of drama. It was recounted in an obituary that Thornton wrote for the newspaper at Hays, Kansas. W. B. was born in 1855 in New Orleans. When the Civil War broke out six years later, his mother was allowed to move her four small children to Washington, D.C., where they were interned for a while. Then they went on to Boston to stay with relatives. From there W. B. went further north to live with another uncle "and learned the meaning of hard work digging stones from the fields of a New Hampshire farm. When he was 15, he shipped with a colonizing company to South America. The company sailed up the Amazon River for a thousand miles, landing at several points, seeking a location for a settlement. The climate, strange people and language, savages, dangerous reptiles, wild animals and a dwindling supply of provisions discouraged the adventurers, who returned to Boston. William earned his expenses both ways as a cabin boy to the captain."

He and his brother Charley then went west to seek their fortunes. "Intending to go to Wisconsin," Thornton wrote, "they eventually landed at Ellsworth, Kansas, in 1872. There they bought horses and rode to Lincoln County where they worked on Bacon Creek. In 1876 William went to Luray to work on a sheep ranch. He soon was made foreman and remained there a number of years. While working on this ranch he became acquainted with Harriet Hilton, to whom he was married in 1879."

Before his marriage he and some friends had gotten a boat and started down the Arkansas River. "They wanted to take a look at the Indian Territory," Thornton wrote. "They were set upon by Indians who stole their provisions and the youths, having their fill of adventure, were content to get back to their homes any way they could."

Ada's mother, Harriet Hilton Daniels, was a great-great-granddaughter of John Hilton, who fought in the Revolutionary War. Ada later traced her ancestry in order to join the Daughters of the American Revolution, which Alice was to join also.

W. B. and Harriet spent most of their lives farming near Luray, where Ada was born in 1882. She and Thornton were married at the Daniels home on June 28, 1903. She had taught school for a few years, but probably didn't teach after their marriage. Teaching jobs were generally reserved for single women.

School terms were determined by how much money the community could scrape up to pay the teachers. In small towns this frequently turned out to be not much. Some years, school might last only four or five months. Thornton would find other work the rest of the winter, such as helping out in stores. He went to college as much as he could in the summer, knowing that a higher-ranking certificate would entitle him to a better job with more pay. He was to be 43 before he finished work on his bachelor's degree, and he was 53 when he finally got his master's.

After he and Ada married, they moved to Lucas, another Russell County town, and he became the principal there. Two days before Christmas in 1904, Ada gave birth to their first child, a girl. They named her Alice Alberta Wells.

The family was living in a house that usually doubled as a hotel.

"The people who owned it had gone away for the winter and rented the house to Mama and Daddy," Alice said. "I was born December 23 in what had been the hotel dining room, during a real severe winter storm. Some people said later that the doctor who delivered me was drunk. I can't say for sure. Mama had some complications during my birth and he injected saltwater in her veins because there was no blood to give her. Mama had rather large scars on her arms from that as long as she lived."

About three blocks away was what was known—and still is—as the Garden of Eden. It was the brainchild of a stone mason, Samuel Perry Dinsmore, who became fascinated with the idea of making unusual figures out of concrete. He built a stone home for himself on a corner lot. Then he began decorating the yard with concrete trees and concrete characters from the Bible—Adam, Eve, Cain, Abel, etc., and various animals. Lots of people came to see them.

"He rigged up something so he could project his voice," Alice said. "He'd cry out, 'Cain, Cain, you son of a gun, what have you done with Abel?' And then a voice would answer 'Am I my brother's keeper?' And things like that."

The Rand McNally road atlas today lists the Garden of Eden in red letters on a map of Kansas, because it continues to be a lively tourist attraction. It ranks as one of the region's best-known examples of what came to be called folk art.

The Wells family lived in four towns while Alice was growing up, all of them within about 35 miles of each other. Thornton was the city superintendent in Lucas, then county superintendent in Russell, then Lucas city superintendent again, then Russell city superintendent, and finally city superintendent in Sylvan Grove just across the county line.

He continued to work toward his degree. For three summers while Alice was in grade school the family lived in Manhattan, Kansas, so Thornton could study at what is now Kansas State University. He was interested in just about everything, and he was always looking for ways to expand his knowledge. Once he caught smallpox and had to be quarantined in one room of his home for three or four weeks. He spent the time teaching himself trigonometry from a book, and the next year he taught trigonometry in school. He learned to weave baskets and make pottery the way the Indians did. He painted, played tennis and volleyball, and when he was 50 he took up golf. When he was 53 he shot a nine-hole round of golf in par.

"He bought a motorcycle when he was county superintendent to ride when he was visiting all the schools," his daughter Helen said. "He had a horse and buggy first, but the horse ran away with him once, and he was afraid it might happen again and he'd kill somebody. So he sold the horse, Old Billy, and got a motorcycle because he felt it would be safer." It might be noted that, half a century later, various of his great-grandchildren were arguing that they ought to be allowed to ride motorcycles but were being told that they were just too dangerous.

While Thornton was spending summers at Kansas State, Ada took some classes in library science. This enabled her to go out into rural schools and catalog their library books scientifically. Her interests were varied, just as his were. She was active in the Methodist Church work. She raised lots of flowers, including some that were unusual for that time and place. She belonged to a Saturday afternoon bridge club and a hobby club.

Thornton and Ada had four girls and two boys. But two of the girls died in childhood, and both boys died as relatively young adults. Ada, who was two-and-a-half years younger than Alice, died during a scarlet fever epidemic when she was in the fifth grade. Harriet died at about six months of what was listed as infantile paralysis, although her parents doubted the diagnosis. Victor was born between them, four years after Alice, but he had rheumatic fever as a child and it damaged his heart. He was to die in his 40s. Kenneth, who was twelve years younger than Alice,

Alice in swing. At left, parents and siblings Victor, Harriet, and Ada

was killed during World War II when the Army glider he was piloting crashed in the India-Burma theater of operations. Helen was born in 1918, when Alice was nearly 14.

"I was the lucky one," Alice said. "I was almost never ill growing up and never with anything serious."

The first playmate she could remember was a little girl named Elma Fose whose parents had come over from Russia, like a number of other people in the community.

"She couldn't speak any English, and of course I couldn't speak any Russian," Alice said. "My folks thought this was a great opportunity for me to learn Russian. But I guess I did all the talking when we played together because she learned my language and I never learned hers."

Alice started to school when the family was living in Russell, the county seat. The school there had a teacher for each grade. After first and second grade, the family moved back to Lucas. The school there had two grades in each room. The teacher would instruct students in one grade, while the students in the other grade worked on their own on their lessons.

Alice was a quick student who liked all her classes (although she was to find out later on she didn't care for Latin). She discovered that when she was in the lower grade in a room, she could often learn what the older kids were learning by listening to the teacher instead of working on her own lessons.

She showed an early talent for music. Her parents arranged for her to take singing lessons even before she started to school. They had an organ at home but someone advised her parents not to let her learn the organ until she knew piano or she'd never take to the piano. When she was about in the fourth grade, they got a piano and she started taking lessons from a local woman. One summer she took lessons from a different teacher, a man.

"I didn't practice like I should and he told me right out, 'You ought to play better than you do.' I also took violin lessons for about a year. My parents bought me a violin for ten dollars. We moved to Sylvan Grove when I was in the tenth grade, and that school didn't have a music teacher. I became the director of what we called our orchestra. There were three of us who played different instruments. If the school was having a program I'd get our little group together and we'd play for it."

She enjoyed the attention she got as a performer and as a class leader. She won a medal in a state voice competition at Hays. When she was a junior, she sang a solo at the graduation for the senior class at Sylvan Grove, "My Laddie."

Of the four towns she grew up in, only Russell was of much size. It has 7,835 people today. But Lucas today has only 452 people, Sylvan Grove 321, and Luray too few to be listed in the atlas.

"We didn't have running water in the first house I remember. We pumped water by hand from a cistern. Before we got electricity we used coal-oil lamps to read and write by at night. We'd bathe about twice a week in a big wash tub, in front of a coal stove. We'd heat water in a tea kettle or in a big pot. We'd take baths on Saturday night to be ready for Sunday school. When one child stepped out of the tub, another would be ready to step in. We didn't always change the water."

They got electric lights while they lived in Lucas, 25-watt bulbs suspended from the ceiling in the middle of the room, "and we felt like we were really living uptown."

When they moved to Russell, Thornton built a house from the same plans W. B. Daniels had used for his two-story house in Luray, except that Thornton's had only one story.

The children had chores such as washing dishes and making beds. They stayed especially busy on washday.

"We children would pump water out of the cistern into a bucket and carry it into the kitchen," Alice said. "It would be heated on the wood or coal stove and poured into a washing machine. It was a big round tublike thing on legs with a device that let you turn the mechanism by hand. You'd wring the water out of the clothes and put them in another tub of clear water. You were supposed to rinse it twice. Mama would put a little blueing in to make the clothes look white even if they weren't. We were considered lucky to have a machine, even if it wasn't electric. Lots of folks had to use a scrub board. We'd hang the clothes outside on a line, and if it was winter, sometimes they'd freeze right in your fingers. People always wore their clothes a lot longer between washings back then. The school always smelled nicer on Mondays."

Much later, when she was living in Guntersville, her father asked her to write down "10 before 10"—10 things she remembered from when she was less than 10 years old. Alice had vivid memories of her childhood, and she recalled many more than 10 things. Here are a few as she wrote them for her parents:

"Those were the days of suffragettes. One Sunday afternoon Luther and Mable Landon drove up in a buggy. He got out and Mama got in to go with Mable to a suffragettes' meeting. The men sort of laughed at the idea of women voting, but they went anyway while you baby-sat."

"There were buffalo wallows in our yard and pasture across the street, and in the spring there would be tadpoles in them when it rained. We used to keep them in buckets until they lost their tails and turned into toads."

"I guess I came as near getting a whipping from Miss DeWald [her teacher] as I ever did at school. She saw me write something on the sidewalk and told me she would whip me if she ever saw me do it again. I had written 'Dale Evans is a big bull.' It was the worst name I could think of to call him."

"We didn't have a telephone so a grocery boy called at the door for our orders each morning. Once he brought us a sample of a new kind of cereal, one you didn't have to cook. It was Post Toasties."

"One Christmas you hired Charlie Harshbarger to drive us to Luray in a big sled (pulled by a horse). We put on extra clothes, wrapped up in blankets and snuggled in together for the eleven-mile trip through the snow to Grandpa and Grandma's. What a thrill that was! It seems to me Mr. Harshbarger had put bells on the harness just for the occasion."

When her little sister Harriet was dying at six months, "you had done everything the doctor said but she kept getting worse. You called us around the baby buggy where she lay, and I watched her slip away."

"How we loved to climb on your lap for a story, especially the true ones that started off, 'Once upon a time when I was a little boy . . .' And as soon as you would finish, we would say 'Tell us another, Papa.'"

"They used to drive herds of cattle to market by our house and we would watch them through the windows. Men on horseback would ride along, keeping them moving in the right direction. I understand stampedes in western movies better because I saw these."

Between Alice's junior and senior years in high school, a woman friend of Ada's needed some help feeding the crew that was going to be on their farm harvesting the wheat. Alice volunteered to stay at her home.

"I was kind of intrigued because I'd never lived on a farm even though we were in farm country. There were 12 to 16 men in the work crew. We'd get up about 4:00 in the morning and go to bed at 10:00 at night and work the whole time. The lady I was working for was pregnant and she had two small children. She asked me if I could make a pie. I asked where she kept the cookbook. She said she didn't have one. She tried to tell me how she did it. She didn't have a measuring cup, just a tin cup. She said, 'Just dip it in the bin of flour.' I asked how much lard and she said, 'Just take a scoop.' Well, the first pie I made you couldn't touch. I called Mama and she mailed me a cookbook and I got along all right after that. The summer before I was there, a girl had made a three-layer cake and frosted it but forgot to take the tin out, and when I heard about that, I felt better. We sliced great big cured hams that they'd prepared the winter before. We'd fry ham and bacon. I learned during that time to slop the pigs with the milk from the dairy the family operated. Once the harvest hands went to town and got caught in a rainstorm. It was up to the farmer's wife and me to milk their 17 cows. I'd never milked before. They had one old cow with great big horns. The farmer's wife said she was an easy milker. She showed me how you pressed on the teats and stripped the milk out. Well, she milked the other 16 cows while I was struggling with the 17th. Somebody heard about it and said they felt mighty sorry for the cow if I took that long."

Sylvan Grove High was a small school, with 13 in the senior class.

"There weren't many girls for the basketball team, so I got to substitute some," Alice said. "About all I could do well was throw the ball a fair distance. Girls' basketball was different then. The court was divided into three parts, with the two forwards at one end, the two centers in the middle and the two guards at the other end. You couldn't get out of your section. I was a guard. We guards played against the other team's forwards and tried to keep them from scoring. As a guard I could never make a goal, but if I needed to I could throw the ball over the center to our forwards at the other end. We wore blue serge bloomers, pleated at the waistline and gathered at the knee with elastic. It was supposed to look like you were wearing a skirt, and not be unladylike. We each wore a middy blouse and a tie with the school colors."

Alice's clothes were mostly made by her mother. She still has the dress her mother made for her graduation from high school, fashioned out of white cotton voile, hemstitched and appliqued with beads. She had a special set of underwear with matching lace, "and I felt like the best-dressed girl in town. Where Mama found the time to make everything, I'll never know."

Alice graduated from high school in 1923 as the valedictorian.

Her first "job" after high school lasted only a couple of weeks, but it's interesting to note that it involved newspapers. She wrote news from Sylvan Grove and mailed it to the nearest paper, the *Lucas Independent*, and they printed it. She had to give that up because the family was moving. Thornton had been appointed assistant state superintendent of education and was already working in Topeka, the capital. Alice and the rest of the family headed east to join him. His term was to last four years. That meant Alice could enroll in Washburn College in Topeka and live at home all during her time in college. It was no small thing for a family with four children living on a school man's pay.

One thing that came up during Thornton's time as assistant state superintendent was the matter of a state bird. The superintendent thought Kansas ought to have one, just as there was a state flower. He asked Thornton to see about it. Thornton devised a plan to let the school children of the state vote. He personally favored the western meadowlark, a species that had been first identified in 1805 by Meriwether Lewis on the Lewis and Clark expedition. Others favored the cardinal or the bob white. Thornton supplied all the schools with materials on the three birds and encouraged the children to cast intelligent votes. The western meadowlark won by about 7,000 votes, and two years later the legislature followed the students' lead. The western meadowlark is still the state bird of Kansas.

Alice had done some debating in high school and she relished it. She thought college might lead to a career as a lawyer. It was a goal she didn't keep long.

"I wanted to stand up in court and argue," she said. "But people told me if you were a woman lawyer, all they'd let you do was sit in a back office and dig up information for men lawyers. I pretty much lost interest in the law when they told me that."

She worked the whole four years she was in college and paid all her tuition and other expenses. Thornton helped her get a four-hour-a-day job in the State Capitol as an assistant to the secretary for the State Board of Education. A lot of it involved documents and reports on schools all over Kansas, and Alice found it pretty tedious going. But it helped pay the bills.

Even with her work she found time to be an honor-roll student and maintain a lively extra-curricular life. She was tapped for Pi Gamma Nu, the national social-science honorary. She was president of Alethean, a literary society. She made the all-state debate team, and she served as secretary-treasurer of the honorary forensic fraternity, Pi Kappa Delta. And she was a member of a social sorority, Zeta Tau Alpha.

If it sounds like a busy college life, it was.

"My economics teacher gave the class an assignment on Friday that we were supposed to bring in on Monday," she said. "It meant going to the library and checking out some books. The class met late on Friday and the library closed before I had a chance to go there. I worked Saturday at the State House so I couldn't go then. When I went to class Monday, I didn't have the assignment. The teacher said, 'Miss Wells, how much are you doing?' I told him the classes I was taking and that I was practicing for the musical 'Pinafore.' I was probably debating too, and I was working half a day in the office. He said, 'Well, if you were a genius you might be able to do all that, but since you're not, you'd better come down to earth and do what an ordinary person would do.' I was embarrassed to death and I was ready to quit debating, which was really what he was upset about. But one of my debate team members graded papers for this teacher and had a lot of influence with him. She talked to him and then she told me, 'I told Cocky (that was what we called him) that I had just dared Alice to quit debate. So you just go right on.' I did keep on debating and doing the other things I was doing."

When she was a senior she tried out for a part in the most ambitious play the Washburn Dramatic Club had ever attempted, "He Who Gets Slapped," by the Russian playwright Leonid Audreyev. "The drama club was sort of politically controlled, or at least we thought it was, and the group I belonged to didn't have anybody in it. But I decided to give it a try. I recited a poem I'd learned for public speaking and I made it. I had the role of Zinida, a woman lion tamer who was also described as 'the unmarried wife of Papa Briquet.' I really enjoyed learning the play and working on it. In fact I got so interested that I quit my job for a while and borrowed money so I could practice. I paid the money back the next fall after I started teaching."

Two reviews of the play were published in the Topeka papers. Charles Matthews, a professor representing the New York Theater Guild, wrote, "Alice Wells' Zinida was charmingly done." The other reviewer said, "She gave the female lion tamer's part a worthy interpretation. . . . Her voice was an outstanding feature of the part."

Alice got a different sort of response from Dr. Karl Menninger, the famous psychiatrist. He had founded the Menninger Clinic in Topeka, just two years earlier. He was to build the clinic into a world-renowned institution. And he himself would be hailed by the American Psychiatric Association as the nation's "greatest living psychiatrist." But in 1927 he and his wife had time to chaperone the Zeta Tau Alpha sorority parties.

"He chaperoned one about the time the play was put on," Alice said. "I was dancing with him and telling him about the play. He was real interested in the psychology of it. He told me he didn't think I had any conception of the feelings or emotions that the woman whose part I played would have had. It kind of took me aback."

As graduation neared in 1927, Alice had been applying for jobs. She had an impressive letter of reference from J. E. Edgerton, a supervisor at the State Department and an old friend of Thornton's. "I have known her since she was a little girl," Mr. Edgerton wrote. "She has been one of the most prominent students in the institution. She is extraordinarily well-poised and sensible. She meets the problems of life with courage and dignity and has great initiative and quick understanding . . . Frankly, I have never known any young person whom I consider more naturally endowed with all the qualifications for teaching."

It's hard to see how any school board could fail to hire such a person, but they all did, and Alice was getting real nervous about it. She graduated in early June and still no job was in hand. In the meantime she hung onto her part-time clerical job at the Capitol. Thornton had gone to Hays in January to join the English faculty at Ft. Hays Teachers College. When school ended in Topeka, Ada and the other children joined him. Alice moved into a dormitory at Washburn for the summer.

"I'd applied at all the larger schools in Kansas. I thought I was too smart to teach in a little bitty school. But I was beginning to think I wouldn't find a job. Then one day Daddy happened to walk across the campus at Hays with Mr. Hite, the superintendent from Dodge City, who was there for the summer. I had applied at Dodge earlier, but they didn't have an opening at that time. Mr. Hite asked Daddy if I had found a job. Daddy said I hadn't. Mr. Hite said an opening had developed, and he told Daddy to tell me to send in another application. I hastened to apply and I got the job. It was just a lucky break for me that Daddy and Mr. Hite happened to walk across the campus together at that time."

She got the job around the Fourth of July but she continued to work in Topeka up to the end of the summer. She took her vacation the two weeks before school was to start. She used her vacation time to move to Dodge and get ready to take charge of her first class.

A friend from work had put her in touch with Maude McComas, another teacher at Dodge, who was to become her best friend. The two of them rented a second-floor room in the home of Mr. and Mrs. Pendleton on First Avenue. They decided to eat at Mrs. Reynolds's boarding house a block or two away.

"About a dozen of us ate there. We sat around one big table and ate family style. The women were all teachers. The men mostly worked downtown. Porter and I had arrived in Dodge City within a week or two of each other. He came into the boarding house with some other fellows. He stood there with his hands in his pockets kind of eyeing all of us, and I kind of eyed him, and that's where it all began."

Porter after high school

Alice as a beginning teacher

CHAPTER 4

GETTING TO KNOW YOU

They got interested in each other pretty quickly.

"In the morning you made your own toast, and one morning he was making toast for me," Alice said. "As he handed me a piece, he looked at my hair and said, in a whisper so no one could hear, 'You're getting more puritanical-looking every day.' It was near the end of the week and the marcel wave was about gone, but I knew he was watching me just as I was watching him and that kindled the fire. A few nights later Porter called up after supper and asked me to go to the picture show if Oel Spellman could also get a date that late. He couldn't, and I went with both of them. As we were walking home, Porter said a real good show was coming up, and he asked me to go with him alone, and I did."

"She had been dating Wallace Emmons," Porter said. "He worked on the Dodge City weekly paper. Maybe she thought she would be stepping up in the world to go out with two men from the daily paper. Anyway, after that I managed to get dates with her by myself, and somehow I beat Wallace's time."

They both roomed on First Avenue. She lived three blocks farther out from town than he did. When Porter's mother sent him oranges or cakes or other tidbits, he would sometimes hide them in the crotches of the trees between his place and hers. When they walked back after the show, he would pick them out of the trees and they would eat them as they walked and talked.

"He liked walks and picnics and so did I," Alice said. "Some were at unconventional times and places. Once he was sick in bed several weeks with sinus trouble and hadn't been able to come to the boarding house for his meals. Then late one night he came by the door and asked me to go walking with him, saying that he felt better. It was a clear cold winter night and he showed me the stars and tried to teach me about the constellations." Once they passed a school playground. "We stopped and teeter-tottered for a while and I hoped none of my pupils saw us."

Alice found that just about any time she showed an interest in a subject, Porter seemed to know a good bit about it. They found they agreed on most things.

He had a daily news and sports broadcast on the Dodge radio station, KGNO, which belonged to the *Globe* and was in the *Globe* building. People around town got a kick out of his Southern accent as he read the news. "Everyone liked to hear Porter talk," Alice said. "One day a woman came into the office and asked to see the announcer. When they pointed to Porter, she was real surprised to see such a young man. She said 'Why he sounds like an old man with mush in his mouth.' Porter tried to teach me to speak 'correctly,' his Southern way, so I could sing dialect. But I never learned."

Neither had had a serious romance before. Many years later, when their granddaughter Anne Harvey was a little girl with a little girl's normal curiosity, she posed a question to Alice. Porter relayed the conversation:

"She asked, 'Grandma, did Grandpa have a skinny leg when you married him?' Alice answered yes and Anne asked, 'Then why did you marry him?' I think I know one answer. It was another lucky break for me. Alice knew a girl in college, and liked her very much, who had a leg about like mine. So Alice wasn't as turned off by a skinny leg as she would have been otherwise."

The girl, Mildred Boggs, had been Alice's best friend at Washburn. She had also had polio. She was in the same sorority as Alice and was on the debate team. Some time after Porter and Alice married, he wanted to write Mildred and thank her.

"I wouldn't let him," Alice said. "I wanted him to know that he had made it on his own."

Porter was the main local reporter for the *Globe.* To advertise the county fair, the paper once put out a 24-page issue, compared to their standard eight pages. There were 40 local stories in it and he wrote 34 of them. He thought a lot of the stories were what he called "hokum," not qualifying as real news. But he was proud of the oversized edition.

In a letter in 1928, he told about an unusually busy week in the news department: "The telegraph printers, over which we get our AP news, have started at 6:00 every morning instead of 8:00, so as to have time to handle all the reams and reams that have been sent out on the [national political] convention. Somebody had to be here at 6:00 every morning to start the machines and edit the copy for the linotype operators to set, and Turrentine [another newsman] and I have taken it turn about. It's been a strenuous week in local news, too, with the taxpayers' league meeting to protest against too much county expense, the county commissioners of western Kansas meeting here to cuss out the state highway commission, a local man being named socialist nominee for governor, the missing bank teller's body being found near Liberal, another storm playing the deuce with the wheat, the 'beautiful, nineteen-year-old former show girl' being acquitted in her murder trial at Liberal, Mrs. Chalk Beeson dying after an hour's illness, and the Dodge City 'bootlegger king' getting caught, sentenced to prison and released on an appeal bond."

Dodge City was on a main line of the Santa Fe Railroad. Trains were the preferred mode of long-distance travel in those days, so well-known people often came through town. Sometimes they would emerge for the public while the train was stopped. Porter met two trains carrying three movie stars within about a week. Lon Chaney came through first, and then action hero Douglas Fairbanks and his wife, Mary Pickford. Porter was especially fascinated by Lon Chaney, the horror-movie champion of silent films.

"Without makeup he looks exactly as he does when he appears on the screen," he wrote. "I suppose I should have had a hot interview for the

Alice decided at this 1928 picnic that Porter was the man she wanted to marry.

Globe, but I didn't try. Although celebrities don't impress me much, I have had an unusual feeling toward Lon Chaney for several years, and I doubt if I could have carried on an intelligent conversation with him."

Alice taught in the junior high her first year. In the spring a chance developed for her to move to the high school. An English teacher who also taught a journalism class was leaving, and Alice was asked to take her place. Teaching journalism would mean supervising the school paper, a prospect that appealed to her but also made her nervous. She decided to spend the summer of 1928 with her parents at Hays so she could take two journalism courses at Ft. Hays College.

Before leaving for Hays, she and Porter went on a picnic with Maude McComas and the man Maude was to marry, Chet Bonar. It turned out to be something of a magical day. Alice said later that it was on that picnic that she decided Porter was the man she wanted to marry.

They each referred to it in the first letters they exchanged after Alice went to Hays.

"My climbing muscles were the sorest things about me Monday," Porter wrote. "But I rather enjoyed being sore. Every time I'd feel a twinge it would remind me of us going up in the tree, and for some reason I got a tremendous kick out of that. If I had my choice of how to spend day after tomorrow, with a dozen Aladdin's genii at my command, I can't think of any way I'd rather spend it than the way I did the last one. That valley south of Ford County stands out in my mind almost as an enchanted spot."

Alice wrote, "I was happier with you that day than I have ever been in all my life, and I had been very happy. I've grown to depend on you for so much that it is going to seem very very strange without you."

They posed for a snapshot on that picnic, standing in front of a rock bluff, Alice wearing a pink jodhpur and jacket that her mother made for her. They liked the picture so well that they had it enlarged and tinted (that was before the days of color photos). They kept it on the wall of their bedroom throughout their married life.

Mail was delivered twice a day back then, and Porter and Alice wrote a lot of letters while he was in Dodge and she was in Hays. Long distance telephone calls were almost unheard of, and then only in real emergencies. They exchanged thoughts on a lot of subjects in their letters.

"I hope you'll excuse this copy paper," Porter wrote. "I came down to the office so I could use the typewriter. My handwriting is not only practically illegible, but it requires such conscious effort that it hampers the free flow of my thoughts, if any."

"The fact that you wrote on copy paper," Alice replied, "added a glamour and romance that not many girls can ever experience. You see, the author of such a letter must be a writer."

Porter's next letter was in longhand, on stationery, and he began, "I'm sorry I can't write this on some glamorous and romantic copy paper, but it's raining pitchforks outside so I think I'll stay here (in my room) this evening."

Porter: "I had my first look at a wheat harvest yesterday. I rode a combine once around a 60-acre field and sure was impressed with the way it operates. To stand up on top, where you can see the blades cutting the standing grain on your left, and the threshed wheat pouring into the bin in front of your nose, seems to me like witnessing just about the last word in mechanical efficiency."

Alice: "Last night I watched some of the fireworks around in the sky but didn't enjoy it particularly. I guess I've acquired a horror of any combination of powder and matches because of the great number of useless accidents."

Porter: "I'm sorry you don't like fireworks. I always get a thrill out of them—not from a big display put on by professionals, but from the kind that boys save up their money to buy and go out in the yard after supper to shoot."

Alice sent him an article she wrote for her journalism class and asked him to critique it. He made several suggestions, but added, "Forgive me, Alice, for saying these things. It's hard for me to find fault with anything you do, but I thought you might get some suggestions that would be useful to you."

Porter: "Sherwood Anderson (the playwright) is right. A man who writes is somewhat set apart from the ordinary run of people. Lots of times I feel resentful that this should be so. I hate to be any different from other people. What Anderson says about a country paper not giving news, but merely 'the small events of a small town people's lives,' is the key to the trouble Turrentine is having with the *Globe*. He is trying to make it a metropolitan paper, but the people here still want their 'small events' played up big and there simply isn't room for both in an eight-page paper."

Alice: "I've always wanted to be set apart, to be able to do even one small task better than someone else. I've studied a little music—piano, violin and voice. I've painted a few pictures, done a little interpretative reading and debating, but in not one of these have I deserved the stamp of more than 'mediocre.' You have set yourself apart in the very act of being like other folks, but in the 'likeness' you have been better without becoming eccentric. In your writings you distinguish yourself by saying the same things perhaps that others say, but you say them better."

Alice: "My reporting class is supposed to be furnishing all the copy [for the school paper] and the editing class functions as copy readers, both editing and writing the headlines. We are keeping examples of heads and leads clipped from daily papers. My folks will hardly let me look at a paper here until all of them have read it because when I get through cutting all I want from it, there's little left except the end lines and the weather."

Toward the end of the summer, Alice and some girl friends took a trip to Creede, Colorado, in the Rocky Mountains. Porter recalled that his father had spoken about being in Creede as a teenager on his own venture out west. "It was a mining town about 1890, and it seems to me that he worked there for quite a while."

Dodge City was getting a new school superintendent, and Porter met him before Alice did. "I sat by Mr. Richards at a breakfast last week and found him to be a very likeable man and enjoyable talker," he wrote. "He did one thing for which I thank him: He put into words the chief reason why I like this part of the country better than farther east, which I had sensed for many months but had been unable to quite define, even to myself. He compared this section with eastern Kansas, but I have found the same difference between here and back home. He said, 'I like western Kansas because it is more unconventional. If you set out to do anything in east Kansas, you find yourself with a mass of traditions hard to get around. This country is newer and traditions have not yet had time to become established.'"

In their letters that summer, they spoke often about the feelings they had developed for one another, and about wishing they were together. But they were also cautious. Alice signed her first letter, "Sincerely yours," and others "Yours, dear," "Yours" or simply "Alice." He signed his "Yours," "Goodnight," and most often simply "Porter." But towards the end of summer, Alice included with her letter a sheet of stationery folded over once and fastened with a sticker like those that were used to decorate Christmas packages. Inside the page was blank except for the words, "I love you, Porter," and signed, "Alice."

They managed to get together a couple of times that summer in Great Bend, where Alice's Aunt Mable lived. Porter used the occasions to go over some of her work for the journalism classes.

"Just before we were to meet in Great Bend the last time," Alice recalled later, "I got a letter from Maude who said our landlady had seen Porter and Chet with some other girls. I wrote him that I had changed my plans and I wouldn't be there." But after reflecting on it, she changed her mind. "I knew I had no right to be jealous, so I wired him, 'Meet me as planned.' And he did."

Porter referred to the dates in a letter. "I can't say that I've really enjoyed a single date I've had this summer. I'll see a girl and talk to her and imagine that I'd like to have a date with her, but I'm always disappointed. I haven't had but a half a dozen, and no two with the same girl. Since I've known you, I haven't been able to take any interest in any other girl. I'm coming more and more to believe that I never will be able to."

The high school faculty at Dodge put on a play each fall. The one that year was *The Goose Hangs High*, and Alice had the romantic lead. The script called for the coach in the play to kiss her.

"I told Porter I didn't feel good about it. He never told me, but one of the other teachers did, that Porter went to the principal to see if they couldn't leave out the kissing. They didn't make any change in the script, and Porter never came to see the play.

"A couple of nights later, on Thanksgiving, Porter asked me if I would marry him when he had saved up a thousand dollars. I told him nothing else in the world would make me so happy."

He knew her feelings for him before he popped the question, but he was still relieved at her answer. "She has always liked security, not adventure," he said later. "At that time in Kansas they didn't let married women teach school. Giving up a job to marry a $30-a-week reporter must have looked like a bad risk, but she agreed to take it."

Alice went home to Hays for Christmas and broke the news by opening the package containing her engagement ring. "Mother smiled and Dad swallowed," she wrote to Porter "and Kenneth broke the silence by blowing a loud blast on his new horn. I'm wearing the ring now and it sparkles and flashes in the light."

Porter wrote her on Christmas Eve after walking downtown among the crowds of people. "There's no other time of year at which I feel so strongly that the world is wonderful, that the general run of people are darn nice folks."

Accumulating the thousand dollars became a much easier goal the next April when Porter got a letter from his father.

"Soon after you were born," Evan wrote, "a little money was put in your name and from time to time more was added. When you were old enough to sell vegetables, that money was added to your fund. As the amount got larger I invested it to where it could earn and increase. A few years ago the total reached $500, which I loaned to a farmer. He has now paid it back and I think I should be relieved of further responsibility (which I have enjoyed very much). So I am sending you herewith a check for $500 and hope it will arrive on your birthday, as I want you to accept my part in accumulating this money as a birthday present. The interest has now been deposited to your account at the National City Bank of Rome. That account now stands at about $200, which you can check out whenever you choose."

The unexpected $700 was equal to slightly more than four months' salary for the prospective groom, who was earning $173 a month or $40 a week. By then he was the telegraph editor of the *Globe*, editing the Associated Press wire and writing the headlines as well as still reporting local news.

They set the wedding for early August. When her school let out in May, Alice went back to Hays to spend the summer at her parents' home. It relieved her of the expense of living on her own. And it let her spend a lot of time working on her wardrobe, linens and furnishings.

They wrote about twice a week. "I had forgotten what a wonderful thing it is to get a letter from you, until I saw it lying on the stairstep as I came home," Porter said after receiving the first one.

"I've never realized," Alice wrote, "how much planning it's going to take to manage even a very simple little wedding."

She thanked Porter for trying to find a job in Dodge for Victor. "I think he needs to get away from home so that he will have to depend on himself a little more. Because of his sickness when a child, he has always been very protected and shielded. I think now he needs some roughness and hard knocks to bring out the best there is in him, even though it will be pretty tough on him at first."

They had arranged to rent a small house still farther out First Avenue from where they had roomed. Porter got to worrying about the fact that it didn't have a front porch. "When it's so hot that a person can't stay in the house, where are we going to stay? Everybody on this street sits on their porches these hot nights.

Porter timed the walk between the Globe and their future home and found it took about 15 minutes each way. "I think I can take 45 minutes off at noon all right, although I don't take but about 15 now." He was trying to find someone to rent the garage that went with the house, since they wouldn't have a car. "Abie Bernstein fizzled out as a garage prospect," he wrote. "Says the wreck he's driving isn't worth protecting, so he's going to park it in the yard. I've got a line on another fellow and am hoping to get $3.50 a month."

Alice made a trip to Topeka during the summer, and one of her friends gathered several of the girls she had known in college. "We sat around and talked about old times and the future," she said in a letter to Porter. "Each one wanted to know all about you and not one hesitated to tell me how 'shocked' she was to hear that I was going to be married. Everyone thought I was cut out for an old maid."

They set August 1, a Thursday, as their wedding day, and Alice's parents' home as the place. Porter had arranged to take two weeks off. His parents had talked about coming to Kansas, but they decided it would be better for Porter and Alice to come to Georgia so they could have a leisurely visit, since they and Alice hadn't met.

Porter had asked Harry Powers to be his best man, and Harry had said he would. But then Harry decided to get married himself, and at just about the same time. A disappointed Porter asked Don Buckley to be best man. Don roomed at the same place Porter did.

Porter planned to work the day of the wedding. He told Alice he figured he could leave Dodge about 4:00 and get to Hays in time for an evening ceremony at 8:00 or 8:30. Then they'd have dinner, change clothes and drive 70 miles to Kingsley in time to catch the train at 12:30 a.m.

Alice thought that might be pushing it, especially if there was car trouble or tire trouble. "I think if you could leave at noon or even 2:00 it might be better," she wrote. "Folks usually practice a wedding. For a small one like ours it might not be necessary, but it would just put me a little more at ease in knowing where to go and what to do."

As it turned out, Alice's caution was well-founded. Porter rode to Hays with Chet, and the car kept losing water. Kansas was in the grip of a heat wave, with temperatures going up to 110 and 115. They had to stop at farm houses all along the way and put more water in. The best man and some other fellows drove up in another car. They tried to talk Porter into going on ahead with them, since he was the one getting married, but Porter felt like he needed to stay with Chet. So the two of them were the last to arrive.

"He was pretty late getting there and I took a lot of teasing about it," Alice said.

It was a simple wedding. Only the immediate family and a handful of friends were there. Maude Bonar was Alice's maid of honor. Alice's sister Helen was flower girl. Alice carried a bouquet of red roses that Porter brought from Dodge. She had picked sweet peas from a neighbor's yard to use for decorations, and their fragrance filled the room. The minister was an old family friend who came from out-of-town. He used a text that Porter and Alice had picked out. In Porter's words, it "doesn't have anything about anybody obeying anybody else. I never did like the sound of that."

After the wedding, everybody ate fried chicken and lemon meringue pie that Ada had cooked. Chet and Maude drove Porter and Alice to Kingsley to catch the train. They made it in time, but Porter had been under such a strain—a day at work, car trouble on the long drive to Hays in hundred-degree heat, the wedding itself, and worry about getting to the train on time—that he threw up outside the station.

They had to change trains the next morning in Kansas City. They had only a few minutes to get from one to the other. Because they had a lot of luggage, Porter hired a red cap. The man struggled with the bags as they hurried to reach the train. When they got there the red cap was really panting. Porter gave him what he thought was a generous tip. The man looked at the coin and threw it back at Porter's feet. "If you're that hard up," he said, "you need it worse than I do."

Porter's family in Rome took quickly to Alice, and she to them. Coley was twenty-one then, while Ellen and Frances were still in their teens. They seemed to Alice like Southern aristocracy, and she felt proud to be connected. Evan and Fanny and other relatives held several dinners to introduce them to people. The whole family went to Mentone, Alabama, about forty miles away on Lookout Mountain, and stayed in the cabin that Evan had recently built on the Little River.

It had a large room, a kitchen and a small bedroom, plus a large porch. Porter and Alice stayed in the bedroom. It was equipped with two sets of bunk beds. "We had planned to sleep in separate beds," Alice said, "but we didn't."

On their way back to Dodge, they stopped in Kansas City to pick out a piano. It was their wedding gift from Porter's father.

"We went around from store to store and tried out a lot of pianos until we found one that pleased us," Alice said. "It was an Elburn upright, the one we still have in the living room. Porter seemed to like to hear me sing."

CHAPTER 5

DIAPERS AND DUST STORMS

In mid-August 1929, the newlyweds set up housekeeping in the little one-bedroom home at 1708 First Avenue. That was on the same street as both of their rooming houses and their boarding house, but a few blocks farther out from town. There was a kitchen with a breakfast nook at one end, and a basement where they sometimes slept and ate in the summer because it was cooler. Porter kept a typewriter on an apple crate in the basement. He strung wires down there so Alice could hang clothes to dry inside in bad weather.

Alice had accumulated a few pieces of furniture before they were married and they bought some more with the money that each had saved up. They didn't have a car. Porter walked the mile or so to the *Globe* office downtown. He also walked home each day for lunch. Alice became a full-time homemaker, a role she had never known before.

They had been married not quite three months when the stock market crash started the country's economy sliding downhill into the Great Depression. Of course, nobody knew then just how bad it was going to get, or that it was going to last more than 10 years. Porter and Alice didn't feel any effect for a while, and they might not have noticed in any case. They were too busy enjoying each other.

Porter had to stay in Dodge and work when Alice went to Hays to have Thanksgiving with her parents. It was their first time apart since the wedding, and they wrote to each other over the holiday.

"I never hated to leave any place as much in my life as I hated to leave our little home and you yesterday," Alice said in a letter to Porter on Thanksgiving day. "Grandma and Grandpa Daniels were here today. When Dad started to serve the turkey, he turned to Grandpa and said he was trying to get acquainted with his son-in-law as Grandpa had done with him, but that you couldn't be here and that was the one thing that kept the day from being complete."

Before leaving Dodge she had left a note telling Porter how much she hated to go without him. "Alice," he wrote, "I pretty near cried when I found the note you left under my pillow." He said they had gotten the *Globe* to press shortly after noon on Thanksgiving. "Had ten pages and a pretty good paper for a holiday. We had to work on it a couple of hours last night." He was hoping to find somebody going to Hays over the weekend so he could catch a ride.

Their house was directly across the street from the high school where Alice had taught the previous year. Just down the street from the school was St. Francis Hospital. By Christmas Alice knew she was pregnant, and she and Porter walked to the hospital over New Year's to check it out.

Porter and Alice's first house, at 1708 First Avenue, Dodge City

"The people at the hospital showed us the delivery room and the babies," Alice said. "They told us how happy they were that we'd be coming there. Of course, we were real excited. We lived close enough to the hospital that when the windows were open in the summer we could hear the women hollering during childbirth, but I don't remember being bothered by the thought."

They still went to movies occasionally, walking down the same street they had walked on during their first dates. Porter's work as a reporter took him to the Courthouse and other places downtown. As he passed a theater he would sometimes stick his head in briefly to see if the film seemed like something he and Alice would like.

They had a baby boy on August 22, 1930, and named him Samuel Wells Harvey. Porter telegraphed his parents in Rome that he "looks like a little pink worm." The *Globe*'s publisher, Jesse Denious, ran into Porter in the hospital. When he found out about the new baby, he had the *Globe* give him a check for $100. That was equal to two and a half weeks pay.

"Mr. and Mrs. Denious were very nice people to work for," Alice said. "They had Porter over to their house for dinner the Christmas after we got engaged, when I was home at Hays. Mrs. Denious had given her husband a watch for Christmas and I had given Porter a watch."

Sam's arrival changed the household routine, especially for Alice. Evenings at the movies became fewer and they spent more time listening to their Philco radio, a living room centerpiece made in the shape of a Gothic cathedral window. They especially liked "Amos and Andy." It came on at 10:00 at night, about the time when Sam had his last feeding.

Alice sometimes called her new son Sammy because Sam "sounded kind of bold for a little bitty baby." He was 10 and a half months old when she carried him to Hays for a visit. "I've just been in to cover Sammy," she wrote to Porter. "He was lying there so sweet. I wanted to kiss him for you and me. He went to town with Mama and me this afternoon and seemed to enjoy his pushcart ride . . . I got two $1 house dresses that are very slenderizing and look nice. I hope you like them."

Porter wrote her a letter that was all one long paragraph but covered a lot of topics—when he expected to reach Hays over the weekend, what he had for breakfast with a couple who had him over, how his sore toe was coming along, what he did the previous evening with some men from the *Globe*, how he won a drawing at a meeting of his Kiwanis Club, cutting the grass at home and eating supper with his friend Don. But without them, he said, "This house sure does seem empty and cold and lonesome."

After a while they started looking for a bigger house, one with more than a single bedroom. They found a two-bedroom they liked and could afford at 1109 Fifth Avenue. It was about seven blocks away, and you had to go down a low hill and back up another to get there. When they moved, Porter carried a lot of their belongings in repeated trips with a child's red wagon. They hired a moving truck for the heavy things.

They called it "the gray house" because of its color, and they were to live there about five years. While it was larger than the one they moved out of, it was also a good bit older, so the rent was less. Alice thinks they paid $15 or $20 a month. "Most of my memories of Dodge are of things that took place while we lived in the gray house," she said.

As the Depression deepened, Porter and other people at the *Globe* sometimes found their hours and their pay reduced. "I got a few pay cuts as things got worse and worse," he said later, "but Alice is a great money manager and she coped with the situation and we got along fine."

"We tried not to spend more than we made," Alice said. "I don't think we ever had to borrow. Porter was never out of a job, unlike a lot of other people. We were never hungry. But our wants were simple. I had a pressure cooker, and I used it to can fruits and vegetables. Our pay went down, but some food prices went down, too."

With fewer hours at work, Porter spent more time in the vegetable garden he planted in back of the house on Fifth Avenue. People who lived there before them had kept a horse—Alice thinks it was a race horse—in the back yard. So the yard was well fertilized, and the soil was good to start with. Vegetables grew well. Just as Porter had sold vegetables in downtown Rome when he was a boy, he tried to supplement his income by selling vegetables in downtown Dodge City. "He would go around to the stores carrying bundles of vegetables and trying to peddle them for 10 cents here and 20 cents there," Alice said. "One of the vegetables he grew was something called Swiss chard. It was a little like spinach. Nobody much liked it but sometimes he could sell some. I don't know that we liked it much ourselves, but we ate it."

In August 1932, Alice took Sam for a visit to see some friends in Hutchinson, Kansas, Ed and Eloise Swearer, who had two children. "I would enjoy it so much more if I didn't know my old Popo was home working hard," she told Porter in a letter. "I feel selfish having a vacation by myself and with Sammy with me, too." Porter wrote that he was scheduled to be the speaker at the next Kiwanis meeting. He was to talk on "Where the Newspaper Comes From and Why."

"I am getting in such demand as an entertainer that I have to turn down offers," he wrote. "Tonight Morris Cannon asked me if I couldn't take a blackface part in the Little Theater's summer festival Friday night. I told him to try Bill Biggers, who I imagine will jump at the chance." In another letter he said he and a friend had tried to get up a poker game "but we got started late and couldn't get enough fellows together. He and I and his wife played three-handed bridge for a while." Then he and the friend went to another home "and they were all drinking Tom and Jerrys. I never knew what a Tom and Jerry was before. It's not much different from an egg nog but it has nutmeg and a few more things like that for flavoring. I would like it pretty well if it weren't for the whisky in it. Maybe the whisky helped my cold . . . I ate the scrapple [cornmeal and ground meat], half of it yesterday morning and half of it this morning. It was fine. Randle [the milkman] hasn't brought any milk since you left. Or if he has, somebody had beat me to it. There was some cream left in the icebox."

The icebox pre-dated the electric refrigerator. It was kept cool by blocks of ice that they bought from a delivery man who came through every day. Alice had a card to put in the front window telling if she needed ice and how much—25 pounds, 50 pounds, etc. The iceman would cut the right amount off the large blocks he carried and bring it into the house with a pair of big tongs. Their milk was placed on the doorstep early each day, before breakfast. "Sometimes in the winter the milk would freeze," Alice said. "It would expand and the frozen cream might stand an inch or two out of the neck of the bottle."

In the fall of 1932, Alice became pregnant again. This time she had some problems, and the doctor was afraid she might lose the baby. He told her to stay in bed for several weeks. They arranged for Alberta Davis to stay with her during the day.

"Porter had to leave for work before Alberta came," Alice said. "That's when Sam learned a lot of the poems in the book 'When We Were Very Young.' He would sit by me and 'read' them to me while we were waiting for Alberta." (Sam's memory of this is somewhat different. He thinks these sessions must have taken place later, when he was older. But Alice is sure it was while she was pregnant with Mary.) The book of poems was known simply as "the little red book." When the back gave out from overuse and it had to be rebound, it became "the little black book."

Mary Margaret Harvey was born July 26, 1933, also in St. Francis Hospital, and also delivered by Dr. Mellencamp, who delivered Sam.

In late September, Alice took the children to Hays for a visit. "We weighed Mary—11-1/2 pounds, according to these scales," she said in a letter to Porter. "I want to measure her tomorrow when she is exactly two months old. She acts older than that. It doesn't seem like she was ever a tiny baby at all. She sure is sweet. We gave her a tub bath this morning in a large pan. She was rather surprised at first, but liked it after a minute. Sam was so happy at seeing her in it that he hardly knew what to do. He misses you and has asked half a dozen times, 'When does Friday come?' and 'Why couldn't Daddy go to work up here?' I read him some stories tonight about monkeys, maple sugar and a little boy who got lost and then was found again. Sam cried as soon as he got lost, but he seemed to forget it as soon as the story was finished."

While Alice was in Hays her brother Kenneth was in Dodge. He stayed in their house a while and worked as a night bellhop in a hotel. "I think you all better come on home," Porter wrote. "Kenneth and I are almost out of dishes. In fact, we are out of cream pitchers and had to wash one this morning. Alberta got our lunch today and I got supper last night." Porter had been to the county fair, "and I pulled a fast one on the Presbyterian ladies. Their concession is next to Slats Walker's beer stand. While I was eating supper at the Presbyterian place I got a glass of beer, one of those glass mugs, and took it to the counter to drink with my supper. I don't think any of the good ladies noticed it, or anybody else, much to my disappointment."

Porter and Alice owned a car by this time, a used Willys-Knight. Porter had driven Alice and the children to Hays, and on the way back to

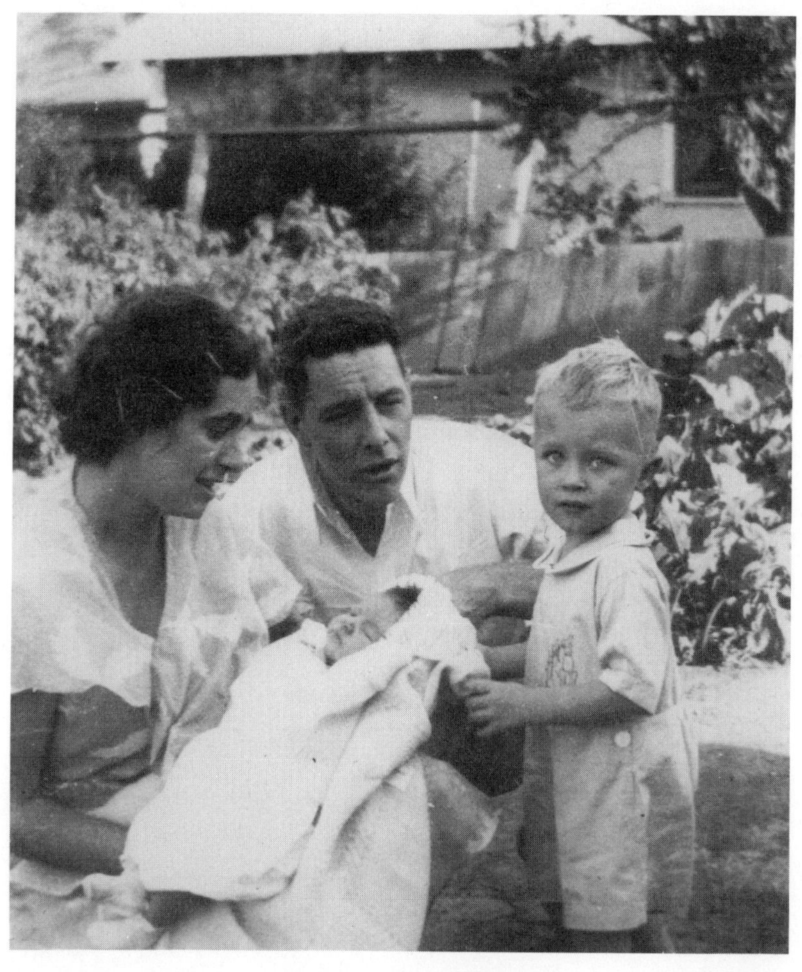

Holding Mary with Sam.

Dodge he and Kenneth "ran into a dust storm, the worst one I was ever out on the road in." It was a forerunner of dust storms that were to worsen as a drought settled over Kansas and nearby states, adding to the economic problems caused by the national Depression.

On another visit to Hays in the spring of 1934, Alice alluded to her two brothers' difficulty finding work: "Porter, you've no idea how thankful I've been that we've had a good job all this time. I think this is telling on all their dispositions. I hope I'll be a little sweeter from now on." Porter wrote her about the same time, "I haven't seen Kenneth since he wrote you this afternoon, so I don't know any more about his job than is in his letter. He is very happy to have it. I'm afraid it may not last. The wheat is getting worse every day, and things are bound to get pretty bad here before long."

When Mary was a year or so old, she developed a severe case of eczema, an itchy rash caused by allergies. The doctor gave her allergy tests to find out what was causing the problem. "I had to hold her down while the doctor was putting the shots in her back," Alice said. It turned out Mary was allergic to many things that are very basic for babies, including milk, eggs, wheat, chocolate, wool, feathers, soap, and a lot more. Being unable to drink cow's milk was especially worrisome. "We went out into the country to buy goat's milk from somebody, but we found out she was allergic to that, too," Alice said. "I bought thick separated cream and gave it to her, thinking it might be different from whole milk. It was thick and she ate it just like you eat butter. I wrote to different companies to see what the ingredients were in crackers and other products." Alice made mittens for Mary to wear at night so she wouldn't scratch herself. The condition hung on for several years before she finally outgrew it.

Porter and Alice thought four children would be just about right. They hoped it would be two boys and two girls. So they were happy when Alice became pregnant for the third time in the summer of 1934. This time she would deliver in the new hospital in town, the one generally referred to simply as "the Protestant hospital" to distinguish it from St. Francis where Sam and Mary were born. It was only about a two-block walk from the house.

But this delivery, on April 17, 1935, didn't go well. Alice, at full term in her pregnancy, woke up during the night, bleeding profusely. They had already arranged for a woman who lived in the same block to stay with Sam and Mary during the birth, so they called her. Porter carried Alice to the hospital in the car. Dr. Mellencamp found that the placenta had started emerging early, before any labor had taken place, a phenomenon known as placenta previa.

"After he examined me," Alice said, "I heard him say to one of the nurses, 'Call Dr. Klein. I don't want to be alone.' That's when I got really scared." The doctors hoped she would still be able to have a normal delivery. She went into labor and they let her continue. They listened periodically to the baby's heartbeat—and then suddenly they didn't hear it anymore. They decided they had to move quickly. They used forceps to deliver the baby, a nine-pound boy. But the ordeal wasn't over. Porter was in the delivery room the whole time, and he had never been so scared in his life. "Right after the birth Alice was lying there motionless," he said later. "She was white as a sheet, looking like she was dead. But the two doctors worked on Alice, and before long she began to show signs of life. I could tell from their talk that they thought she was going to make it, and that was the best feeling I ever had. They had been so busy tending to Alice that they hadn't been paying any attention to the baby. But our doctor's partner went over to where they had laid him. He examined him and said something like, 'Hey, maybe we can save the baby, too.' Pretty soon he was doing all right, and not long after that, so was Alice."

As they were leaving the delivery room, Porter leaned over and kissed Alice and whispered to her, "We're not going to have any more babies."

They named the baby Joseph Glenn, and called him Joe. One of Mary's first recollections is walking along a dusty road with Porter and Sam after being to the hospital to visit Alice and the baby. She remembers their coming home from the hospital and Alice being carried up the steps into the house on a chair. A few months later, Alice went back into the hospital for surgery to correct damage that had been done during the emergency delivery.

Joe's birth wasn't the only dramatic event the family went through just then. Three days before he was born, western Kansas and parts of three other states were hit by what has been known ever since as the "Black Blizzard."

Dust storms had been getting more frequent and more severe for some time, as a drought that began in 1931 continued to hang on. Farmers had long since plowed up most of the prairie grass that held the soil in place. One thing Porter noticed when he first went to Kansas was how the wind never seemed to let up. And when the wind really blew, there wasn't much to keep it from picking up the powdery earth and carrying it along. Dust storms came on an average of once every five days in what was called "the dirty thirties." Alice tried to keep the dust swept off her porches, and she stuffed rags under the doors and around the windows to try to keep it out. Some always got in anyway. "You could write your name in the dust on anything in the house," Alice said. But nothing prepared them for the great dust storm of April 14, 1937—Palm Sunday.

"We were having a beautiful spring day," Alice recalled. "The skies were blue, and it was the first time in a while that people could really take a deep breath and enjoy the air, because we'd had several dust storms just before that. I was standing on our front porch looking out over the town when all of a sudden these big black clouds came rolling along in this lovely blue sky. Almost before I could get into the house and close the door, it darkened everything just like it was night." People on the highways stopped their cars, unable to see even with their lights on. People on foot had to feel their way. Farmers fell to their hands and knees and crawled to their houses. The storm, thousands of feet high and extending as far across the prairie as you could see, came boiling out of Colorado in advance of a cold front, traveling at forty mph. The pall of dust lasted 10 to 15 minutes. "After it passed through and the first rain came," Alice said, "Porter and I stood out back of the house looking up at the sky. Rain started falling and after all that dirt it seemed just wonderful. But the raindrops had picked up so much dirt on the way down that they were like drops of mud. When a drop hit the side of the house, it would make a muddy place the size of a quarter."

The drought spelled disaster for wheat farmers and added to the economic misery of Kansas, where wheat was king. The *Daily Globe* found itself sometimes having to accept clothes and other goods from merchants who had no money to pay for their advertising. Employees would be asked to take some of their pay in merchandise, if they could find something in the accumulation that they could use. Porter got some clothes that way.

After about five years on Fifth Avenue, Porter and Alice moved to a newer house of Fourth Avenue. There was a city park in the next block. The house was a little closer to town and a little closer to the school where Sam had started kindergarten. Distance mattered because the family no longer had a car. A man with no insurance ran into the Willys-Knight, and Porter sold it for salvage for $10. The family wouldn't get another car for about 11 years.

Mr. and Mrs. Rubenstein lived next door and their son Irwin was Sam's best friend, although he was a little younger. The boys already knew each other. Irwin's grandparents, who had migrated from Russia, lived just down the street from the house the Harveys had moved out of. One of the most traumatic events of Alice's life occurred when she invited Mr. and Mrs. Rubenstein to go with her to a Christmas program at the school that Sam was in.

"We walked in and people around me started pointing, and I could hear them say, 'Jew! Jew!' It just killed me to think that my friends and people I knew would behave that way toward people I had invited to be my guests."

Many years later in Guntersville, Sam mentioned Irwin's name and a friend of Porter's asked who Irwin was. Porter replied, "Oh, he was a little Jewish friend of Sam's back in Kansas." It was only then that Sam learned that Irwin was Jewish.

Irwin, Sam, and some other boys were playing in Sam's basement one day when they noticed a box of matches by the furnace. One boy got the idea of setting fire to some brush in the back yard to see what would happen. What happened was that the fire department had to come put the fire out. Porter wrote a small item about it in the *Globe* and told which boy's house it happened at. It was the first time Sam made the newspaper, except for when he was born.

Some of Porter's friends decided one day to bestow a little of Dodge City's reputation on him. The town had gotten famous in the 1870s when the Santa Fe Railroad ended there. Cattlemen from Texas drove huge herds to Dodge to be shipped to markets back East. Buffalo hunters made it their headquarters. At one time the wide-open town boasted 17 saloons. Hollywood kept Dodge famous through the countless movies and later through TV shows including the long-running "Gunsmoke" and "Wyatt Earp." Like a good many other states, Kansas kept the office of constable in existence long after constables had any duties to perform. Porter's buddies got up a write-in campaign and elected him the constable of Dodge City. He went along with the gag and had himself sworn in, and then he promptly resigned. He never arrested any desperadoes or shot it out in front of the Long Branch Saloon. But he gleefully posted a certificate of election above his desk at the *Advertiser-Gleam*, proclaiming that he truly had once been a lawman in the city known as "Queen of the Cowtowns."

For a while he tried his hand at writing fiction. How much of this was in hopes of supplementing his newspaper pay and how much to satisfy a creative urge can only be guessed at. He wrote down dozens and dozens of very brief plot outlines in a notebook he had started keeping at Harvard. And he turned out several complete short stories, some which he hoped to market under the pen name "Ben Rindom." They were adventure-type tales, longer on action and twists of plot than on developing insights into character. In early 1937, after failing to sell them to magazines, he sent two of his stories to a New York agent and writing critic, Thomas H. Uzzell. Mr. Uzzell would give what he called a "full criticism" of a work for $5 for the first 5,000 words, plus $1 for each additional thousand. One story was based on a Kansas weatherman who had become an expert on tornadoes and his encounter with a pack of bandits in the desert. The other told of a mercy killing after a young couple found that their baby was terribly and hopelessly retarded. Mr. Uzzell said the plot of the first was too implausible, while the subject matter of the second would likely make it unacceptable. "But on the strength of the evidence in the two I would say that you should certainly be able to place your work rather satisfactorily," he said. "Your troubles are editorial rather than literary, I would say . . . You write better than average copy. With a closer study of the markets, you should be able soon to straighten out your plots and connect with editors."

He had sold a couple of non-fiction articles earlier. In 1928 he ghost-wrote a piece for *Midwest Sportsman* about a proposal to establish game refuges every 25 miles through the plains country. In 1933 he sold an article to the *National Real Estate Journal* about unemployed men and their families building low-cost homes on suburban tracts with government credit and a system of cooperative labor.

When Alice and the children were visiting in Hays in 1935, he wrote, "I have fixed up my typewriter desk fine, with a shelf through the middle and a hickey like a bread board to pull out and set copy on. I was down here most all day Sunday, fixing it and working on my story, which I started changing in a few places and ended up by changing in a lot of places. I think *Esquire* will grab at it now." It isn't known what story he referred to, but *Esquire* never did grab at it.

In 1974, for Porter's 71st birthday, Alice wrote down some of the things she remembered about life with him in Dodge City.

> "Porter loved Christmases and children too. Once he took Sam and about eight of his little four-year-old friends to the Santa Claus parade. He taught Sam and Joe to box, putting two or three of his fingers into the small gloves. Once he took a lot of kidding from his friends downtown when he had to admit that his black eye was the result of a boxing match he lost [Author's note: well, not really] to five-year-old Sam.
>
> "During the Depression, stores quit delivering groceries free, so Porter would call me each afternoon before he started home and ask what I needed from the store. Sometimes I would walk to meet him, pushing the baby buggy with Mary and or Joe in it. Sam was big enough to ride his tricycle.

> "Porter would always do anything for me. Like the time before Mary was born when I had to stay in bed several weeks. I weighed about 170 and Porter carried me from the cold bedroom where we slept back to the warm bedroom where I spent the day. Then back again at night.
>
> "We had lived in the old house on Fifth Avenue several years and had wondered just what was in an old barrel of rags that had been left in the basement. One day Porter decided to find out. He started pulling things out and a piece of money jingled as it hit the floor. You should have seen Porter dive into the barrel for more. He wound up with between $5 and $10 worth of coins someone had apparently put there for safekeeping and forgot. That's also where he found the old denim jacket he wore for years with the patched overalls.
>
> "We never lived in a house where Porter didn't put up a swing, either in a tree or on a porch.
>
> "Porter drove our car safely through about 15 miles of floodwater where we never saw the road. We were following a highway patrol car all the way. Porter enjoyed danger."

He had gone to Dodge and the *Daily Globe* in 1927. By the middle 1930s he was wondering if he ought to move on. He was still doing some reporting but had been promoted from reporter to news editor, which meant he was responsible for helping decide what wire service stories to carry about state and national events. He also edited wire copy and wrote headlines for it. But prospects seemed limited on a paper the size of the *Globe*. He had three children now, and he knew it was going to cost more to support them as time went on.

Also, the economic outlook in Kansas seemed mighty bleak. Besides the Depression, the long drought had people wondering if the climate might be changing permanently, and if that whole part of the country might be turning into a desert.

So Porter started writing letters to other papers—this time, back east rather than further west—to see if they needed a reporter or copy editor. "I would say to them, 'You probably don't need anybody now, but someday you will. Let me work without pay for a few days and see if you might be interested in me when you do need somebody.'"

He kept a copy of one letter he wrote in 1935, maybe as a guide to use in writing others. "Drought and dust storms continue to grow worse in this section after four years of crop failures, and I can see no future here for some time to come," he told the managing editor of the paper in Cape Girardeau, Missouri. "I'm not a brilliant newspaper man, but I can find news, I can write a fairly good story and I believe I know what it's all about. Approximately half my experience has been on the street and half on the desk. I am steady, honest and easy to get along with . . . The *Dodge City Globe* is rated one of the best smaller dailies in Kansas and I believe I have done my share toward making it that."

At one point Porter gave some thought to starting a daily paper of his own in Russell, one of the towns where Alice had lived as a girl. The town had two weeklies. Porter got some census figures and finally decided the town wasn't ready for a daily. Just how he thought he'd go about starting one isn't known.

Discouraged over his pay and his prospects, he went so far in 1936 as to apply to take a test for a civil service job. Apparently he never actually took it. A letter Alice wrote to her parents said some others who

Joe, Mary, and Sam in last winter in Dodge City, 1936-37.

had also applied were still waiting to see if they were eligible. But it was a striking measure of his worry about his economic situation that he thought at all about abandoning the line of work he loved so much.

In the summer of 1937 the family took a trip by train to Rome. While Alice and the children stayed with Porter's parents, Porter went to Birmingham to check on a job opening on the *Birmingham Post*, a part of the Scripps-Howard chain and a forerunner of the *Post-Herald*. They needed someone on the copy desk. Porter offered to work a while for no pay, but they hired him without taking him up on that offer. They needed him to start as soon as possible. So the children learned that instead of going back to Kansas, they were moving to Birmingham. Sam was almost seven, Mary was nearly four, and Joe was two.

"I couldn't face taking three children back to Kansas on a train and then bringing them back," Alice said. "We got a schoolteacher in Dodge who wasn't working that summer to take care of our things. Between letters and phone calls we decided what she would pack up and send on to us and what she would get rid of there in Dodge."

The *Globe* announced Porter's leaving in a story on the front page under the headline "Stepping Up," under his picture. "Porter has been one of the *Globe*'s old faithfuls ever since he joined the staff and has a large acquaintance in southwest Kansas," the *Globe* said. "From the South and proud of his Democratic lineage, Porter enjoyed the confidence and friendship of persons of every political faith because his stories were fair and always fit the facts. When the *Globe* station, KGNO, was opened, Porter became news broadcaster and the Dixie roll in his diction made this hour one of the most popular programs. When KGNO was reorganized two years ago, Porter inaugurated The Globe Sportscast, a popular sports feature. The Birmingham job is a promotion for Porter. It is one of the outstanding dailies in Alabama, and competition is so keen for places on the staff that applicants usually wait several months."

After 10 years in the West, Porter was back in the South. And Alice got ready to live somewhere other than Kansas for the first time in her life.

CHAPTER 6

BIRMINGHAM AND TRUSSVILLE

Porter started work on the *Birmingham Post* early in the summer of 1937 while Alice and the children were still in Rome. He found an efficiency apartment with a pull-down bed for the family to live in while they looked for a house. It was in a tall building in the Five Points section of Birmingham, a couple of miles from downtown. Coley drove Alice and the children to Birmingham. Alice hired a woman to stay with the children while she went house-hunting.

"I didn't know anything about Birmingham," Alice said. "I'd look at the ads in the paper and try to follow up on the ones that seemed promising. On one trip, when I told the streetcar conductor where I was going, he said, 'Oh, I don't think you'd like that neighborhood.' But he told me about a house I might like instead. He let me off at the right place and told me how to walk there. I liked the look of the house and the neighborhood. I called Porter, he came out, and we decided to take it."

The house was on Eighth Terrace South, on the side of a hill with three flights of concrete steps leading up to it. It was about four blocks from Minnie Holman School, where Sam would be in second grade. Alice went to a second-hand furniture store and bought a few things to use until their other belongings arrived from Kansas. They slept for a while on mattresses on the floor. When the furniture came, eight moving men lugged it up the steps, including a big box that held the piano. It took them a little over three hours, and they were paid, collectively, five dollars. Porter converted the box into a playhouse in the back yard.

A Kelly family lived right across the street. Jackie was almost as old as Sam, and Patsy was the same age as Mary. A little creek ran behind the Kellys' house and Jackie showed Sam how to catch tadpoles and crawfish.

Nature held a couple of nasty surprises.

"I kept noticing what looked like chigger bites all over Joe's little belly," Alice said. "I looked closer and found a little bug. I took him to a neighbor and she said 'You've got bedbugs.' Porter's first big job in the new house was getting rid of the bedbugs. He went to the eradicators, but they were pretty expensive so he decided to do it himself. They sold him the materials. He took the beds apart and put this stuff on everything, even the walls. It took a long time, but we didn't have any more problems."

There were woods all around Birmingham, and Alice found that an enjoyable change from Kansas. The family sometimes went into the woods for Sunday picnics. After one picnic Alice started itching and breaking out and came to find she had been sitting in poison ivy. She went to the doctor on the streetcar but stood up all the way because she was too sore to sit down.

She summarized their first few months in Birmingham in a letter to her brother Kenneth, who was working in the oil fields in Texas. She wrote it one Sunday in the fall of 1937 while Porter was at a meeting of the Newspaper Guild, a CIO union that represented the editorial employees at the *Post*.

> "Sam and his little chum Jackie Kelly are gathering nuts in the woods. Mary is in the doll house and Joe is asleep," she wrote. She went on to describe a typical day: "Alarm at 5:35 or 5:45 a.m. Breakfast at 6:30. Lunch at 11:00 a.m. for all but Porter, who eats a bowl of vegetable soup each weekday except Tuesday when he's home. Dinner at 5:30. Bed for three little Harveys at 7:00 after baths, treatment for the children's impetigo, Sam's foot exercises [for flat feet], teeth brushing, or perhaps a frantic last minute scramble to find something to take to school, or after you think all is quiet a cry from the bedroom, 'I need

Patsy,' 'I want a drink,' 'You forgot to rub my back,' 'Daddy, who's ahead now, Alabama or Georgia Tech?' By the time we've told them a dozen times or more they must stop talking and go to sleep, it's 8:00 or 9:00 and we sometimes are smart enough to go to bed, remembering how soon 5:30 a.m. comes, but more often we just want to look over the day's news, which may take an hour or two. The papers, Porter's and the rival paper, the *News*, average 20 or more pages each so we don't lack for reading material of that kind.

"I haven't seen enough of people to be generalizing too much, but I can't see much difference between our kind of folks here or there. It does sound mighty funny to me to hear grown women singing 'Little Polly Flinda sat upon the cinda . . .' Our children are acquiring the Alabama talk, but my speech habits are too fixed to change.

"Women here dress up a little more—and are prettier in general—than women in Dodge City.

"Sam is getting along very well at school. He rates much better than most of this age and his teacher talked of promotion at mid-year. You're the product of many double promotions. What do you honestly believe about them?

"Mary is still pretty but is in great danger of becoming spoiled from over-attention unless someone more wise than I can tell me how to prevent it. Her uncle John Jervis's young brother saw her for the first time when we were at Rome for Frances's wedding and said, 'What beautiful blue eyes you have!' 'Yes,' she answered, 'and my lashes are long, too,' closing her eyes to show them off.

"Joe is still our clown. He doesn't know any of 'When We Were Very Young' (Sam knew almost all at his age) but he does know a lot more about playing with other children. I believe he is going to be like you, as well as look like you, in another respect—he likes to sing.

"Porter just bought a new pair of pants, having split out the seat of the blue suit he bought from you. He shaves every morning, but in other respects is the same as ever.

"We took the children about half a mile away and up into the edge of the woods during the interruption in this letter. I've seen a few of

> Nature's wonders—Rocky Mountains, waterfalls and the Dust Bowl getting green after the dirt storms of 1935—but I've never stood and looked at anything that thrilled me as the view of the woods turning from many shades of green through all the yellows, browns and reds. Pictures have never caught half their beauty.
>
> "Being strangers in a far-away city on our anniversary last August 1, we thoroughly enjoyed your telegram. It came while we were unpacking and trying to straighten up a bit before time to go to bed. Porter didn't forget for a week that you remembered the day when he hadn't."

Alice and Porter shared an optimistic outlook. They gave the children a large measure of freedom, apparently assuming they would use it wisely. Mary remembers riding alone on a Birmingham streetcar to a birthday party when she was four and getting off when the conductor told her she had come to the right place. Sam and Jackie Kelly spent hours playing along the creek and in the woods without anybody, as far as they knew, worrying about where they were or what they were up to.

Porter's duties at the *Post* were limited to editing, rather than gathering news. As a copy editor—they were called copy readers in those days—he went over what the local reporters had written and tried to improve the writing where he could. He edited national, international and state stories that came in over the Teletype machines from United Press. He wrote headlines for local stories and wire stories, scores of them each day. The *Post* was an afternoon paper and so was the *News*, the dominant paper in town. The *Post* had a smaller staff and less space for stories. Part of Porter's job was to try to make the Post livelier and more appealing through compelling headlines and readable stories. The *Post*—owned by the Scripps-Howard chain—was slowly gaining in circulation on the locally owned News. There was a third paper in town, the *Age-Herald*, a morning paper owned by the *News*.

Birmingham was many times as big as Rome or Dodge City, and Porter and Alice missed the smaller-town atmosphere they had lived in nearly all their lives. They started thinking about the towns right around Birmingham. They were especially intrigued by a government project in

Copy reader for the Birmingham Post.

Trussville, on the Gadsden Highway 14 miles from downtown.

It wasn't at all what New Deal planners had in mind originally. Senator John Bankhead of Alabama had sponsored a bill in 1933 that resulted in what was called the Subsistence Homestead Program. The idea was to provide dwellings with enough land that people having a hard time economically could grow some of their own food and maybe raise some chickens to supplement their income. Congress voted $25 million and Senator Bankhead got $6 million of it for his home county of Walker and the adjoining county of Jefferson, which includes Birmingham.

A committee chose Trussville for one of the projects. It was to be built on 615 acres that had held a turn-of-the-century blast furnace where iron was made. There was still a huge pile of slag, a rocklike by-product. The Trussville project took life on government drawing boards with the romantic name, "Slagheap Village."

The other four Alabama projects went forward as planned. But Slagheap Village languished. The planners had decided the site wasn't suited for subsistence homes and mini-farms. The program manager, a landscape architect by trade, had a different vision. As described in the history book *Trussville Through the Years*, "Instead of housing for the unemployed and those on relief, the proposal was to build a garden-type suburban town, a 'model city'—a community of young families similar in socioeconomic background, interested in their neighbors, their community and its quality of life. [It] would entail buying an additional 175 acres and ultimately investing much more in Slagheap Village than was originally planned."

The program manager sold his vision to the people in charge in Washington, and thus was born "a quality housing development second to none, commonly referred to as 'the government's country club.'" Later the name was changed to the more appealing "Cahaba Village" after the nearby Cahaba River.

In later years the term "government housing project" was to take on a certain stigma. But in 1937 the Cahaba project sounded mighty appealing to a lot of people. Besides nice homes it boasted spacious yards, paved and curbed streets, nice landscaping, a central sewer system, a large park, a community building and more. The government helped pay for a new high school building, since the existing schools lacked the room to handle the new residents. So while there were 287 new homes, including a few apartments, the government received many times that many applications. One application came from Porter and Alice Harvey.

Alabama historian Wayne Flynt wrote about the five "subsistence communities" in the book *Alabama, the History of a Deep South State.* While the original idea may have been to help the needy, "The projects merely skimmed the top off Alabama's bottom class. Lengthy interviews, background investigations, letters of reference, employment records and credit checks assured that most residents were formerly machinists, skilled artisans, professionals or workers in service occupations."

Even more than the other four projects, Cahaba became a community of white-collar workers, many of them with college backgrounds. The rent there was higher because the government had built more expensive homes and had invested more in community facilities. Family income couldn't be less than $1,500 per year, or more than $2,300. Porter's salary at the *Post* put him right about in the middle. Miss Lois Gratz of the project office came to their home in Birmingham and interviewed him and Alice.

"We wanted to be among the chosen ones," Alice said. "And when we found out we had passed, we felt really proud."

They went out to Trussville and looked over the different styles and sizes of homes. They picked a one-floor white frame model with three bedrooms. There was a front porch and partly-enclosed back porch. A driveway of slag, from the big slag heap, led to an outbuilding that held a garage, a storage room, an attic-like storage area, and a space for raising chickens. The government tried to encourage the villagers in that pursuit, in keeping with the original notion of part-time farming. Alice and Porter dutifully kept chickens, but, like most of their neighbors, they didn't keep them long.

They moved to 32 Oak Street in the summer of 1938 after a year in Birmingham. They were among the first families to move into the project, which the government didn't fill up for well over a year. They were still without a car, so Porter paid to ride to work with other men who worked downtown and carpooled. One or two were fellow employees at the *Post.*

Whatever the socio-economic aspects of the Cahaba project, the Harveys found it a wonderful home. They liked being in on the founding of a brand new community, with other people of about the same age and circumstances. Porter had found Kansas appealing partly because it was newer and rawer and the customs less hidebound than where he had grown up. Cahaba was also new and different, although in time it would become pretty much like a lot of other suburban communities.

Mary turned five in July and was enrolled in a kindergarten in the community building on the Mall, a park-like area that the planners left vacant in the middle of the project. The teacher was Roberta Ellenburg, who lived just up the street from the Harveys. She was paid by the government. Public school kindergarten in most of Alabama was still 40 years in the future. When Alice took Mary to an orientation meeting before the kindergarten began, a newspaper photographer from Birmingham was there to cover it. Mary's picture ran in the paper with that of Jeris Garrison, who also lived on Oak Street and who was to be Mary's best friend in Trussville. Sam started to third grade in Hewitt Elementary, about a mile away in downtown Trussville. After a couple of weeks his teacher told Alice she thought Sam should be moved up to the fourth grade. Besides reading well, he was one of the few in the class who already wrote in cursive. The children who had been to Hewitt their first two years only printed, and they were to spend much of the third grade learning to write the other way. Alice and Porter gave their approval, and Sam moved up to the fourth grade.

Alice got active right away in the PTA at school. She had been a member in Dodge City and in Birmingham, and she felt she had learned some things that would help in Trussville. When elections were held the first year they were there, she was chosen as the president. As a teacher she had learned that students do better if they have the right support at home so she organized programs to encourage parents to become more involved in their children's education. She also made time to join a book-study club and became its first secretary.

None of the churches were in easy-walking distance. A delegation from the Presbyterian Church invited the Harveys to attend there and offered to have people come by and pick them up. Alice and Porter accepted the offer, so for the three years they lived in Trussville, they were Presbyterians. The church was a two-story frame structure on Highway 11 that had been built in 1900.

When the government was developing Cahaba, 60 or 70 houses were torn down on the old blast furnace property. Among them were the homes of a good many black families, who were relocated to an area northwest of the project known as "The Forties." A woman who lived there, Julia Washington, worked part time for Alice, mainly helping with the laundry. She preferred using a scrub board even though the family had a washing machine. A survey of the overall Trussville community put the population at 21 percent black, although no blacks lived in Cahaba. So rigid was the segregation of those days that none of the Harvey children can remember even seeing any black children in Trussville, much less knowing them. Nor were they conscious that there was a school for black children, although it was somewhere in the area. Alice remembers that the starting and ending times of the schools were deliberately kept half an hour different so white and black children wouldn't encounter each other on the way.

For Porter's 69th birthday, Alice asked the children—as her father had asked her years earlier—to write down 10 things that each of them remembered before age 10. Some concerned the time in Trussville.

> Sam: "We sometimes took the bus between Trussville and Birmingham. Once we were waiting in Birmingham on a busy street corner for a bus to pick us up. We were pretty tired. Daddy said, 'Let's sit down while we wait.' So all of us (I guess Mama wasn't along on that trip) sat down on the curb in the middle of all the people who were also waiting. They were tired too, but they were too dignified to wait in comfort."
>
> Sam: "I don't know if it was Christmas or a birthday when I got my first real bike (not counting a sidewalk cycle). Daddy bought it in Birmingham and got it to Trussville by riding it about 15 miles along the busy and fairly narrow highway. There was a Christmas when Daddy had to work, and since the men he rode with had a holiday, he had to walk a mile down to the highway and catch the bus. We got up in what

With the children at Mentone after move to Alabama.

seemed like the middle of the night so we could open our presents before Daddy had to leave."

Mary: "I remember Daddy and me sitting in the garage watching our dog Trixie have her first litter of puppies. I also remember the pet ducks that ended up on the dining room table with their feathers in a pillow. For my seventh birthday Mama made cookie dough and all the girls stood around the kitchen table and rolled and cut out cookies."

Joe: "One year we got comic valentines from some kids up the street who had the whooping cough. Mama wouldn't let us touch them until she had baked them on that coal circulating heater to kill all the germs. I still have an aversion to comic valentines."

Sam: "Because he worked at the paper, Daddy used to get passes to things—wrestling matches, the State Fair, and the Lucky Teeter daredevil car show. I didn't realize it then but Daddy's main interest was seeing the monster side of things. At the fair Daddy always took us in the sideshow tent where they had the fat lady, the man with alligator skin, etc. We went to see a fat lady named Baby Ruth about three years running. They said she was over 900 pounds on our last visit. Passes wouldn't work for everything, including the pay toilets. If we couldn't find free toilets, Daddy would look around till we found a place behind some tent and we would all relieve ourselves in the high weeds."

Mary: "Mama got her finger smashed in a door the day she was to ride in an ambulance bringing a friend and her baby home from the hospital. What I remember best is Daddy trying to devise some kind of protection for her hurt finger. It seems to me he put a toilet paper tube over it. And I remember the cozy feeling of having Mama crawl into bed with me in the middle of the night after I woke up from a bad dream. I was terrified of the dark and afraid to walk into a room with the shades up. Mama would walk in ahead of me to pull them down. She put a lamp by my bed that I could leave on all night."

Joe: "Once when we were swimming near that dam on the Cahaba River, Daddy swam or waded out to the dam and sat right under the waterfall, letting the water pour down on him like some kind of nut. Mama nearly died. Mary stepped off into a hole and got strangled, and Daddy picked her up by the ankles and poured the water out."

Mary as you might imagine, also remembers that. "Daddy had told us to quit yelling for help just for fun," she said, "and when I stepped in that hole over my head, at first nobody would pay any attention."

CHAPTER 7

THE FORERUNNER

Trussville was unincorporated, so there was no local government. For people in the project, the closest thing they had was the Cahaba Community Association. It was formed shortly after the project opened, and all residents were encouraged to join. Its purpose was to look after the residents' interests and to work for improvements in the community.

Somebody suggested that the project would benefit from having its own newspaper. The association called a meeting to hash it over. A six-member publication committee was appointed, and Porter was named its chairman. He set about organizing a staff and making other arrangements. They decided to call the paper the *Cahaba Hub* because they saw it as a hub of community life. The first issue came out in December 1938. Porter was the editor, and he was to continue in that capacity for two-and-a-half years, until he and the family left for Guntersville.

Although all the work was done by unpaid volunteers, the *Hub* was a remarkable example of community journalism. It also played a big role in the Harvey family's future.

"I always felt that Porter's experience on the *Hub* had a lot to do with his decision to come to Guntersville and establish the *Gleam*," Alice said. Probably more than anything else, it convinced him that what he wanted to do for the rest of his life was put out a paper of his own.

The *Hub* came out once a month. It was delivered free to homes in the project. It was mimeographed rather than printed, courtesy of the mimeograph machine in the project office. Just about the only expense was buying the paper and the ink. The staff sold ads to cover their costs. The news was typed in two columns, on 8-1/2 by 11-inch pages which were printed front and back. The headlines were typewritten, too, but in capital letters. The front and back covers, also mimeographed, were on blue paper. Mimeographing meant no photographs. But the project was blessed with some artists whose sketches could be used to illustrate stories. A sketch, sort of like a cartoon, always took up the entire front cover. Volunteers typed each story in single space and to the right width. Stories were placed on dummy pages to find out what would fit where. Then everything had to be typed over again, this time on stencils. The pages were run off on the mimeograph machine. Members of the staff got together at a home (sometimes the Harveys'), put stacks of each page on a table and walked around the table picking up the pages and assembling them. Then they were stapled and given to boys to deliver around the project.

From the beginning the *Hub* served up a lively blend of hard news and breezy bulletins about life in the project. The first page of the first issue contained these three items:

"Four New Stores Open: Co-op, Glenn's, Drug Co., Morrison's," with details about each establishment, two of which had been rebuilt after a fire.

"Prayer Meeting Saves Carreker's Automobile, Garage and Coal Pile," about Roland Carreker finding his car on fire just in the nick of time when he went out to his garage to go to church.

"Candid Closeups," half a column of brief reports: "Ted Leath winning a permanent wave at the room mothers' bridge . . . George Walden talking to his white leghorns . . . Meter reader skipping Buck Horton's house because he was afraid of the innocent little Horton dog . . . The Jimmy Hosches scouring the project for a pound of onions after Jimmy Jr. laid them down to play marbles on the way home . . ."

That first issue contained 34 articles with headlines, and the articles contained the names of approximately 200 project residents.

Some articles were straight news stories: A PTA drive to raise money

The Sunday School service was progressing fine at the Baptist Church Sunday before last until all of a sudden the stove pipe began to give way. The stove pipe is a long one, and everybody saw at once that for it to fall during the exercises would be considerable of a calamity.

Well, they got it stopped, but in order to keep it in place somebody had to hold it with a long pole. Wellmer Lamons volunteered, and for the rest of opening program stood there bravely holding the "flagpole".

Between Sunday School and church some of the men undertook to fix it. There was still a big fire going and they had a hard time, but were getting along pretty well until it happened---the pipe crashed around their ears, soot spilled all over everything, the stove belched smoke into the room and it was a mess in general.

They opened the windows and managed to hold church as usual in spite of the catastrophe

P.S. That's no excuse, the pipe has been riveted together now.

HOME GUIDANCE EXPERT TO SPEAK

Dr. Robert G. Foster, family relationship expert from Merrill Palmer School, Detroit, will lecture at the high school auditorium on "Democracy Begins at Home" Tuesday March 24th at 8 P. M.

He is being sponsored in a series of lectures in the county next week by the Birmingham and Jefferson County Councils of P. T. A.

Dr. John M. Bryan will introduce the speaker. There is no admission charge.

Interested in Accounting? Join the Tues night class at the high school. Its free.

COMMUNITY ASSOCIATION MEETING

The Cahaba Community Association opened its March meeting by enjoying three solos--Mrs. Alan Lane at the piano, Geo. Bibb, Jr. on the cornet, Roland Carreker, Jr. on the clarinet--and then proceeded with the following business, announcements and discussions:

STREET LIGHTS--Hugh Hall of the safety committee said several lights were out. "Well," said Mr. Ross, "some like the lights on, and some like them out. But we'll get them attended to." (They have been--some of them, at least.)

TRAFFIC SIGNS--Alex McLendon reported for a committee named to look into this subject. "Traffic men," he said, "tell us that stop signs would speed up traffic on the through streets. They say slow signs in the middle of the block would be better."

Assn. President Ray Hodge asked the committee to do whatever it decides is best about putting slow signs on cross streets.

DOGS--Mr. Hall said there are too many of 'em. "The situation is becoming alarming. All I know to do is appeal to people to keep their dogs up or get rid of them."

TRANSPORTATION--Judge Marshall, transportation committee chairman, said that all he had to report was that the transportation chairman needed some transportation help. The bunch he rides with needed another man to take turns driving their cars to work.

PHYSICAL EDUCATION--Mrs. Tom Fowler announced that a class is to be formed about April 1. Cost will be small. It isn't known yet who will teach it.

DOGS (again)--Dr. Cermak said it's about time to vaccinate them--it's been about a year since the last mass vaccination. "I suggest the day after the April association meeting. Maybe we'd better have two or three sessions, so as to get all the dogs--especially those under foot, Mr. Hall."

SPEED--Mr. Hodge thanked the safety committee again for getting truck operators to cut down their speed, and said the trucks were sticking to their slower

- 1 -

A page from the Cahaba Hub

for school lunches for kids who couldn't afford to buy or bring their own . . . The news that people in the project were about to get telephones for the first time . . . An account of fires in two homes, both from the flues of the circulating heaters that warmed all the houses . . . and many more.

But what really made the *Hub* sparkle were the not-so-serious news items, large and small. The headline "Cahaba Killer Dillers Getting in the Groove" told about six men trying to work up a dance band with two violins, a trombone, a flute, a guitar and a tuba: "They were going to play some tunes at the dance last Saturday night, if they could remember any tunes, which they probably could have, if there'd been a dance, which there wasn't." The headline "Bang! Bang! Bang!" ran over a story with an illustration about people scared out of their wits when slag exploded in their fireplaces. "Street Lights, eh?" told about project maintenance man A. C. Reaves "catching it from the project folks because the street lights had gone blooey, till he discovered that it was the project folks who had done the blooeying. Three of them had cut cables while digging post holes for mail boxes." And "Hi, Big Brother" headlined a story that began, "The *Hewitt Times*, elder brother of the *Hub* in Trussville's journalistic family, reappeared November 22 after several years' absence. Published by students of the Hewitt High School, the *Times* is a newsy, sprightly paper, printed with real type."

Even the filler items were informative: "Mitzie, seven-week-old terrier at the George Bibb home, 139 Meadow Lane, wandered off Monday and at last report had not been found." And there was a long column of personals about who was sick, who had gone on trips, who had entertained company, who had moved, etc.

There were no by-lines in the *Hub*, but the writing in story after story clearly bears Porter's stamp. He kept a typewriter in his bedroom for news he gathered himself, and for writing up information turned in by *Hub* correspondents around the project. He undoubtedly delighted in pieces like, "Don't Argue Over Map on the Cover: The map [of the project] on the cover of this issue is not drawn to scale, so don't use it in an argument over how big your lot is . . ." Since he spent most of his time at the *Post* writing headlines over stories of great importance, he must have reveled at being able to write heads for the *Hub* like "Car Meets Bicycle, Boy Meets Ground," about Kay Lancaster's mishap on his way home from school; "Just One Big Happy Infirmary," over a listing of all the project folks who had come down with the flu, and "Hooray For Cahaba Department" about how few project people were behind in their rent. Even the straight-news stories often included a wry touch. The account of the Community Association meeting noted that H. W. Little, who was appointed chairman of the safety committee, had recently fallen and hurt his arm.

The *Hub* in many ways foreshadowed the paper that Porter would start in Guntersville. The *Hub*, like the *Gleam*, gave lots of details about events large and small, and it reported many with an impish good humor. Both papers testified to Porter's conviction that what mattered was the content, not the looks. Both papers used small, single-column headlines. Both papers stuck religiously to the rule that if it was going to make the paper, it had to be local. Some features from the *Hub* were to be transplanted bodily into the early *Gleam*: Candid Closeups, a mish-mash of small events and observations; Lookalikes ("Vice-president Garner and Tom Stevens of the Woco-Pep station") and fillers that were really worth reading ("Kay Ussery has a green baby chick").

The members of the Harvey family made the columns of the *Hub* from time to time, although Porter was careful not to play them up. Alice's work with the PTA and other civic ventures got her into print fairly often. Joe fell off a window sill and had to have a stitch over his eye. Alice lost some Holmes & Edwards forks at the Fourth of July picnic. "Sam Harvey had the mumps two weeks ago. His brother Joe broke out with them this week on schedule." Mary and Joe attended birthday parties for Bootsie Garrison, Frank Parkel and Joan Leath. Sam was part of the school safety patrol, holding back traffic with flags on long poles while kids crossed the Chalkville Road. "Lookalikes: Porter Harvey and movie gangster Humphrey Bogart." And there was this filler: "Mrs. Porter Harvey and her twice-a-week maid, Julia Washington, can hardly get the housework done for talking over their common problems. Each is president of her PTA."

The *Hub* of April 1941 revealed that Porter had decided to move to Guntersville and start his own weekly paper. In a story written by someone else, the *Hub* said, "One of the first families of Cahaba, moving in a month after the community opened, he and his wife have been active in all phases of Cahaba life . . . It was almost wholly through his originality and efforts that the *Hub* came into being, and his leaving will be most felt by the staff and *Hub* readers."

The new editor initiated a column of editorial opinion, something Porter had always done without. There were two editorials in that issue, including the following:

> **PORTER LEAVES**
>
> Elsewhere in this issue of the *Hub* is a story about the removal of Porter Harvey and family from Cahaba.
>
> There have been other valuable people to leave us, but we of the *Hub* believe that the loss of none of these will be as keenly felt as that of Porter and Alice Harvey.
>
> The *Hub* came into existence through Porter's efforts and has continued largely because of his unlimited enthusiasm.
>
> A former president of the community appraised Porter's worth to Cahaba thusly: "No one has contributed as much to our community life as Porter Harvey."
>
> Tireless, friendly to all and partial to none, he gained the support of every person with whom he associated. Two ideas were fixed in his mind with regard to news writing: How to get the most out of a story and how to word it to spare the feelings of any who might be hurt.
>
> Therefore, with sincerity we speak for Cahaba in wishing Porter greater success in his new venture.

CHAPTER 8

His Own Paper

After about two years as copy editor on the Birmingham *Post,* Porter had once again begun to feel that he wasn't getting anywhere.

"They tried me out for the next highest job, head of the copy desk, but I couldn't handle it," he said.

The Anniston *Star* had always enjoyed a good reputation among smaller Alabama newspapers. Porter heard they had an opening coming up so he wrote them.

"I am 36 years old, married, have three children, am steady, loyal and a hard worker," he said. "I walk with a limp, due to infantile paralysis, but I have never found this a handicap in my work. I believe I can recommend myself as a competent although not a brilliant newspaperman."

Maybe the *Star* was looking for brilliance. At any rate, the job didn't materialize. Whether he applied to other papers isn't known.

His parents had always worried whether he could make it in the newspaper world, especially as a reporter. In a letter to Alice three weeks before their wedding, Porter's mother wrote, "I wonder if he is as unobserving as he used to be. Evan always feared he would fail as a reporter on that account, but as he seemed to get along all right, I guess he's improved."

When Porter was a reporter in Dodge, he told his parents he hoped to try his hand at writing editorials. His father was delighted, "You may not remember," Evan wrote, "but that is what I had in mind when I first spoke of newspaper work as a possible life work for you. I told you that an editor had a fine opportunity to do good by putting out the kind of stuff that would elevate, etc. etc. You said that only a few people read editorials, to which I replied that the few who do are usually the thinkers of the community and really control all the others. I hope you will give the job of writing editorials a fair trial. Strong editors seem to be rather scarce. I suggest that you find out who are considered good editorial writers in your section of the country and study their work. I firmly believe you can make good at it and that once you get the hang of it, you will like it much better than reporting. What would be nicer than to someday own an interest in a good paper and be its editor with a good partner who would be business manager?"

Writing editorials had never really appealed to Porter. But owning his own paper had come more and more to seem like what he wanted to do. His experience with the *Cahaba Hub* helped convince him he would like to run a weekly. It also gave him confidence that he could probably make a go of it.

"I was pushing 40 and decided I'd better try to get a paper of my own," he said. "I couldn't find any way to buy one without money, so I decided to start one."

One thing that helped him decide to leave when he did was the possibility of a strike at the *Post.* Porter and most of the other news employees were members of the Newspaper Guild, a CIO union. Wage negotiations were going on in early 1941 and it looked as if an agreement might not be reached quickly. Porter and Alice tried to put some money aside in case of a strike, but on $40 a week it wasn't easy. Sam asked his mother what they'd do if a strike came. She said they'd cut back wherever they could, maybe have hamburger once a week and skip meat other days, and get by the best they knew how. As it turned out, the Guild did strike not long after Porter left. The *Post* had been gradually gaining ground on the *News*, but it suffered a huge drop in circulation during the months that the strike dragged on. The *Post* never recovered its lost ground and never again posed a serious threat to its bigger then-evening rival. A few years later the chain that owned the *Post,* Scripps-Howard, stopped trying. They worked out a deal to turn everything over to the *News* except the editorial department. The *Post* merged with the *News*'s morning partner, the *Age-Herald*, to form a new morning paper, the *Post-Herald*. Scripps-Howard was to get a small part of the revenue and the *News* got the rest.

In looking for a town to start his own paper in, Porter would go over the weeklies that were mailed to the *Post* on an exchange basis. He wanted to find a town where the economic future looked bright and the established paper seemed weak. The family still didn't have a car, but Porter had a friend who traveled in his work. Porter started going with him on one-day trips to look over some towns. He also visited some places by bus. He gradually narrowed down his choices. The towns he looked at most closely were Fayetteville, Tennessee, and Guntersville, Alabama.

The publisher of the *Guntersville Advertiser*, Yancey Burke, had run the paper since 1914. He had gone into business against what was then the established paper, the *Guntersville Democrat*. In 1928 he bought out the *Democrat*. But Mr. Burke was a printer by background. Porter felt that as an established journalist, he could put out a better product and readers and advertisers would quickly switch. Guntersville itself had just gone through a big change. The Tennessee Valley Authority had built a dam a few miles downstream on the Tennessee River, and in January 1940 a huge new lake had risen and changed the town into almost an island. Like Dodge City and Cahaba, where Porter had gone before, Guntersville appeared to be unique. He picked Guntersville for what was to be the biggest adventure of his life.

"Alice didn't like to take risks and this looked mighty risky," he said. "But she let me do it."

Alice said it never crossed her mind to try to stop him. "It was what he wanted to do, and I was confident he could make a go of it. I didn't think it would be handed to us on a silver platter. But I had taught school and I figured that was something we could fall back on if we had to. The paper was what he wanted, so I was all for it."

Alice may have been agreeable to going to a strange new place, but it was a hard pill for the children to swallow. They loved Trussville.

"When they told me we were moving," Mary said, "I went out and sat down on the curb and cried. I told Jeris Garrison she was my best friend and I had thought she would be my best friend forever and ever, and now we were leaving."

Sam got the news while he and Hosmer Roberson were building a rabbit trap in a vacant lot across from Hosmer's house. Mrs. Roberson came out and told Sam his mother had called and it was time to go home. She also told him that Alice had said they would soon be moving to a place called Guntersville. Sam was almost 11 and too old to cry. But when he got where no one could see him, he cried a little just the same.

Porter knew it would be an uphill struggle that could very easily fail. All his experience had been on the news side. Now, in addition to finding and writing the news, he would have to sell the ads and draw them up, find enough subscribers to make merchants want to advertise, and tend to all the other details involved in running a business. All of these were things he knew next to nothing about. Since he had no money to hire other people, he would have to do practically everything by himself for a while. He would have to do it in a town and county where he didn't know a soul. And he would be up against a newspaper that had been in place since 1880.

And then he found out he wasn't the only one who thought Guntersville was ready for another paper. Randolph Linn of nearby Arab was also getting ready to jump in. Mr. Linn owned the *Arab Advertiser*, with his own printing plant. And he was starting in Guntersville with a huge advantage. He had hired an out-of-town promoter to put on a contest, with a new car as first prize for whoever sold the most subscriptions. It was a powerful incentive, and his *Marshall County Record* started life with more than 1,200 paid subscribers.

Mr. Linn and his paper beat Porter out of the chute by about three weeks. But Porter felt he had gone too far to back out, so he plunged ahead. As his sister Frances once said, of his boyhood exploits, "Porter loved danger."

He had no money of his own, and no banker in his right mind would have made a loan on what looked like the longest of long shots. Porter got his father to lend him $4,000 against his share of the estate. He rented a one-room office on the second floor of the Henry Building over Adams Dry Goods, a block from the Courthouse. He arranged to print his paper ten miles away at the *Albertville Herald.* He lined up several boys to deliver the paper free for a while to homes inside Guntersville, so people could see what the paper was like. He would mail it free to people on rural routes. He quit his job in Birmingham and moved to Guntersville a month ahead of the rest of the family. He rented a room from Mr. and Mrs. A. F. Hinds, just south of the First Methodist Church. He and a couple of other roomers took their meals at the Hinds home.

Given his fondness for language, it's not surprising that he gave a lot of thought to a name for his paper. He wanted something that was short but distinctive, something that went well with "Guntersville." One night as his bus was crossing the Spring Creek causeway, he was struck by the way the town's lights gleamed on the surface of the lake. He was probably familiar with Tennyson's poem, "Merlin and the Gleam," which concludes, "After it, follow it, follow the Gleam," and a 1923 hymn, "Follow the Gleam." He decided to call his paper the Guntersville *Gleam.*

The first issue came out Thursday, May 1, 1941. Whether by design or accident, that was his birthday. The new publisher was 38 years old.

That first issue bears some looking at. In many respects it was an accurate herald of what the paper was to be like for the next half-century and beyond. Porter believed that success for a newspaper depended essentially on two things: giving readers more news than they could find anywhere else, and writing and editing the news in a way that would make people want to read it.

The *Gleam*'s first front page contained 16 stories, even though the paper began life in a tabloid format, half the size of conventional papers. Characteristically, none of those stories mentioned that a new paper was making its debut. That came on page two, under the masthead, where papers traditionally run their editorials. A modest 12-point headline declared, "A Third Newspaper for Guntersville."

The article started out with what might have been considered a plug

100 YEARS
of newspaper publication

The Guntersville Gleam started out as a tabloid, with pages half the size of most newspapers. This was the first issue, May 1, 1941. Porter Harvey, the publisher today, was the publisher then.

The Gleam was circulated free for a few weeks. Then they started selling subscriptions by mail for $1 a year, 60c for 6 months or 35c for 3 months. In town you could take it from a carrier boy for 12c a month.

The Gleam's office was a room on the second floor of the building where the Bargain Outlet is now, across from the First National Bank.

The Guntersville Gleam

VOLUME 1 — GUNTERSVILLE, ALABAMA THURSDAY, MAY 1, 1941. — NUMBER 1.

Commercial Carrier Terminal Moves In With $30,000 Payroll

Commercial Carriers, Inc., moved its southern terminal from Forrest City to Guntersville last week, bringing 35 employes, a payroll of $30,000 to $36,000 a year, and the prospect of expansion in the next few years to a much larger volume of autos and other freight.

The company will get work started immediately on a 50 by 150 foot freight warehouse just this side of the derrick. The building will be all steel construction with concrete floors. At one end there will be 30 by 150 feet of office space. The present dispatcher's office and sleeping quarters for truck drivers from the north will be maintained.

Commercial, one of the fastest growing business concerns in the United States, started bringing automobiles here by barge as an experiment about the first of the year. Since then there has been a barge load about every two weeks. The experiment proved a success, and now the company is getting ready to ship through Guntersville on a really big scale.

The auto hauling business is entering a slack season right now, so the volume of cars will not increase much until fall. But in the meantime Commercial's solicitors are working up business in other lines of freight hauling, and it is for this general freight business that the warehouse will be built.

Starting next September the company expects to bring in a double header barge (two barges towed together) twice a week.

All the barges that have come here up to now have a maximum capacity of 130 cars, but it is planned to put some on this run soon that carry 190. These are what are known as outriggers, four decks and five cars wide.

Commercial opened its Forrest City terminal 16 months ago, before it realized the possibilities of barge-truck haul. It is now abandoning the site at Forrest City and moving that equipment to Guntersville.

J. W. Casey Jones (that's his real name) in charge of operations here, predicts that within two years the line will be handling 70 per cent of all freight that comes up the Tennessee River.

"The company is also working up freight business from the south to

(Continued On Page Two)

"Cotton Week" Observed In County

The week May 14-16 has been designated as "National Cotton Week." The county of Home Demonstration clubs request the co-operation of all urban and rural families in this program. "This is a fine opportunity for individuals, organizations and communities to get behind this important campaign to move a greater volume of cotton goods and thus increase cotton consumption" says Vergie Winn Gunn, Home Demonstration Agent.

The Home Demonstration club women of Marshall county will wear cotton dresses to clubs this month. In each club, a cotton dress revue will be held. Each woman wearing a cotton dress she has made. The three winning dresses in each club will enter the county fashion show to be held at the County Rally in June. The county winner will go to Auburn in August ,all expenses paid, to enter the State Dress Revue that is held annually during farm and home week.

In addition to the women's work 408 4-H club girls will make all cotton dresses and enter the 4-H club dress revue to be also held in June. The 4-H club winner will enter the State Dress Revue for 4-H club girls.

Marshall 4-H'ers To Broadcast

According to Vergie Winn Gunn, Home Demonstration Agent, and H. G. Sims, Assistant County Agent four of our Marshall County 4-H club workers, Myrtice Jones, County Council President, Guntersville Club; Guntersville, Alabama Rt.4 Madge Burns, Boaz, Alabama; Joe Graham, Albertville Club; and H. V. Barnard, Hebron Club; New Hope Rt. 1. Will broadcast over W. A. P. I. Birmingham on Saturday May 10 from 12:30 to 1:00 P. M. These girls and boys will discuss "4-H Clubs as a Democracy"

Music Festival Tomorrow Night

Music by the High School Band and songs by the City School glee club will be among the features of the second annual Music Festival tomorrow (Friday) evening at 8 o'clock in the City School auditorium.

The music Study Club, which is presenting the festival, invites the public to attend. Last year the event drew a capacity audience.

The festival program, arranged by Mrs. Alton B. Brown, follows:

Introductory talk, Mrs. R. A. Brown.

Mutual March, Zenith Overture, Normal March, Ambition Overture (all by Bennett)—High School band

Blue Danube Waltz (Strauss) and About Katy—City School glee club.

Hush, oYur Honey, Hush (Wright—the Collier family.

Diana Waltz (Holts)—Miss Martha Sue Fletcher and Miss Sara Arnold Haden.

The Answer [illegible]—Miss Catherine Jane Jordan.

Trumpet Solo—Mrs. J.L. Cowart.

Luxemburg Garden and Pirate Dream (Hurerter)—Mrs. Oscar Horton.

Pastel Minuet (Paradis)—Mrs. Marshall Henry, Mrs. J. C. Wilson, Jr., Miss Marion Florey and Miss Mildred Williams.

Mardi Gras, from Mississippi Suite (Grofe)—Miss Mary Gene Cox and Miss Beatrice Sulzby.

County High School Will Graduate 49

You could call them the 'Forty Niners" and be right, because exactly 49 Marshall County High School seniors will be graduated at the commencement exercises May 13.

Four events will comprise the graduation program: The senior class play Friday of next week, the baccalaureate sermon the following Sunday, the music recital Monday, May 12 and the graduation exercises Tuesday May 13.

Members of the graduating class are:

Girls—Loyette Adams, Gladys Anderson, Enell Avery, Demress Baugh, Irene Beam, Hazel Burdett, Anna Laura Brown, Desaree Campbell, Julia Mae Chandler, Annette Collins, Mary Cranfill, Mary Gene Cox, Cora Cooley, Opal Cowen, Catherine Garrison, Hazel Goodwin, Lois King, Jessie Mae Mardis, Lorene Mayhall, Dorothy Patterson, Lyndle Powell, Martha Rains, Junior Lee Sims, Beatrice Smith, Grace Walls, Mary Hope Whittaker and Jean Anne Whitten.

Boys— Tolmer Bolding, John Brookshire, Hurschel Burdett, John Hopwood, Jr., Rotha Collins, Charles Hill, Herman Hunkapillar, Reginold Johnson, Gus King, Bill Long, Sam Long, J. C. Mason, James May, Robert Morrow, Ernest Morton, Carl McClendon, Wendell Smith, S. R. Starnes, Louie Starnes, Lincoln Walker, Walker White and John Wilborn.

The play to be given at 7:45 p.m. on May 9, will be a three-act roy-

(Continued on Back Page)

Ball Team Will Open Season This Week

The Guntersville ball team, strengthened with the addition of five new players, opens its season this week-end with two league games against Douglas at Douglas Saturday and here Sunday.

Prospects look good for a winning season, the boys say. Last year Guntersville beat Douglas out for third place in the North Alabama League, finishing only behind Scottsboro and Whitney.

Perk Wililamson is the team's new manager.

The five new players are:

Prickett, first baseman. He played with Whitney last year.

Sokey Walden, a backfield star for Marshall County High School last year.

Milton Heath, another of last fall's M.C.H.S ace backs. Came here from Pineapple. Plays in the outfield.

Whit, from Oneonta. A catcher. Buddy Suttle, centerfielder just come here from [illegible]ville. Weighs only 114 but is a ball hawk from way back.

Last year's players back with the team are:

Joe Barnes, third baseman and the team's sparkplug.

Shirley Davis, the one-man baseball team. Plays all nine positions. (No, not all at once.) Will do his share of the pitching.

Ted Crowson, pitcher. Fast ball and a nice curve. This is his second season with the team. Moved here from New Hope last year.

Sherman Elrod, [illegible] and curve ball hurler. Also utility infielder, a good solid player at any position around the baselines

Fred Baxter, left fielder. A good dependable all-round ball player.

Tom Jackson, second baseman. He's dean of the team, having been on it six years The boys say he's the one they look to to run the club when Perk Williamson isn't around. Tom is 37 but a real player just the same. Batted .300 last year.

Dr. Luck aHn, second base. A good hitter (he's the kind of player who often gets 'em when they're needed worst) and a fielder who lets mighty few get by him.

The team lost three men from last year:

Everett Pitts catcher, now at Camp Blanding.

Robert Martin, center fielder, now with the Leesburg club of the Florida State league. He won a tryout with Gadsden this spring and Gadsden placed him with Leesburg.

John Starnes, first baseman and the best man on the team. Was batting .450 at midseason when the army called him. He was in the officers' reserve corps and is now in camp in North Carolina.

Navy Recruiting Office In G'ville

The Navy Recruting Service from Huntsville will open temporary offices in the Court House in Guntersville on May 7. 8. 9 10th for the purpose of interviewing applicants for enlistment in the U. S. Navy. For further information apply to the Recruting officer at Guntersville on May 7, 8, 9, 10th.

37 Boats In An Hour

It was raining Sunday morning a week ago, but all the fishermen were rarin' to go anyway, and it's believed they set a record for taking boats out ofthe Taylor Camp. In less than a hour 37 boats streaked off, headed for the swift waters below the dam.

It seems everbody was afraid the other fellowwould beat them to the boats, or to the best fishing places, so they all got there early and shoved off in a hurry.

Date To Be Set For Boat Races

The Guntersville Lake Yacht Club will make a cruise to Decatur Sunday and while there expects to set the date for the boat races here this summer.

It is expected the Guntersville and Decatur races will be held close together—probably one on July 4 and the other either the Sunday before or the Sunday after.

The Yacht Club, organized last fall to take charge of holding the races, now has members from Birmingham, Anniston, Talladega, Cullman, Gadsden and Scottsboro as well as Guntersville.

4-H Health Champs Will Be Named

The 4-H Club boys and girls of Marshall county are to be given a free health examination by Dr. Lee Weathington during the month of May, reports H. G. Sims, Assistant County Agent.

This health examination is being given for the purpose of selecting the healthiest boy and girl from each 4-H Club in the county. Those being selected will then compete for the county award. The county winner will enter the state 4-H Health Contest and try for the trip to Chicago.

Meetings are scheduled at the places listed below:

Guntersville Courthouse, May 5, 9 a. m.

Arab School, May 5, 1:30 p. m.

Grant School, May 7, 9 a. m.

Asbury School, May 7, 1:30 p.m.

Liberty Hill School May 12, 9 a. m.

High Point School, May 12, 1:30 p. m.

Douglas School, May 14, 9 a.m.

Whitesville School, May 14, 1 p. m.

All 4-H Club members who are interested in the Health Contest are urged to attend one of the meetings and try for the trip to Chicago.

95 Property Owners File Tax Protests

Of the 685 Marshall County real estate owners whose assessments were raised in the annual reassessment, 95 filed protests during the time allowed. J. W. Musick, tax assessor, says that is an unusually low percentage when everything is taken into consideration.

Assessments on the 685 pices of property were increased a total of about $150,000.

Hearing on the protests will be held by the Equalization Board starting June 2. The Board consists of E. F. Whitman of Boaz, chairman; R. L. Thompson of Albertville and R. N. Cooley of Guntersville.

Doubled In 4 Years

As an indication of how fast business is increasing in this section, Ben Weiler, conductor of the N. C. & St. L. train between Guntersville and Gadsden, says the train's volume of freight is now approximately twice what it was when he came here four years ago.

"At that time our business didn't amount to much, to be right frank about it" he says. "Now we're running a double header train nearly al lthe time."

About half this line's business is through traffic between Gadsden and Huntsville, but Mr. Weiler says most of the increase has been in the local freight.

Lions Meet Tonight

The Lions Club will hold its regular dinner meeting tonight at 7 o'clock at the Glover Hotel. The club plans to take an active part in the district convention at Dothan May 18-19-20. I. B. Woods, club president, says several Guntersville Lions expect to attend.

Paving Project Starting Next Week To Employ 135 Men

Guntersville's $150,000 street paving project has been given final approval by U.S. officials, Mayor E. H. Couch was notified Tuesday by wire from Washington. The approval has to clear through the Montgomery WPA office before work can begin, but city officials hope to get the job under way by Monday.

The project will employ about 135 men and is estimated to last eight months. About five miles of streets will be paved, with concrete curbs and gutters on most of it, and sidewalk improvements where needed.

The City of Guntersville and the property owners will pay between 35 and 40 per cent of the $150,000 cost, with the government paying the rest, it is explained by L. E. Moon, city clerk. H. N. Nelson of Huntsville, a state highway man, has been engaged to direct the project.

The streets will be given a layer of crushed limestone from the quarry at Warrenton, then surfaced with asphalt.

Mr. Nelson expects to start with Obrig avenue, which will be paved from Brown Street to Beard Street.

Cleanup Campaign Showing Results

The cleanup campaign being conducted by the newly organized Guntersville Civic Club has made [illegible] deal of work to be done before the club will be ready to call the campaign completed.

People are co-operating well, according to those in charge of the drive. Many alleys have been cleaned up and other unsightly spots improved. A special effort is being made just now to get owners of vacant lots to clean them up.

Wright Allen, the new driver of the garbage wagon, has promised his full co-operation in the campaign. He assures the public that he will pick up all garbage placed in garbage cans.

"Put it in the can and I'll haul it off" he says. "During the cleanup campaign I'll also haul off any extra trash that anybody wants taken away."

The club hopes to keep the streets permanently clear of papers and other trash by inducing people not to throw them there. Wherever there are alleys, the people are urged to put their garbage cans there instead of out in front.

The Civic Club was formed by committees from various Guntersville women's groups. It is planned to make it a permanent organization to work for improvement of the city.

Civitan Club Elects Offices

The Civitan Club has elected the following new officers: John Sulzby president; P. W. Stockton, first vice president; Doyle Harris, second vice president; B. R. Harbor, executive committeeman; F. H. Yost, treasurer; E. E. Cox, secretary.

A. B. McCormick, the retiring president, will automatically become a member of the executive committee. The new officers will take over at the first meeting in June.

At last week's meeting of the club, Mr. Sulzby and Mr. Cox reported on the district Civitan convention at Gadsden.

Members of the Episcopal church plan to attend communion service at Gadsden Sunday. The service will be at the Church of he Holy Comforter.

The first Guntersville Gleam, *tabloid size, May 1, 1941.*

for the competition: "After many years with only one newspaper, Guntersville now has three. The *Marshall County Record* recently started publication, and this issue marks the first appearance of the *Guntersville Gleam*. Until the *Record* started, the *Guntersville Advertiser* had been the only paper here. . . . "

The announcement said the *Gleam* was being delivered free for a time in the Guntersville trade area, which meant more than 2,000 copies would be distributed each week. That was important for potential advertisers to know.

"We didn't try to sell any ads in this first issue, partly because we didn't have time, partly because we felt that the businessmen might like to see what the *Gleam* was going to be like before they placed any advertising in it. We hope to get around to selling some ads starting with the second issue next week.

"Our office is in the W. G. Henry Building—right across the street from both banks. The phone will be installed in a day or two.

"News of all kinds will be welcome, as well as ads. We expect to have a full staff of rural correspondents before long.

"We hope to get out a paper that will be an asset to the city and county, and will appreciate all the cooperation we can get toward making it that."

The article didn't say who was getting out the paper. To find that out, readers had to look at the masthead. It listed "Porter Harvey, Publisher" along with the information that the paper would come out every Thursday and would cost $1 a year in Marshall County and $1.50 elsewhere.

The front-page articles contained a lot of news: Commercial Carriers was moving to town with 35 employees. A $150,000 street paving project (paid for with federal funds) had gotten final approval and would employ 135 men. A new cleanup campaign was going well. Marshall County High School was graduating 49 seniors. The second annual Music Festival was set for Friday night. 4-H Club boys and girls around the county were to get free health examinations. Tax assessments had been protested by 95 property owners. The Civitan Club had elected officers. The Navy had opened a recruiting office in Guntersville.

And this: "It was raining Sunday morning a week ago, but all the fishermen were rarin' to go anyway, and it's believed they set a record for taking boats out of the Taylor Camp. In less than an hour, 37 boats streaked off, headed for the swift waters below the dam."

And this: "As an indication of how fast business is increasing in this section, Ben Weiler, conductor of the N.C.&St.L. train between Guntersville and Gadsden, says the train's volume of freight is approximately twice what it was when he came here four years ago."

The Guntersville men's baseball team was ready to open its season. The front-page story told a little about each player. Buddy Suttles "weighs only 114 but is a ball hawk from way back." Shirley Davis, the "one-man baseball team, plays all nine positions (no, not all at once)." Ted Crowson, a pitcher, has "a fast ball and a nice curve." And Tom Jackson, the dean of the team, "is 37 but a real player just the same. Batted .300 last year."

The front page didn't carry a picture. That wasn't unusual for weeklies in those days. It was time-consuming to have pictures taken and processed, and then they had to be sent to Birmingham to have metal engravings made before they could be printed in the paper.

One column inside the paper was headed, "All We Know Is What People Tell Us." It was a collection of ten short items, among them: "Rip Barnett's parrot is like children—it won't show off for company. He (or she, nobody knows which) will talk a blue streak when nobody is around, but let anybody come in and Polly goes as silent as Harpo Marx" and "Bruce Long, 11-year-old son of Mr. and Mrs. L. S. Long, has rigged up an apple box wagon so his springer spaniel, Lady, can pull it." In telling about D. C. Segler having returned home from Oklahoma 13 years earlier, Porter couldn't resist adding this, probably thinking about his own experience, "He was born in Marshall County, but like a lot of other young fellows in those days, he had to have a fling out west before he settled down."

Finally, there was this piece:

In the Middle
Of the Night

Scene: Home of W. J. Prickett, the druggist.

Time 2:00 a.m.

The phone rings, and rings and rings, and finally Mr. Prickett gets out of bed and answers it.

Excited voice at the other end of the line: "Is this Mr. Prickett?"

Mr. Prickett: "Yes."

"Well, there's a couple of drunks raising a ruckus up here at my house and I want you to come—"

"I'm sorry but you have the wrong number. You want Mr. Pritchett, the policeman. This is Mr. Prickett you're talking to."

"—and one of them is so crazy drunk he's liable to get hurt if you don't hurry."

"But I'm not the policeman."

"You mean you won't come get these drunks? That's a fine business. Wait till Dr. Couch [the mayor] hears about this."

It seems the name of Mr. Pritchett, the new policeman, isn't in the new phone book. And that's why Mr. Prickett, the druggist, on some mornings looks like he hasn't slept very soundly the night before.

The second issue contained 11 ads. They ranged in size from one column by one inch (for D. W. Scruggs, an optometrist) to four columns by five inches (Woodall's Department Store). Ads sold for 25 cents a column inch. The Woodall ad cost $5.

That issue contained a detailed account of the City Council meeting, where seven different topics were taken up. There was an invitation to people interested in writing news from rural communities to "stop by and let's get acquainted next time you're down this way." And "Candid Closeups" (the heading Porter had used in the *Cahaba Hub*) told about Sandra Hilburn, less than two years old, and her new permanent . . . Mrs. A. B. McCormick having the smallest dog in town, a five-pound Chihuahua ("Anybody know who has the biggest?") . . . and Rev. Jeff

Fletcher confessing he'd been fishing five days straight without a strike. The *Gleam* told how the rival *Guntersville Advertiser* and its staff had been written up in the *Birmingham News* as part of a series on "outstanding weekly papers of Alabama." And there was a column of 26 "Personals" about visits, ailments, births, job changes, etc.

In the fourth issue, the *Gleam* announced that it was ready to start taking paid subscriptions: "We plan to continue free distribution in each neighborhood until we can get around to that neighborhood with our subscription sales. This will apply to the RFD routes and also to Guntersville and the other towns." An ad in that issue describes the *Gleam* as "the handy little paper that tells you what's going on," and it invited readers to sign up at one dollar a year. People who lived in town and who couldn't get up a dollar all at once could take the paper from a carrier boy and pay 12 cents a month. The carriers kept seven cents and paid five cents to the *Gleam*. The first carriers were J. L Patterson Jr., Jack Wright, Buck Woodall, Gordon Ray Moon, Beumen Cook, and Donald Kizzort.

Alice and the children had moved to Guntersville the weekend after the first issue came out. Jack Pickett, who lived just up the street in Trussville, carried them. Two weeks of school remained. Alice and Porter felt that would give Sam and Mary a chance to meet some other children before summer vacation. Sam, who had been practicing for the sixth grade graduation ceremony at Hewitt Elementary, graduated instead from Guntersville Elementary.

They rented a house on Broad Street (now Gunter Avenue) in the first block south of the river bridge. The house was owned by Ben Weiler, the railroad conductor, who lived three doors north. It was about two blocks from the *Gleam* office, making it an easy walk for Porter. A boy in Sam's grade, Glenn Keylon, lived in the same block. Mary quickly made friends with the Carruth girls, Betty Sue, Gail and Tootsie, who lived next door. Neal Smith, who was between Joe's and Mary's ages, lived across the street.

The back windows had a view of the city boat harbor. Alice and the children could watch railroad freight cars being backed onto barges for a

20-mile trip to Hobbs Island, where they connected with the tracks to Huntsville and points north—supposedly the longest over-water railroad transfer in the world. Two sternwheelers, *The Guntersville* and *The Huntsville*, pushed the barges. One day Joe disappeared and Alice had the police and the neighbors out looking, afraid he might have made his way to the lake and fallen in, before she finally found him. He had been on the back porch, watching the trains, and fell asleep under a table.

Porter and Alice knew times were going to be lean, so they reluctantly told the children they wouldn't be getting any allowances for a while. Sam had been getting 21 cents a week (three cents a day), Mary 14 cents, and Joe seven cents. To put those figures in perspective, kids could go to the movie for a dime, an ice cream cone at the drugstore cost a nickel, and model airplane kits (where Sam spent most of his money) cost as little as a dime plus a nickel for the glue.

On July 3, an ad appeared in the *Gleam* with the heading, "Yes, Tomatoes Will Do." It said people who didn't have cash for the one dollar subscription could pay for the paper with produce—"that is if we don't get too much of it. One family can eat only so many beans, you know . . . Better take it to the house rather than to the office. Mrs. Harvey knows best what she can use. We live on Broad Street about the middle of the first block south of the river bridge. We're on the east side of the street."

Behind the house, facing Blount Street, was the home of Tom and Gladys Wiles, who owned a grocery store. Living with them was Mr. Wiles's invalid sister, known simply as "Sister Wiles." She had the mind of an infant. She stayed in a wheelchair and in warm months she was often outside. Sister couldn't talk, but from time to time she would emit what can be described only as howls. They sounded eerily through the neighborhood and kept the Harvey children pretty unsettled.

For months the *Gleam* was practically a one-man operation. Porter's only employee was a teenage boy, Shelley Harris, who lived in the hollow at the end of Taylor Street. He came in on Thursday mornings to help Porter get the papers ready to take to the post office. He was paid 35 cents. Porter got up the news, sold the ads, and did everything else. He knew ads were his weak suit, so he forced himself to concentrate on that aspect of the business. And he discovered as he went from store to store trying to sell ads, he always picked up a lot of news. Stores in small towns are natural collecting points for the latest on what's happening. The people in the stores were generally glad to pass it on to Porter, whether they wanted an ad in that issue or not. It helped him find a lot of things to write about that he would never have learned if he had depended only on public officials and other traditional sources.

He gathered news and ads during the day and did a lot of his writing at night. When he was away from the office, which was most of the time, the office was closed. It was a single room with hardly any furniture. The typewriter—a going-away gift from the people who had worked on the *Cahaba Hub*—sat on an apple crate that was turned up on end.

Porter would send some news and ads to the *Albertville Herald* each Monday by Trailways bus so they could start setting them in metal type. He would catch a bus to Albertville on Wednesday morning with the rest of his copy and spend his day at the *Herald.* While the printers were setting what he had brought them that morning, he would read proof and help put the type into page-sized forms to be put on the press. After the paper was printed, he would catch a bus back to Guntersville, bringing the papers in the baggage compartment. Usually he rode a bus that arrived about supper time. Other times the papers weren't ready by then, and he rode a bus that got to Guntersville about 11 p.m. The bus would let him and the papers off in front of the Courthouse, and he would carry the bundles across the street and up the stairs to the office. Sometimes Alice would meet the bus, maybe with one of the children, and help haul the papers.

The next morning he and Alice would get up about 4:00. To stick the address labels on the papers, he used a flour paste that Alice cooked on the stove. She made it each week because it wouldn't keep. He would take the paste to the office and put it in a hand-operated labeling device known as a Wing Mailer. He stamped the labels on the papers. Shelley, and later other boys, tied the papers into bundles, one for each mail route in Guntersville and the surrounding post offices. They wrapped individual papers for routes that didn't get enough papers to tie up in a bundle and for subscribers outside the county.

Winburn Morgan was the second boy hired, after Shelley got into some trouble with the law. He was the first of three Morgan brothers to work there. Their uncle Cullen Morgan owned the paper in Moundville, Alabama.

"As I remember," Winburn said, "I would go to the office about 6:00 in the morning. Lots of times it was cold standing in front of the building waiting for Mr. Harvey, so we started meeting at Doc's Cafe. It was between his house and the office. Mr. Harvey had a little red wagon with sideboards. We'd stack the bundles in the wagon, and I'd pull them to the post office. I also had a carrier route. I generally delivered my papers in the afternoon rather than before school. On weekends Sam and I would sweep or mop the office. I believe I was paid a quarter an hour. Sometimes Mr. Harvey would give us passes to the picture show. He got them from the theaters, I guess for running things in the paper about the movies." Mary also remembers (at the age of eight or nine) helping sweep the office and the hall outside the office, and being paid a nickel.

Porter hired five people to go from house-to-house in town and try to sell subscriptions. An item in "Candid Closeups" on May 29 noted that Carl McClendon, Bookie Coplin, Mary Gene Cox, Jean Ann Whitten, and Lyndell Powell were "staking off parts of Guntersville as their territories." Presumably, others were doing the same thing in rural areas. The carrier boys in town were signing up customers to take the paper by the month.

The subscription campaign went slower than Porter had been hoping. He had expected people to realize pretty quickly that the *Gleam* was a better product than its competition. When that happened, he figured, the readers would switch and the advertisers would naturally follow. But he discovered that old habits die hard. The momentum of a going concern was turning out to be a lot to overcome. The fourth issue of the paper carried 58 inches of advertising, which brought in not quite $15. And it didn't seem to be improving much. The 10th issue on July 3 contained only 69 inches of advertising, or just over $17 worth.

But Porter was about to get his first big break, thanks to World War II. America wouldn't be in the war for five more months. But young men were already being drafted into the Army and Navy, and one of the draftees was the publisher of the *Marshall County Record*, Randolph Linn. The *Record* still had its subscription contest going on when Mr. Linn got his draft notice. The contest ended June 28. The first-place winner, a lady from Boaz, came to Guntersville that night, got her car and drove it home.

People were no doubt surprised to read about the windup of the *Record*'s contest in the *Gleam*. What they didn't know was that the two publishers had been negotiating what would be described as a consolidation. Mr. Linn was in a bind. He had accepted subscription money from 1,240 people, and he was obligated to provide them with a newspaper every week for the coming year. He couldn't refund their money because most of it had gone to pay for the car and the other prizes. So he and Porter worked out this arrangement: Porter would buy the "name, good will and circulation" of the *Record* and consolidate that paper with the *Gleam*. Subscribers would receive the consolidated paper. Porter would pay Mr. Linn nothing just then, but he would pay $270 when the combined newspaper became eligible for a second-class mailing permit and lower mail rates. That would come sooner than the *Gleam* could have obtained one on its own, because the *Record* had started taking paid subscriptions earlier. Porter also agreed to run $88 worth of advertising that the *Record* had already been paid for.

The agreement was announced in the July 31 issue. Under the nameplate "The Guntersville Gleam" at the top of the front page was now a smaller line of type, "And Marshall County Record." Starting with the August 14 issue, the paper's masthead, on page two, boasted "Biggest Circulation in Marshall County—Most Closely Read Paper in Marshall County."

On September 18, readers got another surprise. The tabloid that had been published since May 1 had given way to a full-size newspaper. That issue contained 220 inches of advertising, which brought in about $55. It still wasn't enough to live on, but it was three times what the *Gleam* had been taking in before it gained the *Record*'s 1,240 subscribers. The rival *Advertiser* that week had only 140 inches of ads.

An ad in that issue of the *Gleam* proclaimed, "An ad in the *Gleam* will reach more Guntersville and more Marshall County people than you can reach in any other way." The tabloids had each contained six pages. The first of the full-size issues had four pages, equal to eight tabloid pages. Guntersville's retail business always picked up in the fall when cotton money started flowing, and the full-size papers that fall often contained six pages, double what the tabloids had offered.

The *Gleam*'s first bookkeeping records were pretty primitive, which wasn't surprising since Porter was the one keeping them. He used a simple ledger book. There was a page for each advertiser, listing the date each ad ran, how big it was, how much it cost and whether it had been paid for.

Joe started first grade in September. With all the children now in school for the first time, Alice began spending some time at the office. That way the office could be kept open while Porter was out getting news and ads. Alice could handle news, ads and subscriptions, and tend to the billing. She started keeping a monthly ledger that recorded the paper's income and outgo. In November, the *Gleam* took in $269, while expenses totaled $167. That left $102 for profit. It was about 60 percent of what Porter had been making at the *Birmingham Post.*

Although things were getting better, it was becoming apparent to Porter and Alice that it was going to be a slow process. The *Gleam* was operating about as frugally as it could. Of the November expenses, $143 went to the *Herald* for printing the paper, and only $24 was spent on everything else. Rent was $12.50. Porter spent 40 cents most weeks going to Albertville—10 cents for the bus going there, 10 cents for the bus coming back and 20 cents for supper. He spent 65 cents that month for three taxi rides, $6.17 for stamps, 35 cents for a day book, 75 cents for a typewriter ribbon, 50 cents for envelopes, and 10 cents for a yardstick. Surprisingly, it cost only $1.74 to mail the papers. In those days, mailing newspapers was practically free.

They decided Alice had better see if she could go back to teaching.

There was an opening for an English teacher at the high school in Guntersville for the second semester of the 1941-42 year, because one of the male teachers was being drafted. The principal wanted to hire Alice, but she didn't have an Alabama teaching certificate. To get one she'd have to take two college courses that she hadn't taken in Kansas.

"They couldn't pay her until she got an Alabama certificate," Porter said. "But they said that if she'd get one, they would go back and pay her from the time she started. She found she could take the courses by correspondence while she taught. She wanted to take both at once, but both the University of Alabama and Auburn told her she could only take one at a time. I guess they thought nobody could handle two at once. So she took one from Alabama and the other from Auburn, and kept on teaching, and kept house, and attended to me and the kids, canned vegetables that we took in on subscriptions, and made flour paste for us to mail the paper with."

She took her final tests in the high school office. The colleges sent the tests to the principal to administer. He left her alone while he went out to tend to other things around the school. It seemed to her that he was almost inviting her to look up the answers to any questions she didn't know. A lot was riding on the results, because if she didn't pass, she couldn't keep the job and she wouldn't get paid for the four months she had already worked.

"But I decided that no matter what happened, I was going to do it without any help," she said. She found out a little later that she had passed with flying colors.

"She got her certificate and she collected her back pay," Porter said. "And we thought we were rich."

CHAPTER 9

The First Years

The *Gleam* almost got into legal trouble soon after it started.

"I used to get the news at the hospital," said Porter, who was allowed to get information directly off the patient charts in the office. "I would tell who was in the hospital and what they were there for. This girl was there for an appendix operation, but I got two items mixed up and said she was there having a baby. She wasn't married. It was much worse back then to have a baby without being married. I went to the hospital and apologized to her, and we ran a correction in the paper. But her stepfather wanted some money. He came to the office to talk about it. They were from around Hebron, north of the river."

A young lawyer, Joe Creel, had his office just down the hall from the *Gleam*. Porter turned to him for help. The man made several trips to town to talk to Mr. Creel.

"He'd come in to see me on Saturdays," Mr. Creel said. "He said, 'This is too serious a matter to rush into any kind of settlement.'"

Porter told the man he didn't have any money. The *Gleam*'s office furniture still consisted of a chair and the apple crate, and the man finally decided there wasn't much to get any money out of. He went back to Mr. Creel.

"He hit my desk with his fist so hard I thought he was going to split it," Mr. Creel said. "He said, 'Young man, I'm ready to settle this thing, but I'm out some money. I've had these trips into town on the bus, and

I've had to buy so many hamburgers and so many Nehis.' He'd paid $5 to a lawyer. It all came to $8.75, as I remember it, and the man said, 'I want every cent of it. I'm not going to compromise.' I said, 'You're being so fair about this that I'm going to write you my check right now. I won't even call Porter. I'll settle with him later.' I wrote him a check and had him sign some kind of receipt saying that settled the matter."

Porter always got a kick out of telling about it: "Joe Creel said it was the only time time he ever heard of an exact monetary value being placed on a woman's reputation."

Some other episodes from the early years were related by four of the first carrier boys. They spoke at a luncheon in 1991 on the 50th-year anniversary of the *Gleam*'s birth.

Jack Wright, who became a lawyer, had a route in the north end of town. He and the other carriers would deliver the paper for four weeks and then collect 12 cents regardless of what time of month it was. It was hard to keep straight. Porter told them to start collecting from everybody on the first of the month. To get the new system going, they would make a one-time collection for however many weeks it had been since the last time each customer paid.

Jack knocked on the door of Mrs. Albert Neely and told her he needed to collect for the paper. "Oh, I don't handle business," she said. "You'll have to see my husband at the motor company."

Jack rode his bicycle to Guntersville Motors, the Dodge dealership, and asked to see Mr. Neely. He was in the restroom. One of the other men, Freelon Manning, banged on the door and yelled, "Albert, somebody here wants to see you."

"Cars were hard to sell in those days, and Albert thought he had a customer," Jack said. "He couldn't wait. He came out, buttoning up, and looked around for somebody, and then he looked down at me, and I was it. He was a big, burly fellow. He said, 'What do you want?' I said, 'I'm the newspaper boy. I'm here to collect for the newspaper.' He said, 'How much is it?' I said 'Three cents.' He said, 'God damn. You got me out of there for three cents?' From then on, if it wasn't more than six cents, I just paid it myself."

Buck Woodall, the real estate and insurance man, was the most successful of the carrier boys. He built up a route that had 140 customers at one point. He and Fred Taylor, another carrier boy who also later went into real estate, sometimes got Porter to tell them how the newspaper business worked.

"We learned how much an ad cost," Buck said. "We could go through the paper and figure up how much money Mr. Harvey had taken in. We used to talk about whether he was going to make it. We were making so much money on our routes that we wanted him to be able to continue. After a few months, we decided that Mr. Harvey was going to make it."

Buck was so good at finding customers that Porter paid him $1 in December 1941 to start a route in Warrenton and then turn the 20 customers over to Wylie Bolding.

"Fred and I went to Arab once to open up an out-of-town territory," Buck said. "We rode our bikes up there and hired two carrier boys." The records show they received $4.35 for that.

Fred Taylor said he and Buck started taking copies to the high school and found them mighty popular.

"We'd deliver to our customers in the morning before school," Fred said. "As soon as we walked into the first class, we'd always take a paper to the teacher. The class wouldn't start till she finished reading the paper, and then the students would start reading it. We'd go to the next class, and she'd read it. If we forgot to take a paper to school on a Thursday morning, we'd really catch the dickens."

Gordon Ray Moon had a route in Southtown. His father, Ed Moon, was the city clerk. Gordon saw Porter for the first time when Porter went to City Hall after some news.

"He was the first man I knew of who ever really covered City Hall," Gordon said. "When he left I asked Dad who that man was that was down there interfering with everybody's business."

Gordon Ray Moon served a term in the Alabama legislature in the 1980s. On one occasion he carried some copies of the *Advertiser-Gleam* and put one in the box of each of his fellow members of the House of

Representatives. "After that," he said, "if I didn't bring down a copy, some of them would want to know where it was."

The *Gleam*'s first office employee was Martha Rains, who had graduated from high school in May 1941. She was hired after Alice started teaching school in January 1942. She worked part-time, and she was paid $6 a week.

"I remember the typewriter and the apple crate it sat on," she said. She used the crate till April, when Porter paid $3.70 for a typewriter table.

She left that summer to marry Gus King, who was in service. Bernice Sulzby took her place in the office for a while, and then Mary Hugh Wood was hired and stayed about four years. By early 1943, the office work load had increased to the point that the job was paying $10 a week.

It didn't take Porter long to find correspondents in lots of the rural communities. His fourth issue on May 29, 1941, had write-ups from Mt. Pleasant, Pleasant Grove, Simpson Point, Grant, Alder Springs and Mt. Carmel. The next week brought Free Home, Mt. Shade, Kings Hollow and Mt. Olive. Successive weeks added Happy Home, Pine Grove No. 1, Fairview, Greenbriar, Jack Webb's Store, and Liberty Hill . . . Cross Roads, Brashiers Chapel, and Haney's Chapel . . . and Pea Ridge, Kirbytown, Clear Springs, and Honeycomb Valley.

The correspondents recorded lots of visits, but they recorded other things as well: whether rain was needed and when it was received; when it was blackberry-picking time; new babies; boys leaving for the Army or Navy (a frequent occurrence then); boys home on leave; sicknesses and recoveries; singings; ice cream suppers at church. The early correspondents generally weren't identified except by pen names—Blue Eyes, July Fly, Brown Eyes, Freckles, Lonesome Girl, and Bootie, to name those in just one issue. Most correspondents wrote every two or three weeks. They weren't paid, but they got the paper free. Rural communities were more clearly defined in those days than they were to become later. Roads were poor, lots of people lacked cars and few traveled into towns to work. The communities were generally centered around church or a store. Most of them had been the sites of one-room or two-room schools at some point, and some still had schools. Porter always felt the need to carry news from all parts of the trade area and not just from Guntersville. Later he would work the names of 184 communities and geographic landmarks into a poem that he used to plug the paper, "That's Where You'll Find the Readers of the *Advertiser-Gleam.*"

One thing that made gathering news harder in those days was that only about 220 homes inside Guntersville had phones, and virtually none outside the city itself had them. Reporters today do a huge amount of their work by talking to people on the phone. In the 1940s a personal trip was often the only way, short of relying on a second-hand account. A city bus company started up in Guntersville during World War II, when tire and gasoline rationing discouraged people from driving their cars. Porter rode the bus a good bit. There were two buses, a red one and a green one, and they traveled back and forth on Main Street. Once in a while, when there was no other way, Porter would take a taxi. Sometimes he went by bicycle.

"One day I rode a bicycle across the old river bridge to Claysville, and it nearly scared Alice to death when she found out," he said.

He had to put in long hours from the time he came to Guntersville. It was soon taken for granted by the family that after supper, Porter would go back to the office and work till close to bedtime.

"Alice used to say that I worked as much after supper as I did after breakfast," he mused.

By the end of the first year, "Candid Closeups" had given way to "The Gleamreel," but it contained the same sort of stuff: "George Halcomb limping on both sides at the same time. He hurt his knee working on the railroad, then strained the other ankle on a trip to Detroit . . . The only man in Marshall County that Big Jim Folsom has to look up to, Dock King, the Sand Mountain giant, 6 feet 9-3/4 inches, home from his work in North Carolina . . . Monroe Kelley of Sims and the 4-1/2 pound black bass he caught. . . ." The collection of longer items still ran under the heading "All We Know Is What People Tell Us."

The paper packed a lot of news into its first pages. The front page of May 28, 1942, carried 20 separate (mostly short, obviously) items with headlines, plus 11 country letters. And there was also a four-column display across the bottom of the front page, headed "Buy It In Guntersville—Here's Where You Can Find It." Underneath were listed about 140 goods and services and the places where each could be found: "Barbizon Underwear—Woodall's . . . Bisma Rex—Guntersville Pharmacy . . . Black Creek Coal—Carl Johnson . . . Blue Horse School Tablets—Yosts . . ." The ad told readers how much it cost to drive to Gadsden or Huntsville or Birmingham and asked, "Do you get your money's worth?"

In June of 1942 the *Gleam* began carrying "News of Arab and Brindlee Mountain" under a three-column heading. The *Arab Advertiser* had died after the drafting of Randolph Linn, the man who sold Porter the *Marshall County Record.* It was doubtful whether Arab at that time was big enough to support a newspaper in any case. But Porter saw it as an opportunity to pick up readers and, hopefully, some advertisers. Arab-area news items, obituaries, and country letters were grouped together, along with a column of personals gathered by Lena Mae Parker. She was paid $1 a week, and she also got a commission on subscriptions she sold.

After about two years on the second floor, Porter moved the *Gleam* to an office on street level. It was directly across from the upstairs office. It opened onto Taylor Street in the rear of the First National building, next to Acey Walls' shoe repair shop. It was also a single room, but a little larger. The new office was a lot more convenient for people who wanted to take out a subscription, place a want ad, or turn in some news. And it was a lot easier not having to carry papers up the stairs for labeling and tying and then back down the stairs for the wagon trip to the post office.

An ad Porter wrote for the paper in June of 1943 carried the headline, "More Than 10,000 People Read the *Gleam* Every Week." The ad went on to explain where that figure came from: The *Gleam* had a sworn circulation of more than 2,000. Surveys showed the average newspaper was read by five people. This number was bound to be higher for weeklies than dailies, he wrote, and even higher for weeklies with all local news. "But to be conservative, let's figure it at five readers to the copy." He concluded with, "That's why *Gleam* advertising, used consistently over a period of time, is such a powerful builder of business."

The message was apparently sinking in. A six-page issue in July of 1943 carried about 390 inches of display ads, plus 14 inches of classifieds. That was about $100 worth of ads—nearly twice what the paper had been carrying shortly after the *Gleam* took over the *Marshall County Record*'s subscription list not quite two years earlier. The *Gleam* by this time had become the dominant paper in town, in both readership and advertising.

Porter was still having the *Gleam* printed in Albertville when Yancey Burke, the owner of the *Guntersville Advertiser,* died on May 31, 1944. He was 62 and had published the paper for 30 years. His father had been in newspaper work earlier, before going into law practice and real estate. Yancey learned the printing trade at the old *Democrat* under E. O. Neely, and in 1914 he started the *Advertiser* in competition with the *Democrat.* He took over the *Democrat* in 1928 and combined the papers. He never married. His closest relatives were a sister in Gadsden and two brothers in Texas and Pennsylvania. After his death the brothers arranged for R. H. Williams, a former probate judge, to serve as acting publisher while they decided what to do with the paper.

Porter had been on friendly terms with this competitor, and he was one of many honorary pallbearers at his funeral. It was held at the First Methodist Church, where both men were members. Mr. Burke's obituary ran at the top of the front page of both papers.

Porter was the logical top prospect to take over the paper. While two-paper towns were much more common in the 1940's than they are today, Guntersville was still pretty small to support more than one. But Mr. Burke's heirs took a while to decide what they wanted to do.

Alice had been planning to go to Kansas after school was out to visit her parents. She hadn't been back since moving to Alabama seven years earlier. She went ahead with her trip, taking Mary and Joe with her on the bus. They were gone about three weeks. While Porter and Sam batched, Porter was getting ready to make a bid to buy the *Advertiser*—if the heirs decided to sell it. He kept Alice posted in letters.

"Yesterday I saw Mr. Burke's brother on the street, the one who was appointed administrator," he wrote. "He said it seems certain now that the paper will be sold, but of course that might mean to him or Judge Williams. He said they plan to do it by private sale rather than by auction as soon as they could get power of attorney from all the heirs. One of them is overseas."

To get an idea of what he should be prepared to bid, Porter wrote to the publishers of three weekly papers in north Alabama and the manager of the Alabama Press Association. After he heard from them, he wrote Alice, "I don't have much more definite idea of the actual value than I did to start with. However, I have a good deal clearer picture of what to figure on. Parker Campbell [the Scottsboro publisher] says it's worth $7,000 to me and $5,000 to anyone else. He may be trying to hold my bid down, as most of the others seem to figure it higher." Porter apparently thought Mr. Campbell might have in mind making a bid of his own.

Two days later he wrote, "Haven't heard anything definite about the *Advertiser* yet, but today somebody told me the Mr. Burke from Texas had gone home to wind up his affairs there preparatory to returning here, apparently for a long stay. Maybe he has decided to operate it himself, at least for a while. Judge Williams is still running it. I understand he hasn't been able to get the backing. The Mr. Burke from Texas told somebody that the paper would be sold to the highest bidder."

Three days after that he wrote, "I keep hearing one thing or another about the *Advertiser*. Lester Johnson [a grocer] said Judge Williams told him he would like to buy it but the family had its price too high. That might be a stall—Judge Williams might be saying that because people know he was wanting to buy it, but maybe he can't get financed. Paul Stockton [a director of the First National Bank] says he can't. J. P. Willis [president of the bank] says the brother who is the administrator indicated that the family would like to operate it a while to see what they can do with it, but the last time he talked to Mr. Willis he sounded as if he were losing interest in operating. He was probably beginning to notice that the money doesn't roll in as fast as most people think. The estate will run over $60,000, I hear, and I guess they figured the paper must be a pretty big money maker to build up that much."

It was nearly two more months before Porter worked things out to buy the *Advertiser* from Mr. Burke's heirs. He got the business and the print shop and office equipment for $8,000. By then his prospects were good enough that he was able to borrow the money from the First National Bank. The shop, which did commercial printing as well as printing the newspaper, included a newspaper press, three job presses, a newspaper folder, an electric paper cutter, a perforator, a Linotype typesetting machine, a casting box, four layout tables known as stones, a proof press, two office desks, a typewriter, a book case, eight cabinets, a coal heating stove, a swivel chair, two straight chairs, and an eight-day wall clock, plus the paper stock and other supplies.

The purchase was announced in each paper on August 31, 1944, under the headline, "*Advertiser* sold to owner of the *Gleam*." The article explained that the *Advertiser* would now be published on Wednesdays and the *Gleam* on Fridays. Everybody who had been getting either paper would now get both. The news carried in one paper wouldn't be repeated

The Advertiser *and the* Gleam *were published as separate papers from 1944 to 1948 at this office on Worth Street, although it was really a single twice-a-week paper. Taken during a rare Alabama snow.*

in the other. Subscriptions would be $2 a year compared to the $1.50 readers had been paying for one. "It will be the same as getting a bi-weekly paper, although each will continue under its own name," the announcement read. Readers would get full credit and more for their subscriptions. Someone who had three months to go on his *Gleam* subscriptions and two months on his *Advertiser,* for example, would now get both papers for five months.

J. J. Benford, the Albertville publisher, had advised Porter to keep the papers separate for business reasons. Out-of-town advertisers (including politicians in state races) often ran ads in every paper in the state. As long as the *Advertiser* and the *Gleam* were technically two newspapers, he stood to pick up two ads instead of one. He also may have hesitated to combine them out of respect for the long history of the older paper. At any rate, the papers were to continue as the *Advertiser* on Wednesday and the *Gleam* on Friday for four more years.

The building was sold to T. Harvey Wright, a real estate lawyer. Before selling it, the heirs had signed a five-year lease with Porter to rent the building for $35 a month. It was on Worth Street between Mr. Wright's law office and City Hall.

Porter was now the owner of the only newspaper in town and the only commercial printing plant. For the time being, at least, he had a monopoly.

CHAPTER 10

Living Downtown

After about three months in Guntersville the family rented a two-story white frame house on the corner of Blount Avenue and Taylor Street. It was only a block from the *Gleam* office. It belonged to two Gilbreath brothers who had given up their Guntersville business and moved to California. A front porch ran the width of the house. Two tall columns framed a small second-floor porch on the first-floor roof. There were five rooms downstairs and two upstairs. The bathroom opened onto the back porch, so getting to it required at least a moment out of doors. The surroundings were right remarkable, even for an era when nice homes often stood next to businesses. The Courthouse lay diagonally across the intersection. Directly across Blount Avenue stood Mrs. Allison's cafe and rooming house. Crain's Mule Barn lay across Taylor Street, with Dee Chamber's blacksmith shop at the back of the mule barn. The Gilbreath and Hawk cotton warehouse stood directly behind the Harveys' house, bordering the back yard. The house just to the north had been hit by a Yankee shell in the Civil War, but, unlike nearly all the other homes in town, it had survived the burning that followed the shelling.

A deep ditch ran across the back yard next to the warehouse. The children and their friends found it an ideal source of mud for mudball battles and a good hiding place in rubber-gun fights and other amusements. They watched mules being shod at the blacksmith shop, and even at night the family could often hear truckloads of mules being put in the barn. The front yard was big enough for passing and kicking a football and even for occasional football games with two or three boys to the side.

For a while they rented out the two second-floor rooms for extra income, with a man and wife in each room. During that time Porter and Alice slept in what was ordinarily the dining room. Sam and Joe slept in the downstairs bedroom, and Mary slept in the kitchen. The rooms were large. The house had several chimneys, and there were small pot-bellied stoves in each bedroom, the bathroom, and the kitchen, with a circulating heater in the living room. They didn't keep a fire going at night. In winter Porter got up in time to make three fires—in the living room, the kitchen, and the bathroom. The kitchen stove had a water jacket connected to the tank that supplied the house with hot water, so there had to be a fire in the stove for baths or for washing clothes or dishes. The stoves burned coal, and for kindling a supply of corn cobs was kept in the garage. The cobs were free at O. J. Walls's granary a short distance away, and they burned fine when started with newspaper. The kids carried coal and cobs in and ashes out. It was a mark of pride to see how cold you could let it get before you built a fire in the bathroom to take a bath.

They didn't rent out the upstairs bedrooms very long, partly because of complications involving some of the roomers' friends. After that Sam and Joe had one upstairs bedroom, Mary had the other, and Porter and Alice moved from the dining room to the downstairs bedroom. Alice would call from downstairs when it was time for the children to get up to go to school. On cold mornings Sam and Joe were especially hard to rouse. Alice would insist on hearing feet hit the floor, and the boys got pretty good at making it sound like they were up when they weren't. "The upstairs bedroom was awful cold," Joe said, "and the trip down to the bathroom on the back porch was even colder. One night I just couldn't make myself take the long trip so I just wee-weed in the little pot-bellied stove in my room. I don't know where Sam was. I didn't tell anyone, but I paid for it later when I built a fire in the stove and the smell almost drove me out of the house."

"Mama and Daddy gave us a lot of freedom, and other kids liked to come there partly for that reason," Mary said. "Mama and Daddy were usually at work so we kids were generally on our own. That didn't seem to worry Mama and Daddy like it would have worried most parents. They just trusted us not to do things we weren't supposed to do."

They gave the kids a taste of democracy by letting them vote on questions that came up, like what the family ought to do during some free time. Each child was given a vote, but Alice and Porter had two votes apiece and they always voted together. The kids finally figured out they didn't really have control.

There was a set of rules which came to be known simply as "The System." Porter and Alice had put it into effect in Trussville after Sam complained that he got stiffer punishment than Mary and Joe for doing the same thing. It carried over to Guntersville. The punishment consisted of standing in the floor and watching the clock for a certain length of time, or keeping silent during meals and other family gatherings. The rules were written down and kept in a glass in the kitchen cupboard for quick reference. Interrupting while someone else was talking was the most common offense, but that brought only one minute of silence. Talking with your mouth full carried a similar penalty. More serious infractions included hitting your sister or brother, talking back to your parents, disobedience, and gross disobedience. Ordinary disobedience (failing to clean your room on schedule, for instance) was either five or 10 minutes in the floor, nobody remembers which. Gross disobedience meant 15 minutes in the floor. That involved being told to do something *right now* and not doing it. If you pitched a fit at being penalized, you risked having your time doubled or tripled.

"They started out making us stand in the corner instead of in the middle of the floor," Joe said. "But we got to leaning on the wall and getting it dirty. So they put us out in the middle of the floor where we could watch the clock. Those hands sure moved slow when you looked right at them."

Kids who were cited for infractions were allowed to plead their case as long as they didn't start repeating themselves. Mary and Joe complained that Sam had an unfair advantage because, being older, he stood a better chance of arguing his way out of trouble. The non-corporal forms of punishment grew out of the teachings of Dr. Gary Cleveland Myers, a leading child-behavior guru of the day. When moments of silence and standing in the floor began to lose their effectiveness, Porter and Alice reluctantly added slaps with a flyswatter which Porter kept on the rungs under his chair at the supper table. The children argued a lot about chore assignments and other things, to the particular dismay of Alice. "I remember Mama saying, 'I'd rather do it myself than try to get you kids to do it,'" Joe said.

Porter worked most nights, and when he didn't have to go back to the office, it was a treat for everybody.

"It seemed like a holiday," Mary said. "Mama would get real excited and say, 'Daddy's going to be home, so we can have family night.' Sometimes Mama and Daddy would read books out loud to us, one chapter at a time. We went through *Cheaper by the Dozen* and *The Egg and I* that way. Or we might play games, like the kind where everybody takes turns asking yes-and-no questions to try to guess what a person is thinking about." Later, on radio, that game was known as "Twenty Questions."

The children had fixed bedtimes, Joe earliest, then Mary, and then Sam. If a radio show came on after bedtime—the Red Skelton show, for instance—a child could go to bed early and then get up when the show came on. But as they got older, set bedtimes disappeared. Most kids who went out had curfews. Sam, Mary, and Joe didn't. Porter and Alice seemingly trusted them to come in at a reasonable hour, and for the most part they did.

During World War II, people were encouraged to grow "victory gardens" to help offset what wasn't being grown by farmers who had gone off to war. The Harveys dutifully had a space plowed up in the back yard where they planted tomatoes and other vegetables. Porter rigged up an irrigation system: shallow ditches that were supposed to carry the water from row to row. They never worked very well and neither did the garden. It produced a modest number of tomatoes but not much else. Porter and Alice were too busy to spend much time battling weeds and bugs. The children seldom could muster the sustained energy the garden required. Mary was on crutches for a while one summer after hurting her foot. Porter, who had spent a lot of time on crutches as a boy, didn't think that should interfere with her garden chores, but she felt otherwise.

"We had a big blackboard on the wall in the kitchen, and Mama wrote the Saturday chores on it," Mary said. "We could take turns picking which ones we wanted to do and marking them off as we got finished. We weren't supposed to play till they were done."

After the *Gleam*'s earnings started to improve, the children's allowances were restored. They were also encouraged to earn money. Joe remembers sweeping the office, the hall, and the stairs at the *Gleam*'s first location for 10 cents an hour when he was six or seven years old. When he was eight, he sometimes helped tie up bundles of papers on mailing mornings as a substitute for some boy who couldn't be there that day. Mary also helped mail. "One morning we carried the papers to the post office and they weren't open yet," she said. "We had gotten mixed up and had gone to work an hour early." Sam helped mail, and he also delivered papers on his bicycle as the substitute carrier on Buck Woodall's route. That was the route that had twice the customers of any other. When Buck gave up the route, Sam took it over, and before long it was back down to the size of most other routes. The route started on Blount Avenue about where Feed Supply & Western is today, swung down to Railroad Avenue, went south several blocks on Blount, cut over to O'Brig and Rayburn avenues, went north to Highway 69 and out that road to about the present-day site of the American Legion. The people who took the paper from carriers were those who couldn't get up $1.50 to subscribe for a year at a time. Sometimes they couldn't get up a month's price either. It was 12 cents at first and 25 cents later on when the paper became twice a week. If the carrier couldn't collect, he took the loss, because the *Gleam* got paid for its share regardless.

One summer the whole family went camping for two or three days. They took a taxi to East Lake, out Hideaway Drive about half a mile past the town's swimming place. They slept in the open on pallets on the ground near a spring that ran down into the lake. "We went swimming and ate and went swimming again," Joe said. "We found some blackberries, some mussels, some crawfish, and a mole. We ate blackberries on our cereal, tried to eat the mussels, and Sam pickled the mole. I believe that was the most enjoyable time I remember from those days."

When Alice took Mary and Joe to Kansas for a visit in 1944, Porter kept her posted by letter on how he and Sam were getting along, in addition to telling about trying to buy the *Advertiser.*

"Tell Joe our garden is really soaked now, with the rains on top of our irrigation," he wrote. "Mary [who was crazy about babies] should have been at the hospital with me last night when I went there to get the news. They had the Purser baby and another and both are unusually cute. . . . Sam has gone home to start the dishes. He washed them after breakfast yesterday, but there is a pretty good pile already. We forgot to send the clothes to the laundry, but it wouldn't have made any difference as the boiler broke down and they can't do any work till tomorrow or later."

Porter brought Alice up to date on Arthur, a goat they had started keeping in the backyard. They thought he might help handle the grass, since Sam always had trouble keeping up with it. Arthur was named for the man they got the goat from, Arthur P. (Stocklaw) Johnson, a firewood peddler, Courthouse Square preacher, and probably the best-known character in Guntersville.

"Yesterday I worked in the garden a while and turned Arthur loose," Porter wrote. "He spent most of the time at the same places we have him tied. Went across to the rear of the mule barn once but came right back. However, I had to chase him out of the garden two or three times so I guess we can't leave him untied except when we are there. The first thing he did when he got loose was to run up on the back porch." In a later letter, "The first day we let Arthur loose he let us walk up to him and put the rope on him to lead him back, but yesterday he was beginning to catch on and would run away. Finally Sam lassoed him. Caught him on one foot as he was running."

And the garden: "I hoed the garden, transplanted some okra and squash where none had come up, dug back bermuda and Johnson grass around the edges, suckered and tied up Joe's and my tomatoes, and put bug dust on everything of ours. Sam is tending to his, more or less."

Sam had a small part in a Town Theater play. He was a last-minute fill-in for James McCain, a grown man, who had to drop out of the cast. "Sam did well except that he talked so fast you couldn't understand him," Porter wrote. "I was about halfway back and caught only two words, 'roller skates.' He had a pair in his hand and I guess that helped me. Everybody laughed when H. A. Smith mentioned that Sam was to be married. It wasn't supposed to be funny but they laughed because Sam was so young [13]."

Porter and Sam were battling bugs in the house and making some progress: "Having conquered the ants with Green Cross and the roaches with a carton of bait on the kitchen floor, we have now made arrangements to get rid of the flies for the summer. We have bought some poison fly paper that is supposed to kill them in droves. You put a little water on it in a plate and the flies sip the water and drop dead. We put some out tonight and up to the time we left, no flies had sipped. Or at least if they had, they hadn't dropped dead."

A couple of weeks into Alice's absence Porter wrote, "We sure were glad to get your letter saying you will be home a week from tomorrow. Sam has the housework in pretty good shape except for cleaning up. We haven't swept or dusted since you left, but it doesn't need it much . . . I took nearly 1-1/2 bushels of Irish potatoes for two subscriptions today. Do you reckon they will keep?" In his final letter he wrote, "I really am by myself today, with Sam at Birmingham (to see a model airplane contest). He left planning to stop off at Trussville and see if he could hint his way into an invitation to spend the night. I gave him enough money to go to a hotel in case he didn't get invited. We had a good poker game last night. I won 84 cents. Tell Joe to find all about how to irrigate so we can do it the right way . . . Lots of people ask when you all are coming home. I guess Mary's strategy must have worked on Sam. I notice he wrote a letter yesterday. Sam and I have proved definitely that there is nothing to the theory that warm water washes cleaner than cold water. We have not had a fire in the kitchen stove [the one that connected with the water heater] since you all left, and we have washed ourselves and the clothes as clean as ever."

Sam did hint his way into an invitation to stay overnight in Trussville with the Elbert Smiths, their former next-door neighbors. On his way home from Birmingham, though, he fell asleep on the bus and instead of getting off in Guntersville he wound up about midnight in Huntsville, the end of the bus run. The bus station had already closed for the night. He didn't know if he had enough money to pay for both a phone call and bus fare back to Guntersville so he didn't phone. He slept on the ground in back of a warehouse near the bus station and caught a bus the next morning. Porter didn't tell Alice about that till she and the other children got home.

CHAPTER 11

Twice A Week

Publishing twice a week was a big gamble. It was tempting in 1944 to combine the *Advertiser* and the *Gleam* into a single weekly. That path offered some economies. There would be only one front page a week—and front pages lose money because they contain no ads, or at least not many. There would be only one mailing operation. Postal costs would be lower. The pressure of closing everything out would come only half as often. Once-a-week was the pattern in the great majority of Alabama towns the size of Guntersville.

But Porter saw opportunity in a semi-weekly. He felt it would help discourage potential competitors. He liked the prospect of being able to get the news out quicker. He figured he would get more ads by giving merchants more choice as to when their ads would appear. Simply being able to publish the paper in his own shop instead of going to Albertville may have made the prospect seem less daunting. And he was never one to shrink from a challenge.

Two papers a week meant Porter would have to come up with more ads and more news. In the past the *Gleam* had usually managed four or six pages. Now it would take a minimum of eight pages for the two papers. And often the timing of the ads would call for one of the papers to have six pages, meaning a weekly total of 10. The six-page papers generally came on Friday. Advertisers liked to get their messages to customers close to the weekend. Saturday was the big shopping day, the day farmers and their families came into town, the day people with jobs had money from being paid.

For a while Porter continued to handle just about all the ads himself, in addition to the news. Mary Hugh Wood had moved from the *Gleam* office to the new office. A little later, Martha King, who had worked at the *Gleam* previously, rejoined the staff. Alice was still teaching school, and she had also started working on Saturdays at Wiles Grocery half a block from home. One day in early 1945 the owner, Tom Wiles, had a suggestion for Porter.

"He asked me if Alice wouldn't be worth more working on the paper than what she was making teaching school," Porter said. Tom's wife, Gladys, had worked with him at the store for many years.

Porter and Alice talked it over. Alice was already a little concerned about teaching the next year because Mary would be moving up to the seventh grade, which was part of the high school. Alice didn't think it would be a good idea for her to have her own children in her class. When Sam was in junior high she taught senior high classes. As Sam moved up she moved down. But in 1945-46 Sam would be in the 11th and Mary would be in the seventh and Alice wasn't sure she could schedule around both of them. She and Porter decided to give up the sure thing of a teaching salary for the gamble of working in the newspaper office. She was to work alongside Porter 28 years.

"It was a great move," Porter said. "She could do anything. At different times—or even all at the same time—she sold ads, wrote news, was bookkeeper, circulation manager and I don't remember what else. And through it all she was the steadying influence that kept me from going off the deep end oftener than I did."

Interviewed once by the *Birmingham News* along with other Alabama newspaper wives, Alice said newspaper work was a lot of fun. But it was also a lot like housework: "You work at it all the time and you never get it done."

All three of the Harvey children worked at the paper. Sam, who turned 14 the month Porter bought the *Advertiser*, started working in the shop after school and on Saturday mornings. His main job was running the newspaper press. It printed two pages at a time. The standard schedule was to print the first two pages of the *Advertiser* on Monday, then turn them over and print the other two on Tuesday, when the paper was mailed. The *Gleam* was printed on Wednesday and Thursday, with an extra run Wednesday night if the paper was to have six pages instead of four. The press required a catcher as well as a feeder. Long wooden fingers deposited the papers on a table. The catcher had to keep them in a straight pile, so they could be turned over and fed through the press again, or through the machine that folded them. Both Mary and Joe caught some until Porter was cautioned about letting them work there because of their age (Mary was eleven and Joe was nine). Both jobs were pretty monotonous, but the feeder at least had the challenge of putting the papers into the press just right to avoid the disaster known as a roll-up. That happened when the paper came loose from the grippers and wrapped around the rubber ink rollers, where it usually tore itself into small pieces that had to be laboriously cleaned off. Catching was pure drudgery. Joe remembers throwing a metal tool known as a quoin key on the floor so Sam would hear it and stop the press, thinking something had come loose from the page forms. "That way I got some rest," Joe explained later. More than likely he was just bored and inspired by the prospect of shaking up his older brother. Before long Porter bought a newer second-hand press, a Lee, still a two-pager but with a mechanical jogger that kept the papers straight as they were printed. It could also run faster, to better keep up with the increasing circulation of the *Advertiser* and the *Gleam*.

Sam was running the press one afternoon in April 1945 when his friend Earl Hammer came into the shop and told him that Franklin D. Roosevelt, the only president either of them could remember, had died. The war ended shortly after that. Joe remembers walking home from the office with Porter when R. A. Brown, who owned the Chevrolet dealership across the street, stopped them. The men talked about the end of the war that had so dominated everyone's lives. Mr. Brown got an automatic pistol out of a safe in his office and talked Porter into firing it into the air in celebration. Joe also watched while someone in the sheriff's office stood in front of the jail across the street and fired a machine gun into the air, the bullets tracing patterns in the evening sky.

When Porter bought the *Advertiser*, it had only two full-time shop employees, the foreman, Emmett Reynolds, and the Linotype operator, Aileen Williams. Printers were scarce during the war, like people in all other trades, because so many men were in service. Emmett built ads out of handset type, laid out pages, printed all sorts of forms and supplies for businesses, supervised the mailing and did anything else that needed doing. Aileen spent almost all her time operating the Linotype, which converted melted lead into "straight matter," the small type that news articles were printed in. It was a wondrous machine, incredibly faster than setting the tiny type by hand the way it had been done early in the century, but nowhere near as fast as the electronic "cold-type" devices that would replace it later. Emmett had been born with club feet and, like Porter, walked with a limp. So he was ineligible for the Army. Not long after Porter bought the paper, Emmett got an offer to work for a newspaper in another town. The prospect of trying to replace him was frightening, and Porter simply didn't know how he would manage to get the paper out if Emmett left. But Emmett decided to stay, and he was to remain in charge of the shop for more than thirty years.

When the war ended, the economy picked up steam and so did the newspaper business. Men came out of the services looking for work, and Porter gradually added people in both the office and the shop. Katherine Duncan had worked at the old *Advertiser* in 1917 when she was in high school, addressing newspapers by hand before they went in the mail. In her new job she waited on customers, edited country letters, and read proof. She was given some advertisers to call on. She started the column "Chatter," the closest thing to a society page that Porter would allow. She frequently used her lunch hour to go through the files of old newspapers to compile a column, "Yesteryears." She also made notes that ultimately led her to co-author the book *The History of Marshall County*.

Fay Starkey began working in the office in 1946 after she finished high school, replacing Mary Hugh Wood. She was to work there 19 years. She "did a little bit of everything," as most employees did, including keeping books. She wrote a headline on a country letter that Porter (a superb headwriter himself) thought may have been the best the paper ever ran for reader appeal and for getting right to the heart of the story: "Pig Drowns in Slop." Faye recalls the time some of the shop employees came to work with a jug of home brew, and some of the men took turns nipping from it till Porter finally found out and made them quit. It was illegal then to have alcohol in Guntersville and the police station was next door. He didn't think it would look very good if the law found out, not to mention what it might do to the men's ability to set type or run presses.

Porter didn't write editorials in the paper's early years. He admired the motto of the Scripps-Howard chain, owner of the *Birmingham Post* where he had worked, "Give Light and the People Will Find Their Own Way" (not that the motto ever kept Scripps-Howard from editorializing). Porter saw his job as reporting what went on, rather than trying to tell people what to think about it. But in 1946 the papers began carrying a front-page column in most issues, "Did You Ever Stop to Think." It was signed only "Bud." It was written by R. A. (Bob) Conard, who had come to town with TVA and then became the part-time manager of the Chamber of Commerce. He earned a nominal $20 a month from the paper. As the name implied, the column primarily tried to draw readers' attention to things they might not otherwise think about. It was an approach Porter felt comfortable with. Sometimes the column used conversations between two fictional men, Hal and Steve, to make points about public issues.

The column often tackled three or four topics in an issue. On January 9, 1946, "Bud" noted that servicemen were trickling back to the community: "This is as it should be. We need new blood to carry on." Golf was one activity that the returning young men and the elders could enjoy together: "Come on—let's have a golf course!" A fifteen-minute parking rule in front of the Post Office would be a great convenience. Housing was becoming critical, with servicemen coming home, and Guntersville needed to do something about it: "A first and important step is opening up new streets, making more building lots available. The next step is the extension of sewers and water mains to such property. It is believed with these two steps, the houses will follow. The city and the property owners must get together on those two steps. Yours till next time, Bud."

"Did You Ever Stop To Think" was invariably positive in its approach to public issues. Porter frequently suggested topics that "Bud" might want to write about, and the column remained a part of the paper's front page for seven years. It inspired a similar column in a paper in faraway Seward, Alaska, published by Chrystine Rouse. Her sister Mary Rouse worked in the newspaper shop in Guntersville and her sister Lucille, a teacher, wrote the paper's personals. Chrystine called her column, "Did It Ever Occur to You?"

The newspaper continued to give readers a lot for their money. A typical issue on January 11, 1946, carried 17 news stories on the front page—plus a *Gleam*reel, correspondents' reports from Wesson Branch and Haney's Chapel, "Did You Ever Stop To Think," and a two-column ad for Economy Furniture. Front-page ads were generally frowned on in journalistic circles, but Porter couldn't see any reason not to run them, especially at the premium prices which that space commanded.

A feature began in the summer of 1946 that was to appear off and on for years, the "Quiz." Porter would pose a question one week and answer it the next. "What Guntersville man spent last summer at a place where the sun didn't set all summer long?" asked the Quiz of July 10, 1946. The answer was Stuart Stone, a Guntersville lawyer who had been in the Navy Seabees at Barrow, Alaska. The answer took nearly a column, relating the details of Mr. Stone's time in the frozen north. The next Quiz reflecting Porter's lifelong fascination with words: "What Guntersville man has five capitals in his name?" (Answer: R. F. B. St. John.)

Porter got up his first special edition in 1946. He was convinced it was going to make a lot of money. The first postwar running of the annual Guntersville Boat Races was set for that summer, and people were expecting a huge crowd. "We will print about 20,000 copies and expect the souvenir edition to be read by 80,000 to 100,000 people," an ad the previous month proclaimed. "We'll need to sell a good many ads but we won't have much time to do much soliciting. If you'd like to put an ad before 80,000 people, many of them frequent visitors to Guntersville, let us know and we'll fix you up. Because of the large circulation, the rate will have to be higher than the regular rate."

The special edition was a 16-page tabloid. Porter had it printed in Birmingham, with color on the front page. The red ink turned out to be reflective of the issue itself. Businesses didn't exactly break down the doors to buy ads. And most of the 20,000 papers remained unsold after the races were over. Porter and Sam loaded the papers into the 1939 Ford the family had recently acquired. Waiting till almost dark so nobody would see them, they hauled them to the city dump. Porter, who disliked asking businesses to buy ads that he didn't think would do them much good, remained forever leery of the special editions that some newspapers put out with astonishing frequency.

He had no hesitation, however, about accepting some ads that other papers might quibble over. A regular ad in the 1940s and 1950s featured the palmist Malawha, who lived and held forth on the road to Arab. "Consult One Who Knows," the two-column ad stated. "By a natural gift she is able to tell you everything in a clear and intelligent manner, demonstrating that her power is little short of supernatural . . . No orthodox Christian, professional alienist, student or professor of psychology nor judge upon the bench should fail to consult this woman of mystery."

Chiropractors' ads were welcomed too. Most contained the testimony of patients who had found blessed relief on the chiropractic table. Porter got a kick out of their claims and figured his readers probably would too. "I Was in a Nervous Jerk All Over My Body," proclaimed one long-running ad.

All weekly newspapers found it hard to attract national advertising. In 1947, Porter and the publishers of seven other papers went together in a venture known as "Alabama's Greater Weeklies." They offered advertisers 19,000 paid circulation in Guntersville, Haleyville, Fayette, Geneva, Homewood, Sylacauga, Winfield and Alexander City. The combined rate was $5.02 per column inch. Like most other attempts to market weeklies outside their own towns, this one had limited success and was soon dropped.

Not that the Guntersville paper's ads lacked pulling power. The front page of September 12, 1947, carried a picture of J. W. Higgins and Maude Southerland with the headline, "He Found Her." Mr. Higgins had run a 50-cent classified ad for a wife. He kept the ad going for several weeks (a point Porter always liked to stress) and "he received 37 replies before he finally found the lady he wanted for a wife. They are shown here after their wedding."

By this time Porter was frequently getting up 12 pages between the two papers, six on Wednesday and six on Friday, with an occasional eight-page whopper on Friday when the ads were booming.

In 1948, an ad in the paper boasted, "Audited Circulation More than 3,400." The word "audited" was significant. Weekly papers were sometimes given to stretching the figures when asked how many subscribers they had. Porter signed up with the Audit Bureau of Circulation, the national agency that verifies the circulation of practically all major magazines and daily papers. Very few weeklies, even those that were honest in their claims, wanted to go to the expense or the trouble of being audited. But Porter thought it was important that advertisers know he was telling the truth. So he signed up, and the paper has remained a member ever since. At times it has been the only ABC weekly in Alabama.

In early 1948, Porter got some competition. The weekly *Marshall Times* was started by three men who owned the Anchor Cafe across from the Post Office—L. C. Stewart, E. C. Smeds and S. M. Olson. They felt, among other things, that the *Advertiser* and the *Gleam* were failing to reach newcomers who were living in lakeside cabins and homes, either full-time or part-time. One feature of the *Times* was a column, "Around the Lake." But the new paper never attracted many subscribers or advertisers, and after four months the partners gave up. They gave their subscription list to Porter, and he agreed to provide their readers with a newspaper for the rest of the time they had paid for. The announcement also said the papers would carry a new column, "Life On The Lake," which before long would give way to "Chatter." It was the last challenge Porter was to face in the form of hometown competition, despite occasional rumors that somebody was thinking about it.

While absorbing the *Marshall Times*, Porter was trying to decide whether to combine the *Advertiser* and the *Gleam* into a true semi-weekly with a single name. Alice made a trip to Kansas in June of 1948 to see her parents, and Porter wrote to her about a possible complication involving postal rates if he changed from two papers to one. "I am writing to some semi-weeklies to see how they handle it," he told her. "We may decide to keep the papers separate after all."

The question was resolved, and on October 1, 1948, readers received the first issue of the *Advertiser-Gleam*. Beneath the new nameplate on the front page was the line, "Successor to: The *Democrat*, established 1880; *Advertiser*, 1914; *Gleam*, 1941; *Marshall Times*, 1948."

"The paper will continue to have the same news and ads as before," the announcement said. "The schedule will continue the same, two issues going out each week, Wednesday and Friday. The only change is that instead of the Wednesday paper being named the *Advertiser* and the Friday paper the *Gleam*, both will be named the *Advertiser-Gleam*."

Sam had continued to work in the shop while he was in high school, although he worked fewer hours than he had worked during the war when grownup help was hard to come by. He wrote for the high school paper, the *Wildcat*. When he finished high school in 1947, he enrolled in the journalism department of the University of Alabama and worked on the student paper, the *Crimson-White*. He worked summers at the *Advertiser-Gleam*. By then he had moved from the shop to the office, where he did a combination of news, ads, clerical work, and other chores.

Mary helped out in the back shop on mailing days, tying up small bundles and wrapping single copies. She was 14 or 15. Teenage boys handled most of the mailing operation. "I liked it because I would be the only girl working there," Mary said. "Emmett once told Daddy that I talked too much. I started working in the office in the summers from about my senior year on through college. For a while I wrote a column called Chatter Jr. I was probably a senior then. Frances Smith had written it first, and she graduated a year ahead of me." In the summers Mary would work half a day and Alice the other half, to give Alice a breather. Mary read proof, edited country letters, went through the mail, answered the phone, and went to stores to pick up ad copy. At times she called people at random in search of news for the "Personals" column, a task she hated but Porter insisted on.

Joe worked some at the shop, but not as much as either Sam or Mary. He was an athlete, unlike Sam, and baseball, football, and basketball took up a lot of his spare time. And by the time Joe got old enough to work legally, the wartime manpower shortage was long since over.

CHAPTER 12

'Behaving Reasonably Well'

The civil rights movement that followed World War II brought tense times to Alabama, especially in areas with large numbers of blacks. The black population of Marshall County was less than two percent, but the county didn't entirely escape some of what was going on elsewhere. A cross-burning in 1949 got Porter and the *Advertiser-Gleam* written up in some daily papers around the state.

Actually there were two cross-burnings. The first took place at East Lake. Nobody knew what to make of it. Porter wrote in the *Gleam*, "This is the first incident reported in the county in years smacking of terrorism. If there is any Ku Klux Klan organization in the county, we haven't heard of it." The next issue contained an explanation: A cross with 12 candles had been used during a worship service at a picnic by the young people from the First Methodist Church. The cross caught fire. The kids put it out but left it there, where it was found and thought to be something entirely different. "The burning wasn't an indication that Marshall County may be in for some of the terroristic mess that is disgracing a few other counties in the state," Porter's story concluded.

Early the next morning somebody burned a cross in the Harveys' front yard.

"It was a crudely made cross about three feet high, wrapped with tow sacks soaked in kerosene," the *Gleam*'s next issue reported. The bottom was nailed to an old washboard that lay flat on the ground and served as a base to hold the cross upright. Porter and Alice were awakened about 3:00 a.m. by their dog barking at the flames and went out to see about it. Nobody was in sight. After the fire had burned down and they had gone back inside the house, a car or truck drove slowly along Gunter Avenue a block away with the horn blowing almost constantly. It went around the Courthouse square and then left.

In Porter's story in the *Gleam*, he quoted himself, "Mr. and Mrs. Harvey don't know whether to regard the cross as a joke or a serious warning of some sort. 'The only thing I can think that might have brought it on,' he said, 'is that we have mentioned the Klan and other such groups in the paper a couple of times lately. In one piece I said that if there was any Klan organization in this county, I haven't heard of it. The cross might have been an answer to that, either as a joke or otherwise. None of our mentions of the under-cover activities have been exactly complimentary. I have always been opposed to any group of people who try to take the law into their own hands and are too cowardly to show their faces or take the responsibility for what they do.' He claims he doesn't know any personal reason for the cross being burned in his yard. He insists he has been supporting his family and behaving reasonably well."

Much later Porter heard that the cross had been burned in the yard simply as a prank by a man from East Lake. In future years there would be attempts from time to time to establish a Klan in Marshall County, but none of them lasted very long or made much headway.

Porter enjoyed using superlatives. He liked being able to say that Dock King was the tallest man in the county, that Zeke Boyles's funeral drew the biggest crowd of any local funeral in history, and that Leon Kennamer was the world's leading authority on outdoor portraiture. In June 1949 he wrote an ad for the *Gleam* whose headline bragged, "The Biggest Advertising Bargain in Marshall County History." The text said the *Advertiser-Gleam* now had more than 3,500 paid circulation, verified by the ABC. "That means our local advertising rate (50 cents per column inch) is less than 15 one-thousandths of a cent per paid subscriber. That is lower than it was before the war. In 1941, an ad in either the *Advertiser* or the *Gleam* cost more than 17 one-thousandths of a cent per paid subscriber. When you consider the difference in the value of a dollar now and then, you can see what an unprecedented bargain our circulation represents." The *Advertiser-Gleam* now had, he wrote, "more paid subscribers than any other Alabama paper published in a city this size."

Merchants were slowly becoming more advertising-minded. By 1950, full-page ads were no longer all that rare. Guntersville that year got its first real supermarket, an A&P, which ran pretty big ads and ran them every week. The town's first radio station, WGSV, opened in April of that year. Although he was a little uneasy about the competition for ad dollars, Porter joined other businesses in an opening day program welcoming the new station. Later he concluded that ads on the radio didn't really hurt the newspaper and, by making people more ad-conscious, might even have helped. The paper and radio station started out on good terms and remained that way.

Alice was one of the nominees that fall for Guntersville Woman of the Year, an honor that went to her friend, Annie Virgie Barton.

The fall of 1950 found three newspaper editors in the family. Mary was editor of the *Wildcat* at Marshall County High School. And Sam had lucked into the editorship of the *Crimson-White*, the student paper at the University, when the elected editor was recalled by the Army during the Korean War. Sam caused something of a stir in one of his first issues, a week before he was promoted from acting editor to editor. He wrote an editorial which he titled "The Southern College and the Color Line." In it he predicted that blacks would be admitted to the University before too long, adding, "We fail to see what would be so terrible about it." The wire services sent out pieces about it that ran in a good many dailies around the state. It even got a couple of paragraphs in the *New York Times*.

The *Gleam* continued to print intriguing news of a kind that didn't often make it into other papers. A headline on February 7, 1951, stated simply, "Ear Bitten Off." "We keep hearing about a fight that happened at a party the other night at Pleasant Hill," Porter wrote. "As near as we can find out, the results were approximately as follows: Bill Davidson of Pleasant Hill lost part of his ear. We understand it was bitten off. Dub

Kay of Mountain View was cut twice across the chest and stabbed in the back, but it seems that none of his wounds were very bad. The boys have always been real good friends, and still are. We have conflicting reports as to what became of the piece of ear. One report is that Bill was carrying it around in his pocket, and said he was a good mind to make Dub eat it. Another report was that Dub had it in his pocket. Still another was that a lady slipped it from them and buried it."

The family in 1950. Seated, Alice, Porter, and Mary. Standing, Joe and Sam.

On September 7, 1951: "The day after her marriage, Mrs. Willard Wade of Guntersville was found in the woods with her face severely bruised and her body almost covered with 150 to 200 whip marks [from a switch]. Her husband was found guilty in City Court the next day of assault and battery. Judge Williams fined him $100 and gave him six months. He did not deny whipping his bride but said he didn't remember hitting her in the face."

After 22 years of renting and 10 years across from the Courthouse, Porter and Alice moved in 1951 into the only house they ever owned. It was a one-floor, three-bedroom house on Alves Road in Carlisle Park, a postwar subdivision on the west side of the ridge that splits the Guntersville peninsula. They had considered building and had looked at a good many lots. But they decided to take the easy way out and buy one that was already built. They bought it from Mr. and Mrs. A. B. Marsh when it was three or four years old.

At work Porter and the staff got up a special edition in 1951, selling ads to businesses so they could show the pictures of all the people who worked in each place. It turned out to be a 24-page issue with ads from 149 businesses. The businesses had their people go to Bill Kroelinger's photo studio to have their pictures made. Mary was working that summer, and part of her job was hounding the stores to send their people in for their pictures. The *Gleam*'s own ad listed 20 people, full-time and part-time. The title under each name was followed by "etc." to indicate that everybody did more than one job. Porter was listed as "editor, etc.," Alice as "business manager, etc." and Mary as "reporter, etc." Others were Bill Mahan, printer; L. G. Morrow, mailer; Fay Starkey, circulation manager; Dona Riddle, Arab reporter; Billy Grant, Linotype operator; Lucille Rouse, reporter; James Patterson, Jr., pressman; Kenneth Cornelius, mailer; Jean Goecks, printer; Katherine Duncan, society editor; Emmett Reynolds, shop foreman; Shorty King, ad salesman; R. A. Conard, "Bud" columnist; J. D. Looney, janitor; Mary Rouse, Linotype operator; Glema Richardson, Graphotype operator, and Jesse B. Allen, Addressograph operator.

Porter listed himself as editor rather than publisher, just as he did in the masthead in each issue, although he was both. He said people knew what it meant to be editor, but they weren't sure about the role of publisher.

In the spring of 1952, the paper ran dozens of pictures of people with stockings over their faces, their features all distorted. Readers were invited to guess who each person was. The picture would be rerun the next week along with a normal shot of the person. "We got the idea from Life magazine," Porter conceded.

The paper also got up a list of eligible bachelors for Leap Year, since that's the time for ladies to pop the question. Readers were asked to send in the names of bachelors and also to rate them on finances, behavior, type and attitude. On finances, for instance, they would be categorized as one of the following: A, needs help to spend it; B, has enough; C, can scrape by; D, you'd better keep your job; and E, poor as an editor. One bachelor who made the list was Sam, who was listed as "already spoken for." He was out of college and in the Air Force by then, and while in Washington he had met Valerie Yencha of Latrobe, Pennsylvania, whom he was to marry the following year.

After a couple of months of listing bachelors and their ratings, the paper announced the list was complete. "We have listed 538," Porter wrote. "If you haven't found one to your liking among all these, you must be mighty hard to please." He noted that the total was 50 more than a bachelor list the paper had gotten up four years earlier.

Photographs were showing up more often in the paper, but it still wasn't unusual for a front page to be printed without one. Porter felt that a picture ought to show something and not be run just for the sake of having a picture. He delighted in pictures like the five he ran in June 1952 of Buddy Taylor's duck. The duck had taken up with the family dog and apparently thought it was a dog. If another dog came up, the duck would run it off. Later that month Porter ran a picture with the caption "Where Is It?" and a warning, "There's a trick about this." It was a picture of Army trucks lined up near the barge dock in Northtown—but Porter ran the picture upside down, giving it a weird, surrealistic look.

The editorial column "Did You Ever Stop To Think," was discontinued in 1953. The writer, R. A. Conard or "Bud," had moved back to his home state after his eyesight failed. Later that year Porter began writing his own editorials, at first only occasionally, and then more frequently. Like Bud's pieces, they ran initially on the front page, under the overline, "As the editor sees it." One of his first appeared February 12, 1954, and it dealt with blacks and the right to vote. Some local blacks (the term used in those days was "colored") had tried to register "but for one reason or other they were all turned down." Porter noted that it was a hard thing for the registrars, because of the long Southern tradition against blacks voting. "Yet by all principles of justice they have a right to . . . We don't bar them when it's time to pay taxes, or go to war. There isn't any sound reason for barring them when it's time to vote, either . . . It will be far better to welcome them into full citizenship than to have it forced on us from the outside." It was to be 11 years before Congress would pass the Voting Rights Act, which guaranteed blacks everywhere the right to vote. But three weeks after the editorial appeared, the *Advertiser-Gleam* reported, "The first colored people to qualify as voters in Marshall County, at least in modern times, registered at the Courthouse Monday. They were a Guntersville couple, Joe D. (Shank) Moore and his wife Odell Moore. She had paid her poll tax before the deadline February 1, and he is exempt because he is a veteran."

Partly to encourage rural correspondents to report things besides visits and illnesses, Porter started putting news headlines beneath the small community headings. The issue of January 29, 1954, contained "Home Burned" over the Preston column, "Now She's a Nurse" over Pine Ridge and "Home Burglarized" over Radio Hill. Other country letters in that issue were from New Harmony, Mountain View, Jack Webb Store, Nixon Chapel, Douglas, Preston, Anderson Ridge, Georgia Mountain, Swearengin, Polecat, Red Hill and Kings Hollow. The paper totaled up the rural correspondents in 1955 and found there were 102 of them. "They are an unusually good bunch," Porter wrote. "In fact, they frequently send us so much news that we can't get it all in the paper and have to hold part of it over till the next week." A house ad asked people to tell their community correspondent of any news they knew about. If nobody in that community was writing news, "Maybe you can help us get somebody. A good correspondent is a big asset to a community. How about helping us out?"

The paper by the mid-1950s was averaging about 16 pages a week, usually eight on Wednesday and eight on Friday, with an occasional 10 or even 12 on Friday. The two-page press had given way to a four-page. A second Linotype had been bought to help keep up with the greater volume of news and also to help set small type for ads. A machine known as a Ludlow offered an alternative to handset type for the larger type in ads and commercial printing.

Competitors continued to get the friendly treatment. On February 17, 1954, the paper carried a front-page feature story on the four-year-old radio station, WGSV, with six pictures. One photo showed announcer Ray McClendon with mouth wide open and the caption, "From the cavern above comes Guntersville's best known voice . . . Long before Guntersville had a radio station, he started training his voice by reading newspapers out loud." In April 1955, a front-page story announced that Marshall County was getting a daily newspaper, a five-day-a-week tabloid called the *Sand Mountain Reporter*, to be published in Albertville. It would be the first paper in Alabama printed by the offset method. It would emphasize pictures, which the offset process excelled at. Its publisher, Albertville radio station owner Pat Courington, saw it as circulating throughout the county, including Guntersville. And in June of that year Porter reported that Arab was getting a paper, the *Arab News-Record.* His story described the new paper as "well written and well edited, with a good volume of ads. For a long time Arab has felt the need of a paper of its own. Alan Barker, editor and publisher, is going to do everything he can to fill this need . . . The *Advertiser-Gleam* extends to Mr. and Mrs. Barker, and to Arab, sincere wishes for the success of the *News-Record.*"

Rival ideas also got equal time. Porter wrote an editorial March 5, 1954, suggesting it was time to number and rename some of the streets to make it easier for people to find their way around town. "Bud" had proposed the same thing several years earlier, without getting anywhere. The notion didn't sit well with Guntersville old-timers, including Katherine Duncan of the *Gleam* office. In the paper after Porter's editorial, the front page carried a much longer article she wrote, "Let's Keep Historic Names of Our Streets." The street names stayed as they were.

A photo of two men in stocking masks appeared in the issue of May 28, 1954. As a gag, Tom Grimes and Forrest Shields had knocked on several people's doors while dolled up that way. Virginia McGowin took their picture and brought it to the paper. "For the peace of mind of *Advertiser-Gleam* readers who lived through our series of stocking face pictures two years ago," Porter wrote, "we want to assure them that this isn't the beginning of another series."

In 1953 Porter, Alice and Mary flew to Pennsylvania for Sam's wedding. Sam was out of the Air Force now after 21 months. He had graduated from the University in May 1951 with a journalism degree and an Air Force officer's commission from ROTC. The Korean War was on and new lieutenants were being called to active duty as soon as they graduated. He was in Washington being trained at Georgetown University in psychological warfare when he met Valerie Yencha. They were introduced by Barbara Burrow, who had finished in journalism at the University the previous year. She was working in Washington for an Alabama congressman, Carl Elliott. Val was working for a congressman from Indiana and was shortly to move to the office of her own congressman, Gus Kelley of Pennsylvania. She and Sam drove to Guntersville in December after his time at Georgetown was over and she met his family. He was sent to Idaho and then to the Philippines. They got engaged in the spring of 1952 during his pre-embarkation leave. Val found out that she and Porter had the same favorite comic strip, Walt Kelly's "Pogo." The Birmingham paper at that time carried it only on weekdays. While Sam was overseas, Val would clip "Pogo" out of the Washington Star every Sunday and mail it to Porter.

In November of 1952 Val and her sister Marge flew to Alabama to spend Thanksgiving with Porter, Alice, Mary and Joe. Another Yankee visitor was there at the same time, a University of Alabama senior from New Jersey whom Mary was dating, Gay Talese. He was destined to be the most famous journalist the University of Alabama ever produced—a writer for the *New York Times* and *Esquire*, author of several books and pioneer of a form of journalism that used many techniques of fiction in telling factual stories. Joe was a senior in high school. He had been captain of the football team and was looking forward to the basketball and baseball seasons.

Sam got out of the Air Force the next spring, and he and Val were married on April 25, 1953, in the archabbey church at St. Vincent College in Latrobe, Pennsylvania. They left after the reception for their honeymoon, while Alice, Porter, and Mary went to the Yencha home in the coal-mining village of Marguerite. There Val's mother, Anna Yencha, and the rest of the large Yencha clan introduced them to halupkes, nut rolls and other Slovak dishes.

Val and Sam spent the summer in Washington, where he found a temporary job. That fall they headed to Tuscaloosa for a year at the

Gay Talese (left), who later gained journalistic and literary fame, spent Thanksgiving with the Harveys in 1952. Alice plays, seated next to Sam's future wife, Valerie Yencha. Others standing are Joe, Porter, Joe's future wife Jo Kirkpatrick, and Val's sister Marge Yencha.

University. They stopped in Rome so Val could meet relatives there. Porter's father Evan had died 11 years earlier. The heart trouble that had been detected when he was 41 finally killed him, but not till he was 70. His mother Fanny had cancer and was living with her daughter Frances Wood and her family. Porter and Alice had told them about Val's singing voice, and Fanny asked her to stand by her bed and sing "Let There Be Peace on Earth." She died a couple of months later. Sam and Val spent ten months at the University, he in graduate school and she as a special student, taking courses mainly in music. They went north in the summer of 1954 with Sam still lacking a thesis for a master's degree. He found a job as a reporter on the *Evening Dispatch* in Columbus, Ohio. By then, they were expecting their first child.

Mary was a junior at the University during that year, majoring in home economics. She had long since shed the poundage that had caused friends to nickname her "Tubb" and as a junior she was voted one of the 20 Corolla Beauties, with a half-page portrait in the University yearbook. She was president of her sorority, Zeta Tau Alpha, just as Alice had been president of that sorority at Washburn. Mary by then was again dating Don Woodward of Harperville, Mississippi, who had spent two summers in Guntersville with his cousin Lamar Majure Jr. while Mary was in high school. Don had been a student at Mississippi State when he enlisted in the Air Force to keep from being drafted into the Army. He was out of service and Mary was a new graduate of the University when they married June 18, 1955, in the First Methodist Church in Guntersville. Don lacked a year and a half of finishing college, so they started their marriage in Starkville, he in business school at Mississippi State and she working as a home economist for the local electric co-op.

Joe was a freshman at the University of Alabama the year Val and Sam were there, so all three of the Harvey children were on the campus at the same time. Joe was studying to be an industrial engineer. His dormitory was close to Val's and Sam's apartment, and he found the quickest and cheapest breakfast he could get was to dash by their place, down a couple of raw eggs in a glass of milk and head for the engineering building across a big field from where they lived. Most of his weekends were taken up traveling to and from Montevallo where his high school sweetheart, Jo Kirkpatrick, was attending what was then called the Alabama College for Women.

Joe had worked less at the *Gleam* as a youngster than either Sam or Mary, and he was to be the only one of the three who didn't eventually migrate back to Guntersville and the paper. He knew when he finished high school in 1953 that he wanted to be an engineer. He got a job that summer working at the Redmer machine tool plant in Guntersville, but he stayed there only two weeks. "The company lost a contract with the Arsenal and I got laid off," he said. "Then I went to Detroit. I said it was so I could work, but it was really so I could be with Jo, who was spending the summer with her sisters and earning money for her own college. I got a job at the DeSoto plant (part of Chrysler Corporation) but after two weeks at that job they laid everybody off and the plant folded. I worked the rest of the summer at the Packard auto plant helping x-ray jet engine parts." Packard didn't last much longer either, and Joe later said he helped wipe out three companies in just one summer. In college he was an A and B student and was elected president of the Engineering School student body. In 1957, he received the "Outstanding Engineering Graduate" award.

He and Jo got married August 31, 1957, in the Church of Christ in Guntersville, soon after he graduated as an industrial engineer. He took a job with American Air Filter, trained for six months in Louisville and then was assigned to their plant in Moline, Illinois. AAF transferred him to their plant in Morrison, Illinois, 44 miles away, and then to Brownsville, Tennessee, when the Morrison plant closed. In 1968 he started a long career with the Carrier Corporation, the air-conditioning company, at a new plant in McMinnville, Tennessee. Although he and Jo never moved back to Guntersville, they raised their four children only a two-and-a-half hour drive away.

Porter published his paper for 11 years in the building he took over when he bought the *Advertiser*. With the business growing, he clearly needed more room. He also thought he'd do better in the long run if he had a building of his own. He bought a lot on Taylor Street, just across the alley from the back of the two-story building where he had started out in 1941. He hired Mack Gilbreath to oversee the construction of a 35-by-110 foot brick and block building. "Here We Come, Ready Or Not," said the headline on a story June 10, 1955. The new building wasn't quite finished, but he had to move because the old building had already been rented out for the county's commodity-foods program. The move was set for that weekend. "The roof is of hollow concrete slabs, the first in Guntersville," the story said. The building was half-again as big as the old one. And it had air conditioning, something that only movie theaters had been able to boast of just a few years earlier.

As luck and the construction schedule would have it, the move took place only a week before Mary's and Don's wedding. Alice's parents had come from Kansas with Alice's brother Victor and his children, Carl and Jeanette. Sam and Val had come from Columbus with five-month-old Kenneth. Margaret Nicholas, the maid of honor, was up from Dothan. They all stayed with Porter and Alice in their three-bedroom, one bath house or with neighbors, and they all ate at the Harveys'. So Alice was dealing simultaneously with all the details of her only daughter's wedding, a slew of out-of-town guests, and helping get out a newspaper in a building where everything was in a brand new location. If it rattled her, she never let on.

While Joe was in college, he came across the idea of profit sharing by businesses, a concept that was also known as incentive management. The idea intrigued him. He asked Porter if he thought profit sharing might work at the *Advertiser-Gleam*. Porter was intrigued too. He felt that if the employees shared in the rewards they would have a powerful incentive to do a better job. It also appealed to the egalitarian streak that always ran through his bones.

"It was unusual to have profit sharing in that small a business," Joe said later, "especially a family-owned business, and especially that long ago."

Porter got in touch with two organizations, the Council of Profit Sharing Industries in Chicago and the Profit Sharing Research Foundation in Evanston, Illinois. They sent him a good bit of literature. Porter

Advertiser-Gleam *employees enjoy their own product in this ad promoting the paper in the early 1960s. From left, seated: Bill Mahan, Arnie Bradford, Emmett Reynolds, Katherine Duncan, Theola Green. Standing: Billy Grant, Bo Artis, Alice Harvey, Porter Harvey, Don Woodward, Neal Dispennett, L. C. Mitchell, Lucille Rouse, Glema Hall Baxter, and Freeman Elliott.*

sent the Council an outline of what he had in mind, along with some details about the *Advertiser-Gleam.* The executive secretary, Joseph B. Meier, sent him a lengthy letter with some advice on how to go about it and what to watch out for. Porter put profit-sharing into effect April 1, 1965. He told the employees that the profit would be calculated every three months, and they would get a share. It was apparently the first plan ever established by a paper that small in Alabama, and it has been in effect ever since.

The middle 1950s found Porter writing editorials with increasing frequency. They were always on local issues, like everything else in the paper. One month, August 1955, brought these: August 5, the need for year-round recreation for teenagers; August 10, "Let's Put Teeth Into the Parking Meters" (instead of letting some people get by without paying); August 12, a multi-topic editorial that called for safety lessons for bicycle and motor scooter riders, congratulated Arab on passing 2,000 population and asked that everybody be given an equal shot at the new reserved-seat football tickets; August 26, a call for great care in picking a new county school superintendent; and August 31, another multi-topic piece on double parking at the Courthouse, speeding by boaters near Jaycee beach, and the need for low-rent housing.

In October of that year Porter put a highly personal touch into an editorial. A boy on a bicycle had ridden out of a side street and smacked into the side of Porter's car. The boy wasn't hurt, "but if he had been a fraction of a second sooner I might have hit him and there's no telling what it would have done," he wrote. He said it pointed up the need for the safety-education program he had called for in August.

In the adjoining towns, ownership and operation of the *Gleam*'s competitors went through some rapid changes from 1954 to 1964.

The *Sand Mountain Reporter* was in direct competition with the *Albertville Herald*, the weekly where Porter had printed the *Gleam* from 1941 to 1944. In October 1956, J. J. Benford agreed to sell the *Herald* to Ed Richberg and Percy Hamilton, who were newcomers to the county. Four months later the new owners, who were making payments to Mr. Benford, worked out a so-called merger with the *Reporter*: Each paper would publish once a week, giving Albertville in effect a semi-weekly, the *Reporter* on Tuesday and the *Herald* on Thursday. Advertisers received combined bills. In the meantime, Jack Thompson and his brother-in law Frank Reed had opened Thompson Printing in Albertville. "The *Herald* and the *Reporter* couldn't really merge because both were too heavily in debt," Jack said. "Not long after the 'merger' Mr. Richberg and Mr. Hamilton found they weren't making enough money to keep up their payments. I told Frank that Mr. Benford was going to walk in our office one day soon and say, 'Do you boys want to buy the *Herald*?' Well, before that day was out, Mr. Benford came in and carried us to the back and said, 'Do you boys want to buy the *Herald*?' We said we'd take it before we even asked the price. We came to terms and took over his print shop and published the very next issue of the *Albertville Herald*." That was in March 1957. The *Reporter* immediately became a semi-weekly, publishing Tuesday and Thursday, while the *Herald* came out on Thursday.

That competition continued for seven years—and the *Advertiser-Gleam* played an indirect role in ending it.

"Porter brought some printing forms up to our shop in 1966 because his press was down," Jack said. "The forms had some hollow-core castings in them that we didn't know about. We tightened the forms too much and the castings broke while the press was running. It left a groove in the bed of the press and pretty much disabled it. Pat Courington had already been talking to us about a merger. I had bought Frank out by this time, and he had gone into education for a career. When our press went out, I gave Pat a price for the name and circulation of the *Herald*. He counter-offered with some cash, plus a four-year contract for me as a 'consultant.' I took the offer." That left the *Reporter* as the only paper in Albertville, which by that time had passed Guntersville as the biggest town in the county.

On the other side of Guntersville in Arab, the newspaper scene had been feeling ripples from events in Albertville. The *Reporter* in late 1955 bought out the *Arab News-Record*, which had been started the previous June by Alan Barker. Subscribers began receiving the *Reporter* five days a week instead of the *News-Record* once a week. Editor Jesse Culp said the *Reporter* would maintain an office in Arab "as part of our extended service to your area." But the *Reporter* never really took hold on Brindlee Mountain or in other parts of the county away from Sand Mountain. In March 1957, Glenn Hewett began publishing the *Arab Journal* in still another attempt to establish a paper in that growing town. The *Journal* got a boost six months later, at least psychologically, when Gov. Big Jim Folsom bought a one-third interest. But the paper died while still in infancy despite its famous partner. Ralph Reed—a brother of Frank Reed, who for a time was a partner in the *Albertville Herald*—moved from Albertville to Arab and opened a printshop. He intended to go into the newspaper business after he got acquainted with people in town. Jack Thompson and his brother Jim were partners in the Arab printshop that Ralph was running. In March of 1958, Ralph published his first issue of the *Arab Tribune*. It made a good impression, and it appeared that Arab might at last have a paper of its own. But only two months after the

Tribune's debut, Ralph was killed in a wreck while chaperoning a busload of Union Grove students on a field trip to Tennessee. Ralph's brother, Ewell Reed, left the FBI to take over the fledgling paper. The *Tribune* weathered its traumatic start and became the first Arab paper to survive into maturity.

By the middle 1960s, the newspaper scene in Marshall County had settled down with a single paper in each of the major towns—the *Advertiser-Gleam* in Guntersville, the *Sand Mountain Reporter* in Albertville, the *Tribune* in Arab and the *Boaz Leader*, published by Leroy Sumner, in Boaz.

Porter ran a picture in 1959 of Dago Walden, who claimed to be the oldest continuous subscriber to the Guntersville paper. "He isn't sure when the subscription was taken out," Porter wrote. "But he moved here in October 1898 and he got his finger cut off at the basket factory in 1901, and it was between those dates."

CHAPTER 13

A Family Affair

Alice, besides working full-time at the paper, put a lot into civic projects. "She always made me proud of her because she did everything better than anybody else ever had," Porter said. She had been a PTA leader in Trussville and she got active again in Guntersville, serving as PTA president and helping organize PTAs in several rural schools. She helped organize Family Life Conferences, which brought in specialists in raising children. She helped put on community concerts with visiting professional musicians. The Alabama Red Cross gave her an award at their Birmingham convention for recruiting record numbers of blood donors (including herself—she had a two-gallon pin, and gave blood as long as they let her). After surviving a bout with breast cancer she served as a volunteer in the Reach to Recovery program, working with other women who had undergone mastectomies. She belonged to a women's service group at the First Methodist Church, sang in the church choir, helped organize the 20th Century literary club and, like her mother before her, joined the Daughters of the American Revolution.

She always did some writing at the paper, and once she wrote a feisty editorial under the heading, "As the wife of the editor sees it." The *Gleam* had carried a piece about the birth of 18 puppies. They had to be delivered by Caesarean. Some readers complained that the article contained details which had no place in a decent newspaper. Alice was incensed.

"Someone even said the Ku Klux Klan should ride us out of town," she wrote. "To those we offended, we are sorry. We are sorry people can't read about the reproductive processes of a little animal without embarrassment. Sorry because it probably means that they have the same attitude toward human behavior. There is nothing vulgar about nature's way of bringing new life into being. And there should be no stigma attached to open discussion of the problems relating to it. We should get away from the feelings of guilt and shame where sex is concerned. Children who are brought up in this atmosphere, where their questions about the great mysteries of life are answered as they are asked, will have fewer problems of adjustment to make toward those of the opposite sex. They will be more mature adults and make better husbands, wives and parents. All this may seem a far cry from a simple news story about a mother dog that had a record litter of 18 puppies. But we believe it is the real issue raised in the objections of some of our readers."

Alice's finest hours, probably, came without warning in September 1959. She waited two days before telling the children. Sam got the call while writing a story in the newsroom of the *Louisville Times*, the only time she ever phoned him at work. "I don't want to upset you," she said, "but Porter had a heart attack." She hadn't called the children until she could tell them Porter was better. Sam wanted to take off work and go to Guntersville and help her get the paper out. "No," she insisted, "I'm getting along fine."

She and Porter had driven to Opelika for the weekend to baby-sit their two grandsons so Mary and Don could go to Florida with some friends over Labor Day. Because the paper had to be gotten out, Porter rode a bus back to Guntersville on Sunday, leaving Alice to drive back Monday after Don and Mary returned. Porter found that a lot had happened over the weekend that needed to be covered. The county jail had recorded its biggest weekend in history with seventy-five arrests. A former "boy preacher" who was one of the county's best known evangelists had been found dead in a corn field after a search by hundreds of people, and nobody knew what happened. A new city bus had gone into operation. Sixteen-year-old Rayford Tucker had been shot at East Lake, and one arrest had been made. A car dodged a dog and five people were hurt in the wreck. Plus the normal run of deaths and other news, and the ads and other things that had to be tended to. So he was under a lot of stress. When the paper was put to bed about noon Tuesday and he and Alice went home for lunch, he was unusually tired. He told her he didn't feel good. Alice got a thermometer, put it under his tongue while he sat at the table, and went into the kitchen. When she came back,his eyes were closed, his mouth was hanging open and the thermometer was drooping. She managed to get him onto the floor. Then she started trying to find some help. There was no 911 in those days and no trained medics were standing by for emergencies. She began phoning doctors' offices. It was noon and no doctors were in, but she left word at each place. On the floor, Porter was starting to turn blue. Three doctors happened to live close by, and all of them came to the house—Dr. Walter Alves, Dr. A. G. Finlay and Dr. John Boggess. Dr. Finlay brought an oxygen bottle and let Porter breathe from it. From across the street came Vicki Carter, who was a registered nurse, and her husband Clayton, who had been a medical corpsman in the Navy. Once help arrived, Alice got so weak she had to lie down on the floor herself. Finally, Porter started coming around.

"Alice didn't panic," Porter said later, calling it just another instance of the luck that he felt had followed him all his life. "She did what needed to be done. When I came to, there were three doctors in the room, an RN, a former Navy medic, and two or three doctors' wives. No wonder I survived."

Porter was 56, the son of a man who had died of heart trouble. He stayed 10 days in the City Hospital, part of the time under an oxygen tent. Mary and her two children stayed with Alice while Porter was in the hospital.

As worried as she was, Alice managed to keep the paper going with the help of the others who worked there. The next issue went to press on schedule Thursday with a full run of news, including a paragraph in the City Hospital column that Porter Harvey was improving after a heart attack. The front page carried a lot of news. Automatic Sprinkler Co. was getting its new plant ready. A $125,000 gym was being planned at the DAR School. An eight-year-old boy's hand had been mangled in a hay baler. A 94-year-old man had broken his hip. And the mother of Katherine Duncan, the other main news writer at the *Gleam*, had died the day after Porter went into the hospital. Two more issues were put together and published before Porter went back to work, and they also carried a respectable run of news.

Mary sent carbon-copy letters to various members of the family a week after Porter went into the hospital. "Mother is doing fine at the paper," she reported. "She got a four page issue out today without using any house ads and had three galleys of type left over. She is trying to do as little rewriting as possible and other things to save time. Somebody called here at the house at 5:45 a.m. today to give her a 50 cent want ad. I think I would have refused the ad."

The paper of September 23 included an item in the Personals column that Porter was at home after 10 days in the hospital. "At first it seemed that he had had a heart attack, but now they aren't sure what it was," the paper said. "He expects to go back to work at the *Advertiser-Gleam* a little at a time this week." It may have been a "little at a time," but the front page of that same issue included some stories whose style showed clearly that Porter was already at the typewriter.

A heart specialist in Gadsden, Dr. J. O. Finney, ran some tests and concluded that Porter's spell had probably been caused by fibrillation or fluttering of the heart, and not by a coronary thrombosis. There didn't seem to be any heart damage. But Dr. Finney found that Porter's cholesterol was high. He prescribed a strict low-cholesterol diet, exercise, a 30-minute nap after lunch and a daily tranquilizer. Porter began to follow the advice religiously. He was to live 35 more years, and he never had any serious heart trouble again.

The scare prompted talk within the family about the work load Porter was carrying. He and Don had already talked about the possiblity of Don's someday going to work for the *Gleam*. The paper had never had a trained salesman in charge of advertising. In the early days, Porter had tended to all the ads as well as the news. As time went on, others took on most of the load of selling and laying out ads. Robert Bain, who had started working in the back shop, had been shifted to the office to work on ads before Porter had his heart spell. He and Porter had been scheduled to go to an advertising meeting of the Alabama Press Association on a weekend when Porter was in the hospital, so Porter asked Don to go in his place. Don had been selling soap for three years for Procter and Gamble. He had graduated from Mississippi State in 1956 with a degree in marketing. He and Mary lived in Opelika, where he was in charge of sales in about seven counties. He called on the wholesale houses that supplied the grocery stores, and he called on the stores themselves, big and little, trying to convince them to put more Tide, Comet, Crest, etc., on their shelves.

"I knew I didn't want to work for Procter and Gamble all my life," Don said. There was a lot more detail work than he liked. And there was always pressure from above to sell more than he sold last month or last year. After Porter's heart spell, he and Mary talked some more with Porter and Alice about joining the paper. Sam and Joe were sounded out. Everybody agreed that it seemed like a logical move. Porter and Alice were delighted at the thought of having some of their family in Guntersville.

"We sort of firmed it up at Christmas that we'd come back," Don said. "Daddy talked to Carmage Walls (a chain newspaper owner who lived in Guntersville). Carmage said it would be easier to teach a salesman about advertising than to teach somebody who knew advertising how to sell. I think Carmage volunteered to let me go through a training program they had for ad people at the *Tuscaloosa News*. I left Procter and Gamble in February of 1960. We brought our furniture to Guntersville and stored it in the front bedroom and the garage of Mama's and Daddy's house. We took a furnished apartment in Tuscaloosa and spent four months there while I learned about the advertising business." He was like any other trainee at the *News*, calling on customers and prospects and laying out ads. Porter put him on the *Advertiser-Gleam* payroll to supplement the one dollar an hour he was paid by the *News*. When the four months was over, they moved to Guntersville and he became the

Don Woodward, Mary's husband, took charge of the advertising in 1960.

advertising manager of the paper in late June. They rented a house on Carlisle Avenue near Gilbreath Street for them and their sons, Craig, four, and Steve, one. Robert Bain, who had been selling ads for the *Gleam*, got a job selling ads for the Guntersville radio station.

That summer and fall found a hot controversy going on in the county, the first wet-dry election in 12 years. Marshall County had always voted heavily dry—4,463 to 1,193 in 1948. But some people thought that this time it might be different. Sheriff Warren Jones was cracking down on people caught with beer or whiskey and his controversial campaign fueled the wets' determination. Porter decided to come out editorially. "There are some mighty good arguments on both sides of this question," he wrote. "I've lived where liquor is legal and I've lived where it's illegal, and I believe it does less harm where it's legal . . . Just look around. Liquor has been illegal in Marshall County for about 60 years, and if there's any place with more alcoholics to the square foot than we have here, I'd hate to see it." His endorsement startled a lot of people, not so much for the stand he took as for the fact that he took one at all on an issue that packed so much emotion. The vote failed again, 7,005 to 3,348. But it carried in Guntersville 942 to 658. It left the wets wishing for a city-option law that would allow cities to decide the question for themselves—a right they were to get 24 years later.

In July 1963, Porter and Alice took off for a week—Porter's first real vacation since coming to Guntersville 22 years earlier. Sam, Val and their three children came to Guntersville and Sam spent the week handling the news in Porter's absence. Among other things, Porter and Alice attended the summer convention of the Alabama Press Association on Dauphin Island. For Sam it was a chance to get a better idea of what it was like to work on a country weekly. His work up to then, except for high school and college days, had been for metropolitan dailies. He had spent four years as a reporter for the *Columbus Dispatch* in Ohio and five years as a reporter and assistant city editor for the *Louisville Times*. Returning some day to Guntersville had always been in his mind and Porter's, but the two of them had never actively kicked the idea around. Porter left a fair supply of copy before going on his vacation, and Sam managed to get two papers out. But observant readers may have noticed that the run of news was pretty skimpy, especially by the time the second paper made it to press. The experience left Sam without any clear notion as to his future career.

Porter was never one to enter newspaper contests. But Alice was especially proud of two editorials he had written in 1962 on hot local controversies—whether to close the City Hospital and whether county commissioners should be doing work on private property. She sent them in to the Alabama Press Association's annual contest. And at the summer convention in July 1963, it was announced that Porter had won first place for editorial writing. He quietly put the winning plaque in a desk drawer where he kept resolutions and "awards" that newspapers frequently get from organizations whose causes they have publicized.

Less than a month later the paper carried one of the most interesting editorials Porter ever wrote. The small community of Union Grove had been accused of operating a speed trap, aimed mainly at the hundreds of people who drove between Guntersville and their jobs at Redstone Arsenal in Huntsville. Porter wrote the editorial in a very personal way:

As the editor sees it—

Union Grove as seen from the outside

I went to Union Grove Tuesday night to attend the meeting of the Town Council, but I was told that I couldn't go in.

I asked if I could go in long enough to say something to the Council. I was told that I couldn't go in at all.

I had gone there for two reasons. One was that three officials of the American Automobile Assn. had announced that they would meet with the Council and I felt that I should report the meeting. The other reason was that I wanted to mention something to the Council from the standpoint of people living outside Union Grove.

Since I couldn't speak to the Council in person I am taking this means of saying what I had in mind.

I'm sure the Union Grove officials have reasons for the policies they are following. I assume the people of Union Grove understand the situation and know what the officials' reasons are.

But people outside the community don't know. Since the controversy about the police activities started a few weeks ago, many people have heard a great deal said in criticism of what has been done but have hardly heard anything in support of it. The officials felt that if they said nothing, the controversy would die down. They also felt it would be best if there were no newspaper accounts concerning it.

However, when a mass meeting was held over the issue, when rocks were thrown at the mayor's home and when the AAA started an investigation, I felt that this was news that should be published. In publishing it I tried to give both sides but found this to be impossible because those on one side wouldn't say anything. I have used only a small fraction of what I have been told by critics of the police activities but even so the reports have been one-sided because I have been able to get almost nothing from supporters of the policies. One reason I especially wanted to attend the meeting Tuesday night was that I hoped the discussion between the Council members and the AAA officials would give me a chance to get something of the Council's side of the situation.

As an outsider I certainly won't presume to suggest what the Union Grove officials should do about presenting their side, or about anything else. But I do hope they will give consideration to the impression that is being received by people outside the community.

Porter getting a story over the phone.

Porter possessed a rare gift for knowing how people were likely to feel about something. Blasting the Union Grove officials would have gone over very well with many of his readers. But he knew it would be resented by many residents of that tiny community. So he never accused the officials of misconduct. He didn't say they broke the law by meeting behind closed doors, as so many papers are quick to do despite the self-serving way it always sounds. He gave the officials the benefit of every doubt. But it's hard to imagine an editorial calculated to make a stronger overall impression. The Council responded with a long statement saying it was trying to do the right thing and people outside just didn't understand. But the ticketing slacked off and the controversy died, at least as far as public charges and counter-charges were concerned.

In February 1964 a half-page ad for the paper asked readers' help in finding news. "It doesn't have to be something big," the ad said. "Most of the news of the county papers like ours is made up of happenings that a large city paper wouldn't consider important at all. But our readers are interested in the doings of people they know, and they want to read about them in the paper. Let us know any time you: Move—Change jobs—Get married—Get sick—Get well—Go off on a visit—Have visitors from off—Buy a home or farm—Build a home or business place—Go into service—Get your discharge—Buy a car, truck, tractor, sewing machine, refrigerator, etc." Readers were invited to call or write the paper's office "or tell any of our correspondents."

The *Advertiser-Gleam* was a member of the Alabama Press Association, and Porter and Alice enjoyed going to the APA conventions when they were able to get away. It was good to swap ideas with other publishers and editors who were wrestling with similar problems. In 1965 the nominating committee asked Porter if it could propose him for second vice-president—the first step on a ladder leading to the presidency. He agreed, and in 1967 he became the president of the organization representing virtually all the papers in Alabama, daily and weekly, big and small. The APA had a full-time manager in Tuscaloosa, Jim Hall, but the president was still called on frequently when difficult situations came up. Porter presided at several meetings a year of the board of directors. And he presided at some of the sessions at the twice-a-year conventions, always careful to have a yarn or two to lighten things up.

In the meantime Alice and Porter had taken on some major added responsibilities at home. Alice's parents had come from Kansas in 1964 to live with them. Ada, who was 82, was paralyzed on her left side from a stroke. Thornton's problems were mainly mental. In Hays he had sometimes wandered from home in confusion about where he was and who he was with. Alice and her sister Helen, who lived in Texas, went to Kansas and packed up their parents' belongings. Ada and Thornton flew with them to Alabama and they moved into the middle bedroom of the house. Thornton's physical condition was also deteriorating and he died after 10 months in Guntersville on May 15, 1965, at the age of 88. His tombstone in Crestview Cemetery in Guntersville bears the legend he asked for, "From Pilot Rock to Picken Hall," for the one-room school where he started teaching as a teenager and the college building where he taught till he retired at 75.

Ada made her home with Porter and Alice until her death seven years after Thornton's death. She was in a wheelchair most of the time, but she could walk with help, and she stayed mentally alert all her life. She loved to go see places. Porter and Alice took her on rides around the county, folding her wheelchair and carrying it in the trunk of their car. She attended the First Methodist Church and one of its women's circles. Alice carried her to musical events, flower shows, plays, etc. Because Alice was still working at the paper, they arranged for ladies to stay with Ada during the day and when they had to be away on weekends. They enclosed a breezeway between the house and the garage to make the garage part of the house. They put a second bathroom there, next to what became a sort of office (and a play room for visiting grandchildren).

Early 1967 found Sam giving serious thought to returning to Guntersville. Besides his job at the *Louisville Times*, he was writing copy for a small Louisville advertising agency, a part-time job that kept getting bigger. The owner of the agency, Jack Doyle, was talking about needing someone full-time. Sam didn't want that, but he could see the part-time job playing out. He and Val and their four children had come to depend on the extra income. He was 37. He decided that maybe he ought to try weekly work while he was still young enough to go back into dailies if it didn't work out. He and Val and the children spent a long weekend in Guntersville that spring and he and Porter talked it over. They studied the paper's financial records to see if the *Advertiser-Gleam* could afford to take on another newsman. They tried to be realistic. No matter how Sam looked at the figures, he couldn't see that the paper was making enough money to handle it. He told Porter they'd better forget it. He and Val and the children headed back to Louisville.

As they drove, Sam realized he was feeling let down. Aside from any other reason, he had always wanted to work with Porter, and he didn't know how much longer that option might be available. Val asked if he didn't think the financial prospects in Guntersville would improve with time. Sam said he supposed they would. It had occurred to him that changing the way the profit sharing was calculated might allow the paper to squeeze in another salary. They talked some more and agreed not to give up just yet. Sam called Porter from a pay phone in a small Tennessee town and went over what he and Val had been talking about. One effect of changing the profit sharing would be to reduce the amount going to Porter and Alice as the owners. Porter said they could handle that. Sam and Val talked some more and decided to make the move to Guntersville.

Sam assumed he would simply be a reporter, possibly with a title such as news editor. "No," Porter said, "when you come back I want you to come back as editor." They would both spend nearly all their time working as reporters, but Sam would edit Porter's copy before it went to the typesetter, and it would be up to Sam to write most of whatever editorials were to be written. In July 1967, Porter announced that Sam

Sam and Porter shared the news duties from 1967 until Porter's death in 1995. Photo by Tom Riordan.

was going to be the editor and that Don was being promoted to general manager. Sam and Val sold their house and moved to Guntersville with their children: Kenneth, 12; John, 10; Anne, seven; and Mary, three. They rented a house on Lusk Street that Alice had found for them.

From then on Porter was to say he had turned the paper over to Don and Sam. But he was still the owner. As soon as Sam arrived, Porter proposed that they get up a picture edition, and they all got right to it. It was like the one he had published in 1951. Businesses were invited to run ads with individual pictures of all their employees. Don and Porter sold them. This time, instead of having a commercial studio take the pictures, Porter, Don, and Sam went to the businesses and took the pictures with Polaroid cameras. For news to go with the ads, Porter contacted clubs and churches and invited them to turn in writeups of their histories. This special edition turned out to have 32 pages in four sections. It was printed over a couple of weeks' time in between the regular issues. There were photos of 603 employees and writeups on 54 churches and clubs. It made interesting reading. And it allowed the *Advertiser-Gleam* to have some money to hand out to employees at the next quarterly profit-sharing. Porter confided later that the fear of a profitless quarter right after Sam was brought into the business had convinced him to publish the special edition.

The paper was operated as if it were a three-man partnership. Whoever could get one of the others to agree with him would win whatever argument had come up. Don complained that Sam and Porter, both being on the news side and being blood kin, had him at a disadvantage. But serious disagreements were to be pretty rare.

The three set out to increase the paper's circulation, which had fluctuated between 3,300 and 3,800 for more than 15 years. Twice before when circulation had been climbing slowly—in 1951 and 1963—increases in the subscription price had knocked it back down. There were two people gathering and writing news now, and they figured that ought to give the paper more appeal. The population of the *Gleam*'s territory was growing, even if Guntersville itself was pretty static for lack of room to expand. They mailed out sample copies to non-subscribers and invited them to take the paper free for a few weeks and then decide if they wanted to stay on. They began plugging the paper in ads on the radio, a swap-out for ads the radio station ran in the paper. The radio ads stressed the fact that you could subscribe over the phone and let the paper bill you later, rather than having to make a trip to the office. While the three weren't ready to concede the merits of radio advertising in general, they knew it was one way to reach people who didn't already take the paper. In 1969, the circulation crept over 4,000 for the first time; in 1971 it topped 5,000; and in 1973, it went above 6,000. Higher circulation made ads in the paper pay off better for stores, car dealers, real estate companies, etc. It turned out that raising subscription prices could lead to even more subscribers instead of fewer, if you advertised the increase ahead of time and urged people to beat the price hike. A 1978 campaign when the price was going up $2 brought in 675 new subscribers. Single-copy sales were promoted by installing more racks. Circulation continued to grow pretty steadily, and in 1993 it went over 12,000. At 12,034 paid circulation, the *Gleam* had become the biggest non-daily in the state, edging out its Albertville-Boaz neighbor, the *Sand Mountain Reporter*, which had been the state's largest for years. Shortly after that, the *Reporter* put on a circulation drive and got back out front. Albertville and Boaz had a total population three times Guntersville's, so the *Gleam* folks didn't feel too bad. And before long the *Gleam* was back on top again.

The *Reporter* had been the first paper in Alabama and one of the first in the South to use the printing process known as offset. That was in 1955. Offset caught on fast, especially among weeklies, and by 1970 the *Gleam* was one of the very few papers in Alabama still using lead type and the process known as letterpress. The *Gleam*'s move to offset was forced by a growth in advertising in the early 1970s with the opening of the Southgate Shopping Center. That brought Guntersville its first discount department store, Big K, plus a Kroger supermarket and SuperX Drugs. The paper gained four or five pages a week of advertising almost overnight. The paper also began getting more ads from stores in Albertville. Bigger papers plus the increasing circulation meant more work than the average four-page letterpress could handle, even running nearly full-time. And the extra ads put a severe strain on the shop's ability to compose them with lead type. Offset printing offered some clear advantages. The reproduction was a lot sharper, especially when it came to pictures. News and ads could be set faster and cheaper with a process known as phototypesetting. Old ads, and ads from other papers, could be reproduced photographically without setting new type. But offset presses, while fast and efficient, were also very expensive. Most publishers with offset presses felt they had to print more than just their own product to pay for them. That meant hustling for printing business far away from your own town. Porter, Don, and Sam decided to farm out the press work but to keep doing their own composition. They took proposals from publishers in several towns and were real happy when the best offer came from the *Reporter* just 10 miles away. There was the obvious travel advantage in printing close to home. In addition, many stores liked to advertise in both papers. With one plant printing both, each paper could pick up ads from the other without having to build them from scratch. A lot more Albertville businesses advertised in Guntersville than vice-versa, so this arrangement was especially to the *Gleam*'s advantage. The change to offset took place in May 1972. All the employees managed to make the switch to the new technology except for one man, a deaf Linotype operator who wound up retiring on a disability. The old pressroom was converted into a mailroom. The *Gleam* kept its hot type equipment for several more years because of its commercial printing work, but ultimately that too gave way to all-offset.

A new kind of competition appeared in April 1981. Bob Bryan, owner of the daily *Cullman Times* and some other papers, began publishing a countywide free-circulation paper, the *Marshall Shopping News*. It was an outgrowth of the *Boaz Leader-Dispatch*, which he had bought a year or two earlier. The *Shopping News* was mailed to 35,550 addresses. It held some appeal to stores that tried to draw from more than one part of the county, and especially to those with locations in more than one town.

The other three papers in the county—the *Gleam*, the *Sand Mountain Reporter* and the *Arab Tribune*—all began publishing weekly shoppers of their own. The *Gleam*'s was called the *Bargaineer*. It consisted of four to six pages lifted bodily from the paper, plus pre-printed inserts. It was mailed each Wednesday to everybody with a Guntersville address or north of the river who didn't subscribe to the *Gleam*—a little over 4,000 in all. It contained ads from businesses who were willing to pay a higher rate for the extra coverage. The shoppers let the three established papers give advertisers blanket coverage in their territories, just as the *Shopping News* was doing countywide.

The *Shopping News* died after exactly two years. Mr. Bryan announced on March 30, 1983, that he was folding it: "We thought we saw a need for complete coverage of Marshall County to serve the multi-outlet discount stores, groceries and others, but it didn't work out that way." Its death left Boaz without a paper, a gap which the *Reporter* was happy to fill. The *Gleam* continued publishing the *Bargaineer*, and the *Reporter* and the *Tribune* kept their shoppers going too. They felt the shoppers gave them some protection against growing competition from direct-mail advertisers.

As Porter approached seventy, he decided to start transferring the *Advertiser-Gleam* to the next generation. He talked to some people who advised him that the simplest approach would be to incorporate the paper and give out shares of stock. A corporation was formed in 1970, and over the next few years Porter gave equal shares to Sam, Val, Don, Mary, Joe, and Jo Kirk. He and Alice kept slightly fewer shares than each of the others had. He became president of the corporation, Don became vice-president, and Sam became secretary-treasurer. Jo Kirk joined them as a director, which got Joe's family on the board and also kept the board from being an all-male stronghold. But incorporating left the operations of the paper essentially unchanged.

A few years after they incorporated, Porter wrote Jo Kirk that he had good news and bad news. "The good news is that the *Advertiser-Gleam* has been doing well, and at least for a while, is going to distribute more of its money than it has been doing," he wrote. "Wade Hyatt [a CPA] watches after our finances and on his advice some of the increase will be in bigger annual dividends and some will be in directors' fees. We decided on $1,500 a year per director, so you will be getting your check soon. The bad news is that Wade says one reason corporations pay fees to their directors is to compensate them for the fact that they are subject to being sued . . . The *Advertiser-Gleam* had never had a lawsuit against it until this year, but now everybody seems to want to go to court and there's a case pending against us. Fortunately it's a small one. The fellow is only suing us for five million dollars. He's doing time in prison. He was sentenced as a habitual offender, and in reporting it I listed the crimes he committed before and by mistake included rape as one of them. He says that damaged his reputation. We don't see how a little thing like rape could hurt anybody's reputation, but he says it did. We have a million dollars worth of libel insurance and are confident the case won't cost us any more than that. His suit, like practically all suits, doesn't mention the directors. But you never know what the next one may be, so be ready to dig up five million dollars any time." The lawsuit died a natural death when the man never followed up, possibly because he couldn't get out of prison to appear in court and push it. He had never been able to get a lawyer to take the case and push it for him.

Porter was a master at disarming people who felt the *Gleam* had done them wrong. A man might storm in, wave a copy of the paper and demand to know who wrote some three-inch police story. Porter would get up from behind his desk, look at the story, and say softly, "I did. Did we get something wrong?" You'd better believe it's wrong, the man would say. "We'd be glad to tell your side of it," Porter would reply as he took out his note pad and asked the man to sit down. Pretty soon the irate reader would be appeased. And the next issue would have a piece that might run several times as long as the original and be several times as interesting.

Porter and Sam divided the news beats. For most of the time they worked together Sam covered city and county government, the city police, the Guntersville schools, and the sports. Porter had the courts, the sheriff's office, the county schools, and the obituaries. When Sam joined the paper, he was concerned that he might have a hard time writing stories the way *Advertiser-Gleam* subscribers were accustomed to seeing them. He had spent 13 years on big-city dailies, and he felt some of the rigidities of those papers were probably too ingrained. But reading the *Gleam* over the years paid off. He hadn't been back more than a month or so when his sister Mary told him, "I can't tell which stories are yours and which ones are Daddy's." Sam took it as a high compliment and decided the move to Guntersville was probably going to work out all right.

Alice's mother, Ada Wells, died at age ninety on September 22, 1972, after living with Alice and Porter for eight years. Alert to the end, she was listening to a radio broadcast of the Guntersville-Arab football game when she suffered a stroke like the one that had crippled her 15 years earlier, only this one was almost immediately fatal. She was buried in Guntersville next to her husband.

Alice decided to retire the following year. The *Alabama Publisher,* a newspaper issued by the press association, reported it under the headline, "Mrs. Harvey to Take A Few Days Off." The article said she had "worked continuously at the twice-weekly for 28 years—or 32, if some people's calculations are considered. Her title at the paper was circulation manager. In the early years of her career, that meant she would have to get up at 4:00 every Thursday morning and cook the flour paste to be used on the mailing labels. The spritely Mrs. Harvey is 68 now and she doesn't

Alice checking subscription records.

mind who knows it. She just thinks its time to let someone else do the work at the office so she can putter around the house and yard. . . . "

There was always a good bit of family at the paper, and frequent visitors noticed something else, especially in the shop. An unusual number of people who worked there had some sort of disability. Porter, probably because of his own experience with polio, was inclined to hire people who had been dealt hard blows by fate. At one time in the 1960s the work force included a foreman with crippled feet, two deaf-mute printers, a printer with a speech impediment, and a woman whose burns had left her hands partly crippled.

The best-known handicapped person associated with the paper was a short, retarded man, Arnold Bradford Jr., known affectionately to most people as "Little Arnie." His father was an accountant who for years did the *Gleam*'s tax returns. They lived near the business district, and Little Arnie was often in the *Gleam* office and in other business places while he was growing up. He became the *Gleam*'s last newspaper carrier. The paper's bookkeeper, Johnnie Couch, patiently made time each month to go over Arnie's records with him so he would know who had paid him and who he still needed to collect from. When he had to give up his route in 1979 at the age of 43, the paper ran a picture of him and his wagon and Porter wrote, "For more than 25 years one of the most familiar sights in Northtown has been Arnie Bradford Jr. and his wagon, delivering his newspaper route or delivering things printed at the *Advertiser-Gleam*. It's a sight that won't be seen anymore. Arnie has had to retire because of his health. He has muscular dystrophy. . . . Arnie is going to be missed as very few others in Guntersville would be. Through the years hundreds of people have taken a special interest in him. They have commented many times on his friendliness, his politeness, his ability to joke with people and take it in good humor when they joke with him. . . . We have had lots of carriers over the years, maybe a hundred or so, but as time went on more and more people subscribed by mail, and there was less need for hand delivery. One by one the routes shrank until they were dropped— all but Arnie's. His customers liked to have him come around twice a week. And years after all the other routes had disappeared, he still had about 70 people taking the paper from him when he retired."

In gratitude for what Porter had done for Arnie over the years, Arnold Sr. set up a trust fund of several thousand dollars, to be divided eventually among Porter's grandchildren. He told Porter not to try to talk him out of it because he had already done it and the trust was non-revocable.

Everybody in Porter's family had worked at the paper, and so did everybody in Don's and Sam's families, to one extent or another.

The boys—Craig and Steve Woodward and Kenneth and John Harvey—all helped with the mailing operation on press days. As the papers came off the press and were put through the folder, they had to be addressed, tied in bundles, put into mailing sacks and hauled to the post office. High school boys were hired for this, generally three or four of them. The job called for accuracy and speed, to make sure the papers were labeled properly and at the post office by the deadline. It also

Porter's and Alice's Guntersville grandchildren all worked at the paper in high school, mostly in the mail room. From left, Anne Harvey, Steve Woodward, Craig Woodward, and John Harvey.

required strong backs for handling the heavy mail sacks. Boys also worked after school on other days, making the metal address plates for the Addressograph machine that stamped subscribers' names and addresses on the paper. A new plate had to be made every time somebody subscribed, and the plate had to be changed whenever someone renewed his subscription or moved. Diligence was essential to keep the system from getting fouled up, and speed was a definite asset. Generally, boys signed up for one of the vocational programs which allowed them to leave school early in order to work.

The oldest boys, Kenneth and Craig, undertook a special project for the paper in the summer of 1969, before they were old enough to work regularly. Kenneth was 14 and Craig 13. The paper had an old Plymouth station wagon for hauling papers to the post office. The boys were at the Woodwards' house one day when Don mentioned that the station wagon needed painting. He said it might be a job the boys could do. They asked if they could paint it the way they wanted. That took a little more thought on the part of the *Gleam* management, but finally they said OK. Kenneth, who had taken some art lessons in Louisville, drew up a design that he and Craig thought was pretty cool 1960s pop art. The *Gleam* bought paint, brushes, primer, and tape. Over a couple of weeks the boys transformed the drab and aging vehicle, painting broad red and white stripes down the sides from top to bottom. They painted the hood, roof and tailgate solid yellow. They lettered "The *Advertiser-Gleam*" on the sides in black, duplicating the paper's nameplate as closely as possible. On the back they painted the proclamation, "News Is Our Bag." The boys weren't old enough to drive, but with a 16-year old friend at the wheel, they and some of their friends rode in it during the high school Homecoming parade. The psychedelic Plymouth served the *Advertiser-Gleam* a couple more years before it finally wore out. An older employee in the mailing operation bought it, repainted the yellow parts blue, and drove it a while longer.

"We had been going to paint it red, white and blue ourselves, but the grownups said that wouldn't be respectful of the flag," Craig remembers.

The girls—Anne and Mary Harvey and Coley Woodward—all

Red and white stripes, a yellow roof, and "News Is Our Bag" marked the station wagon that carried the papers to the post office after a design and paint job by Kenneth Harvey (left) and Craig Woodward about 1970. Kenneth later became an industrial designer.

worked in the office for at least a time. They answered the phone and helped people who came in to buy want ads, take out subscriptions, leave some news, etc. They helped file subscription records. They read proof on type that had been set for news, ads or commercial printing jobs. They sometimes worked in the shop on mailing days when there were advertising fliers to be inserted into the papers. Anne also worked one summer as a reporter while studying journalism at Auburn. She took a picture of a bunch of dead cows on Grant Mountain, lying on their backs with their legs in the air, after lightning struck the tree they had huddled under in a storm. The picture caused some merriment at Auburn where her fellow journalism students put it down as just another strange-animal report in the *Advertiser-Gleam*.

Mary Woodward, who had worked in the office as a teenager, found herself called on to help out from time to time after she and Don moved back to Guntersville. She filled in on occasional days or weeks when one of the women in the office needed to be gone. Once she worked about three months when the bookkeeper, Mrs. Couch, had to be out because of her husband's illness and death. Mary never claimed to be a bookkeeper, but she measured the ads in the paper, calculated the bills, typed them up and sent them out and did other things necessary to keep the records current from day to day. In 1986, she started working in the office each Monday, keeping track of the legal notices and handling the bookwork and the billing they needed, besides helping with general office matters on the busiest day of the week.

Val had gone to work full time when Kenneth started college in 1973. She worked first as a teller at the First Alabama Bank and then at First Federal Savings & Loan. In 1977 she started working at the *Gleam* as the circulation manager and receptionist. Two years later she switched to writing news on Mondays and Tuesdays while handling the front desk the rest of the week. That made her the first person besides Porter and Sam to work as a reporter at the *Gleam* on a regular basis. She did the obituaries for the first paper of the week and wrote feature stories. Writing an obit meant contacting the family, getting information that wasn't available from the funeral home, and trying to write what amounted to a small feature story on the deceased. It was a practice Porter had developed out of a feeling that detailed obits ought not to be limited to big shots. As the children got through college, Val cut back her work, first to four days a week, then to two days, and in 1987 to part of a day at home, doing obits for the Wednesday paper. In 1991, she retired completely, shortly after the paper hired a young reporter, Anthony Campbell, to work part-time while he was going to college. In 1992, Anthony graduated from the University of Alabama in Huntsville with an accounting degree. But he had decided by then that newspaper work was more interesting than keeping track of figures. After a three-month crash course in journalism at Auburn, he became a full-time reporter for the *Gleam*. Porter cut back his own schedule to about twenty-eight hours a week, but he often fudged by getting up news while he was at home.

CHAPTER 14

Breaking the Rules

It only took a glance at the front page to know that the *Advertiser-Gleam* was pretty much of a journalistic oddball. Its small headlines and vertical columns of news were throwbacks to a much earlier time. And the peculiarities went beyond layout. The news wasn't segregated into sections of the paper. A football story might appear next to a crime report or the county agent's column, and a wedding story might run alongside an editorial. Legal notices ran wherever they fit (and came in mighty handy when making up pages). The definition of news went beyond the traditional fare. Porter once wrote a piece about a column of ants he observed in the bank parking lot across from the newspaper office. ("I thought that was a wonderful story," Jerry Brown, a journalism professor at Auburn University, and later head of the department, said in a letter).

The writing was often casual, with the editorial "we" showing up often in news stories (as in "We couldn't find out much about that"). A headline might begin with a verb ("Claims he stabbed her") or have no verb at all ("Biggest crowd ever") in violation of all journalistic dogma, as long as the writer felt that was the best way to tell the story and get people to read it. Numbers were written 2, 3, 4, etc., instead of two, three, four. People in the news were given courtesy titles, because most people talked that way. It was "Mr. Smith" or "Mrs. Jones." Someone who was known by his nickname got called by his nickname , and not only in parentheses. When the late Sheriff Colbert decided he liked "Big John" better than

"Walter" he became "Sheriff Big John Colbert" in the *Gleam*. C. A. Langford was Rabbit. Bill Moss was Bimbo. Jerry Lang, at least part of the time, was Peckerhead.

When Sam became the editor in 1967, Porter told him to feel free to make changes. "Don't wait too long," Porter cautioned, "or you'll get too used to the way we're doing things now." Sam hadn't arrived with a lot of changes in mind, but he gave some thought to modifying the physical appearance of the paper. He got the printers to set some headlines in larger type and in multi-column width. He pasted them on dummy layouts to see how they'd look. but the more he thought about changing, the less sense it seemed to make. He left the layout the way it was.

The *Gleam* had run ads on the front page since the late 1940s, at nearly three times the standard rate. Porter couldn't see any logical reason not to do it, and neither could Don or Sam. Don could brag at newspaper meetings that he had the only front page in the state that paid for itself. They imposed an arbitrary rule that no more than a third of the front page could be advertising. It was a rule that almost never had to be called into play, although right before elections they sometimes had more front page ads than they could use.

Some less conspicuous changes were made after Sam joined the paper, primarily because there were now two people working on news, and they could spend more time on each story. Sam had been a city hall reporter in both Columbus and Louisville, so his ideas were somewhat skewed toward governmental coverage. The *Gleam*'s reports of City Council, County Commission, and School Board meetings got longer and more numerous. A typical meeting might wind up in half a dozen stories, scattered through three or four issues of the paper. Sam picked up Porter's dialogue technique. An amused Frank Sikora of the Birmingham News did a 1972 piece which referred to the paper's "word-by-word accounts" of meeting including such illuminating passages as this:

> JONES: "What are we going to do about the two new trucks we need?"
>
> SMITH: "I don't know."

Sam experimented with different formats for editorials in order to set them off from the news. He ran them in two-column measure, and for a while he even ran them on the front page. But he settled back into doing them the way Porter had done them, single-column measure, placed anywhere in the paper that they happened to fit. It seemed more in keeping with the paper's character.

If some really big event came along, Sam could spend full time on that while Porter tended to the rest of the news, or vice-versa. Or both of them could pool their efforts. When Sam covered the Jeff Newsome murder trial in 1988, he wrote six full columns for the Saturday paper and seven columns for the Wednesday paper, taking notes in court all day and writing each night and during court breaks. Whether anybody waded through so much verbiage was an open question. Porter kept trying to get Sam to cut it down, but he had gotten so accustomed to blow-by-blow coverage of city and county meetings that he had a hard time leaving anything out.

Big weather events—snow storms, ice storms, floods or tornados—generally resulted in lots of individual stories by both writers (or all three after Anthony joined the staff). A blizzard in 1993 was reported in 14 stories and 19 pictures in the Wednesday paper and 15 more stories and four more pictures in the Saturday paper. A tornado ripped through part of Guntersville on a Sunday in 1994, and the three writers produced 23 stories and 18 pictures for the Wednesday issue.

As on most weeklies, the people who wrote for the *Gleam* also took the pictures. They used Polaroids because of the darkroom time they saved, and also because the reporter could tell right away if he needed to take another one. The Polaroid photos fell short of conventional photos in some ways, but from the paper's perspective, the advantages outweighed the drawbacks. The *Gleam* continued to be more of a word paper than a picture paper.

Porter and Sam resisted a growing trend in weeklies to departmentalize the news and create separate pages or even sections for sports, society and expressions of opinion. Except for grouping the obituaries together, they let things run pretty much wherever they fit. It vastly simplified the job of making up the pages, freeing that time for other things. And they felt it encouraged readers to look at all parts of the paper and not just some of it. For one thing, a reader who scanned every page was more likely to see the ads on every page. They figured this made the ads more effective, and they would sell more of them.

The *Gleam* covered high school football and basketball, which both drew big crowds. But the coverage of other local sports—high school baseball, track, volleyball, etc.—didn't go much beyond telling who was on the teams and running the team pictures. If coaches called in the results of games, they got written up. Tournaments and playoffs held in town got some attention, but that was about it. The coverage of little league baseball and soccer was generally limited to running the team rosters and telling who made the all-stars, plus an occasional picture.

On most newspaper staffs, obituaries tend to be an afterthought, a chore often passed off to clerks or handled in desultory fashion by reporters. Porter had always tried to contact relatives to get more than the bare facts provided by funeral homes. After Sam came and Porter had more time, the writeups got longer and more detailed. For years the paper had run all the deaths on the front page. But by 1969 they were taking up so much room that they were moved inside for the prominent and the obscure alike. In 1975, Don suggested that since relatives were being contacted anyway, they should be asked to bring in pictures. Before long about half of the obituaries were accompanied by photos. When Val wrote deaths in the late 1980s, she began asking about hobbies and pastimes as well as occupations and memberships, and that became standard practice for Porter and Sam too.

Porter could find something interesting to say about almost everybody. He used different techniques for enticing readers into the stories. Jay Reeves of the Associated Press did a piece on the *Gleam*'s obituaries in 1993, observing that they "include the kind of gossip you'd hear in hushed tones on the back porch of a small-town funeral home." The following 10 leads are all from three consecutive issues in 1993—July 7, July 10, and July 1:

Lee Burroughs

• He was one of the few remaining veterans of World War I.

• In recent years he was a familiar sight walking around Guntersville's business and residential districts. He'd walk two or three miles.

• He had been a brick mason many years.

Andrew Lee Burroughs died in the Marshall Manor nursing home Saturday at the age of 96.

James Lang

A survivor of the most dramatic shooting in the history of Marshall County, James Sidney Lang died Sunday in his home in Albertville. He was 72.

Sheriff Zeke Boyles, Chief Deputy Washington Bennett and Boaz Police Chief Leonard Floyd were killed in the shooting in 1951, along with Aubrey Kilpatrick, owner of the home near Boaz where the shooting took place. Mr. Lang, a deputy sheriff, was seriously wounded, but recovered . . .

T. L. Johnson

After a day at a flea market, Thomas Lennie Johnson died Sunday night at his home at the top of Baker Mountain. He was 85. A retired carpenter, he had been making wooden chairs and benches and selling them . . .

Louella Nix

Although she was in a wheelchair the last 13 years until six months ago, Louella Taylor Nix kept on going to church in Guntersville and doing part of the cooking in her home at Welcome Home on Grant Mountain. Mrs. Nix, who was 92, died Friday night. She was a seamstress.

Ricky Norris

Lightning was thought to have struck him, but later the doctors said it appeared that he had a heart attack. An autopsy was performed to find out. William Richard Norris Sr. was cooking steaks on the back porch of his home at Horton when it happened . . .

Alvin Lackey

He bought the old Nixon Chapel School house in 1968, tore it down and used the lumber to build the house he lived in until he entered the Marshall Manor nursing home. His wife still lives there. Alvin Ward Lackey died in the nursing home Friday after three years of failing health. He was 83.

Mrs. William Pritchett

In the same community where she and her husband were born, Ina Kathleen Rice Pritchett died Wednesday in her home at Waverly Hills between Grant and Swearengin. She had been sick about a year. She was 65 . . .

Red Johnson

He had not been sick until a heart attack hit him in his home Sunday and he died there. Benny Wayne (Red) Johnson, 39, had lived in Huntsville since he moved there in September from Swearengin . . .

Bob Rogers

He fought in several countries of Europe in World War II. He was wounded three times. The last time in Germany, a shell burst near him and the shrapnel left him partly disabled for the rest of his life. Robert Montgomery Rogers of Diamond died in the G-A Hospital Wednesday, two months after he had an aneurysm in his neck. He was 80...

Herbert Hitchcock

"It was just like he went to sleep," his wife said. Herbert Hugh Hitchcock died quietly in bed Sunday evening in his home at Pinedale Haven near Warrenton. He had had cancer since March. He was 79 . . .

When it came to detailed descriptions of the death itself, the high point may have come in 1977 when Porter told how retired grocer Ralph Rogers dropped dead during a Wednesday night revival service at the Victory Baptist Church: "Mr. Rogers was standing between his wife and Russell Spray. As they started the fourth verse of the second song, 'Since I Have Been Redeemed,' he fell into Mr. Spray's arms. An ambulance was called and took him to the hospital, but he had apparently died instantly. The service was resumed after the ambulance left. Three people were saved that night."

Relatives were generally glad to tell the *Gleam* in considerable detail just how the departed left this world. Not so in the case of suicide. Traditionally, when someone took his own life, the paper said so, as part of telling the news. But Sam and Porter finally concluded they were causing too much pain for people who were already going through enough pain, often mixed with feelings of guilt. They decided in 1993 that they would withhold the cause of death in suicides if the family requested it.

The most frequent requests to hold something out of the paper had to do with drunk-driving arrests. When Guntersville voted to become legally wet in 1986 (a move the paper had endorsed), Porter, Don, and Sam talked it over and decided that printing the DUIs might have some deterrent effect on that deadly practice. Every month or so somebody would ask to have his DUI arrest suppressed, usually saying it was going to cost him his job, or because "it's just going to kill my mother." But they all got printed, even some involving close neighbors and substantial advertisers. One businessman pulled his ads after his arrest ran in the paper, but he eventually came back. The only driver whose DUI was knowingly covered up was a man who died before the paper went to press. Sam felt that was cause for an exception to the rule.

Surprisingly, for every request they got to keep something out of the paper, they got dozens of requests to put something in that they couldn't use. Most often it was something that ran afoul of the "local news only" rule. "What do you mean it's not local?" went the typical response when the *Gleam* wouldn't run a letter about some alarming bill in Congress or the state Legislature. Or, "If they pass this tax they're going to be collecting it right here in Guntersville." Sam or Porter would point out that they were going to be collecting it everywhere else, too, but the explanation didn't always satisfy.

Mothers who had grown up in Guntersville and moved away had a hard time understanding why their daughters' weddings couldn't be written up in full just because the daughters and their intendeds had always lived somewhere else. People living in Marshall County but outside the *Gleam*'s coverage area were even more perplexed, especially since the paper sold a lot of subscriptions inside the other towns. ("We've been taking your paper for 20 years. You mean you're not going to write up our 50th anniversary just because we happen to live in Albertville?")

There were arguments over the *Gleam*'s refusal to print some kinds of pictures they saw in other papers—club presidents or businessmen handing out checks or awards, mayors signing proclamations, athletes signing scholarships in front of coaches and kinfolks, etc. The *Gleam* looked on those as artificial events, usually staged only to get a picture in the paper. The paper's policy was to run a picture of the people receiving honors, but not the donors. It was a hard policy for some to understand, especially for businesses that ran a lot of ads in the paper. Sometimes they could be assuaged by running the picture in the form of an ad and not charging for it.

A heavy-equipment operator named Earl Rollings came to be one of the best-known men in the county almost entirely through his letters in the *Advertiser-Gleam*. He wrote hundreds of them from the early 1960s until his death in 1986. He saw himself as speaking for ordinary people who felt unfairly treated by society, which was the way he usually felt. He railed against contractors who wouldn't hire local workers, county commissioners who ignored the roads he traveled, school officials who favored other parts of the county, doctors who charged too much, hospitals who kept him waiting too long in the emergency room, etc. He was not a learned man, and his letters usually required a lot of editing. Many times he would call Porter, at the office or at home, tell Porter what was on his mind and let Porter write it down. When he died, Porter wrote, "He didn't hesitate to say what he thought. His blunt statements of his views and his down-to-earth way of expressing himself made many people look forward to his letters." Porter was careful to say "many people" and not "everybody" because he knew some readers cringed at the sight of "another Earl Rollings letter." But he also knew Earl spoke the sentiments of plenty of people who felt aggrieved but who would never step forward to say so.

The best-known picture the *Gleam* ever ran was one that some people thought had no business being in a newspaper at all. On a cold

January day in 1978, a man burst into the office, steaming with indignation. A state road-striping crew had come to a dead dog in the middle of Highway 431 about three miles north of Guntersville. Rather than moving the carcass, they striped right across it. Sam drove out, took a picture, ran it on Page Two with brief cutlines and didn't think much about it. But the picture touched a nerve in a lot of readers.

"For what macabre reason did you publish the grotesque picture of a dog lying dead on the highway with a highway stripe painted over him?" asked Dr. Richard Huie, a pediatrician. Elizabeth Clark wrote, "The disgusting picture was a complete waste of space and an insult to my intelligence."

Those letters brought other readers to the paper's defense. Mrs. William Denyer: "It was gruesome that the machine ran over the dog, but not that you showed what happened. The people who wrote you missed the whole point." Jerry Pace: "My only regrets are that the dog is dead and that the caption should have said, 'Our tax dollars at work.'" Sam Hendrix: "Your photograph was a humorous and thought-provoking satire of just how human we are." Jimmy Ashmore: "Continue to show us and tell us like it is."

Nancy Gross Hamilton, a former Guntersville resident working for Paramount Pictures in New York, couldn't understand why anybody defended the use of the picture. She agreed with one writer that "error and neglect are part of the human condition" but added, "So is diarrhea, but I don't want to see a picture of it in the paper."

The episode grew into something of a legend. For years afterward people came into the paper office wanting to know if copies of that issue were still available (they weren't). And word spread around the state. When Porter, Don or Sam went to a meeting of newspaper people, they could usually count on someone asking, "Aren't you the guys who ran that picture of the dead dog in the road?" The folklore came to include the notion that the Associated Press (or somebody) had picked up the picture and sent it to papers all across the U.S. In fact, the only attempt to publish it outside of Guntersville ended in failure. Sam's son John, who was then a junior at the University of Alabama, sent the picture to the *National Lampoon* in hopes they'd use it in their "True Facts" section and pay him $15. They didn't use it and they didn't send it back. Since it was a Polaroid, that was the only copy there was. Years later, the *Lampoon* ran a similar picture from some other part of the country. Still later, in a listing of 10 things they didn't want readers to send them any more of, the Lampoon included pictures of dead dogs that had been striped over in the road. The *Gleam* reprinted its photo in 1989 under the headline, "The Most Famous Picture We Ever Ran"—with an apology for the poor reproduction, since it had to be taken from the 1978 newspaper and not from the photo itself.

Many years after the original photo ran, Sam was taking a picture of a highway crew at work. One employee moved quickly out of camera range, explaining, "You nearly cost me my job once." He was the operator of the machine that had striped over the dog. Somebody had sent the paper to his bosses in Montgomery, demanding to know just what kind of people they had working for the state anyway.

In 1994, the *Mobile Register* ran a picture of a road stripe across a dead armadillo. Editor Stan Tiner said in his weekly column that it "set off a huge volume of pro and con comments around town," and he referred to the *Gleam*'s experience. He said the Mobile picture would soon be available on T-shirts and invited readers to help come up with a good caption: "Please write to Stan Tiner, c/o 'Cultural Icon,' PO Box 2488, Mobile, Alabama 35530." The winning slogan was, "Damn the Armadillos. Full Speed Ahead."

Gleam readers found themselves on both sides of another issue involving the paper in 1988. Carole Brown of Warrenton clipped out an article that Sam had written about a grease fire in two homes. She pasted it on a sheet of paper and critiqued it, phrase by phrase, like an English teacher grading a theme. She found a lot not to like: five points off for saying one of the homes was "mostly destroyed" ("Something is either totally destroyed or partially damaged"). She deducted five points for capitalizing "Fire Department" and four points for saying "2 homes" instead of "two homes." The story lost two points for saying Mr. Harris didn't have to stay in the hospital ("absolutely no relevance to the article") and three points for saying Mrs. Walden in the other house was cooking hamburgers when the fire broke out ("Does it really matter what the woman was cooking?") The final paragraph cost the *Gleam* 15 points for not one but three offenses: Being too wordy, being too informal and changing tenses twice. It all added up to a grade of 53 and a bold "F" for "overall poor journalism and butchery of the English language."

"Is this the best writing of which you're capable?" Mrs. Brown asked. "Or are you trying to 'talk down' to your perceived audience? Why don't you hire someone who can write? You represent your readers as a bunch of uneducated bumpkins . . . Stop doing what you're doing."

The paper spread Mrs. Brown's critique across four columns, above her letter. It spurred a dozen letters from other readers. Practically all of them defended the paper, at least to some extent. "I'm sure the editor was aware of the grammatical mistakes," said Joseph Darnell, "but I kind of like the way it reads." Polly Coker Benson said Mrs. Brown lacked sensitivity to the paper's overall personality: "It is not the New York Times." Glenna Baxter said Mrs. Brown would give an "A" to most of the writing in the *Huntsville Times:* "Well, it is dull, dull, dull." Johnny Mastin commented, "Mr. Harris not having to stay in the hospital may have no relevance to Mrs. Brown but I sure bet it did to his family and friends . . . If this makes me a bumpkin, well at least I'll be an informed bumpkin."

Nancy Larson, on the other hand, thought Mrs. Brown had made some valid points. "The people and the stories are what make the *Advertiser-Gleam* unique," she wrote, "and not the infamous poor use of grammar. If it is perfectly acceptable that our newspaper continue to sacrifice grammatical correctness for whatever reasons, then we waste our time sending our children to school."

In an editorial, Sam came to Mrs. Brown's defense: "It took gumption for her tell us to our face how she feels, and I salute her . . . If people think we're falling down on our job, we'd like for them to let us know. Just like Mrs. Brown did. Maybe I ought to rephrase that to read 'Just as Mrs. Brown did.'"

Porter had always believed in writing the way most people talked, within certain limits. Burglars didn't pry doors open; they prized them open. Defendants pled guilty, rather than pleaded. In the *Gleam*'s early days Porter once reached back into Chaucerian English for a phrase he still heard occasionally in Marshall County. He reported that a man had "holp" his neighbor bring in a crop. Alice, who after all was an English teacher, convinced him that he was going too far, and from then on, Porter simply wrote "helped." But speaking in the vernacular was to remain a firmly-established part of the *Gleam*'s way of telling the news.

Shortly after Sam joined the paper in 1967, the receptionist, Charlene Jordan, was reading proof on one of his stories. She found something that wasn't clear and asked him if it shouldn't be reworded. Sam said it seemed clear enough to him. Porter, whose desk was at the far end of the room, overheard the conversation and looked up.

"Now, Sam," he said. "She's an average reader. If she's having trouble with it, other people will, too."

Charlene was amused at being labeled an "average reader." But the wording got changed.

Porter once got to playing around with the names of places in the county—communities, streams, mountains, streets, etc. Always a bit of a poet, he put some of the names together in an ad for the paper titled "That's Where You'll Find the Readers of the Advertiser-Gleam." Then he used more place names in another ad. Nobody remembers how many ads there were, but Don and Sam decided to put them together in a single ad and run it on a full page, with all 184 names. Porter argued that it would be so long nobody would want to read it, but they did it anyway, and it appeared several times over the years. They figured it would help convince readers that the paper was produced for more than Guntersville alone.

[The poem appears on page 255.]

CHAPTER 15

Attracting Attention

Despite its penchant for doing things in strange ways—or maybe because of it—the *Gleam* came to be looked on with a certain fondness by a good many people working on other papers, or teaching journalism in college.

"If you and your father ever feel down and out," *Birmingham News* writer Carl Sanders Jr. said in a letter to Sam in 1979, "remember y'all are well-loved here in the newsroom. I cannot begin to count the people who are *Gleam*ers and read it on a regular basis." He had written a piece about the *Gleam* and about the way Porter had started the paper thirty-eight years earlier. "Theirs is more than a newspaper," his story said. "It is a celebration of average folks in homilies and grit, with a minimum of gilt. No news story rates more than a one-column headline, 14 point. This is about twice as tall as the characters you are now reading. As for editorials, 'We try not to write anything unless we have something to say,' says Porter."

His article relayed some figures Sam had compiled showing that in a typical issue, the *Birmingham News* devoted 109 square inches of its front page to headlines while the *Gleam* used 18, leaving the *Gleam* 91 more inches of useful space for telling stories.

Another *Birmingham News* writer, Frank Sikora, had described the paper in 1972 as "probably the favorite weekly in Alabama—at least among newspaper people. Everybody in the business likes to read the *Advertiser-Gleam*."

At a 1979 seminar on newspaper layout, University of Alabama professor James Stovall gave this critique: "The *Advertiser-Gleam* breaks just about every rule, tenet, commandment and piece of common knowledge concerning modern newspaper design. Yet the paper does it with such grace, style and consistency that, in Shakespeare's words, the rules are more honored in the breach than in the observance . . . If the design leaves much to be desired by the modern newspaper reader, other qualities of the paper stand out as excellent by any standards. The paper is tightly written and edited; it is packed with interesting and useful information. The paper exudes a sense of purpose which the reader must take seriously." He said the *Gleam* "might want to consider broadening the paper's sports coverage and instituting an opinion page."

Washingtonian magazine contained a blurb in 1982 by Vic Gold, a D.C. author who had been a columnist for the *Crimson-White* at the University while Sam was editor: "My own favorite for down-to-earth news coverage is the Guntersville, Alabama, *Advertiser-Gleam*. Following are some items from recent issues: Hollie Walley is recovering from surgery. Bertha Fultz's son-in-law put new shingles on her back porch. Mrs. Claude Snelling and Jerry Snelling spent a day with Mr. and Mrs. Odell Ennis at Brashers Chapel and helped them butcher two hogs. Just before Red Lang was going to have six remaining teeth pulled, all but one were knocked out in a wreck. And finally, Dimple Hunkapiller has been to Talladega to see a new grandson. There it is, everything about Guntersville you ever wanted to know. *Post* Style section, eat your heart out." Mr. Gold had gotten the items from Leo Willette, another former Crimson-White columnist who took the *Gleam* for a while.

Columnist Linda Quigley wrote in the Florence, Alabama, *Times Daily*, "The *Gleam* is like a letter from home, even to me, and I only lived in Guntersville for a year. A friend still sends me an occasional copy and I read every word and I call people and read items to them and I show it around . . . I remember an obituary from a couple of years back that ran with a picture of the deceased and his dog. I can't remember the man's name but I remember that his Chihuahua was called 'Tiny' and he had predeceased his master."

35¢ **The Advertiser-Gleam**

Saturday, March 30, 1996 - Guntersville, Ala. 35976 - Our 116th Year, No. 26

Save $18.40 a year. Take the Advertiser-Gleam by mail. Just call 582-3232	SUBSCRIPTION PRICES In Marshall County $18 a year. Outside Marshall County $32 a year.

Announcements

Red Hill Baptist **singing** Sat., 6:00, Chosen from Huntsville.

North of the River Ministers Fellowship— including Claysville, Grant, Pine Island, New Hope, Owens Cross Roads and Woodville. Banquet room of Triple K Restaurant in Grant, Thurs., 6:00, dutch treat.

County Democratic Club Tues. 6:30, Catfish Cabin in Al'ville, all invited; speakers, Democratic candidates for tax assessor and tax collector.

Vegetable growing workshop Thur. 10:00-2:00, Rec Center, sponsored by A&M Extension. All invited.

Compassionate Friends support group for parents who've lost a child, Tues. 7:00, Hospice office, 501 Blount Avenue. For more info, call 582-2111.

Grant Mountain Saddle Club Thur. 6:30, Triple K Restaurant, prospective members invited.

Fairview Baptist at Nixon Chapel, Bro. Jeff Edwards speaker Sun. 11:00; young people in charge. Basket lunch at noon. Revival April 3-5, services 7:00; Rev. Greg Gibbs evangelist, Rev. Bruce Jones pastor.

AARP Thur. 10:00, Catfish Cabin; speaker Jeannie Lyle, community health organizer.

GHS Athletic Booster Club meeting Mon. 7:00, Reid's Restaurant.

Free movies at museum: Sat. 1:15, "How to Marry a Millionaire" with Marilyn Monroe & Betty Grable; Sun. 1:15, "Love Me Tender" with Elvis Presley. Free popcorn. 930 O'Brig Avenue.

Sid McDonald for U.S. Senate barbecue Mon. 5:00-7:00, Civitan Park; tickets $25 at Collins Auto Parts or call Dan Smalley, 1-800-586-5408.

Claysville Church of God special musical guests "Pure Heart," Sun., 5:30.

Easter Musical, "Calvary's Love," First Methodist, Sun., 8:30 and 10:55.

Lake Guntersville Computer Club meeting Sat. 2:00, Library. Open to the public.

Grant VFW Post meeting Tues., 7:00, with dinner at 6:00. Members and Auxiliary invited.

Spring craft show by Marshall County Craft Club Sat. 9:00-5:00, Boaz Outlet Center main parking lot, next to former Childcraft building. Over 40 craft booths.

Bethel Methodist on Georgia Mountain **singing** Sun., 5:00, Southern Revival, Brooks Sisters and others.

Red Hill Baptist **singing** March 30, 6:00, Chosen from Huntsville.

Bids a little high on U. Grove water project

Bids were opened Tuesday on a Union Grove water project consisting of adding a new storage tank, pumping station and 5 miles of 8-inch line.

The Union Grove Water Board got a community development block grant to make the improvements, which are designed to increase water pressure throughout the system, particularly on the Brocks Chapel end.

The project was budgeted for $621,535 with half the money com-

2 ladies found dead in the same house

It never happened here before, as far as anyone can remember — 2 people were found dead of natural causes in the same home, at the same time.

Audrey Pack, who was 82, apparently suffered a heart attack at the shock of finding Donna Lavigne dead.

Mrs. Lavigne, who was 65, had come here about a year ago to stay with Mrs. Pack in her home at 100 Pine Street in Warrenton. Mrs. Pack had been in frail health.

Coroner Dempsey Hibbs said Mrs. Lavigne suffered from diabetes and died in bed during the night of a diabetic attack and heart failure. Mrs. Pack evidently found her the next morning and had a fatal heart attack, Mr. Hibbs said. She was sitting in a chair when she was found.

Mrs. Pack was a retired nurse and the widow of Rev. L. D. Pack, a minister whose last pastorate was at the Victory Baptist Church here. She apparently tried to call her brother Hoyt Holcomb of Albertville after finding Mrs. Lavigne dead. He wasn't there but he found a message on his answering machine from Mrs. Pack, asking him to call back immediately. The ladies ordinarily didn't get up till the middle of the morning, and it's thought she placed the call then, Mr. Hibbs said.

The Guntersville police went to the home about 8:00 Tuesday night after receiving a call from Mrs. Pack's daughter Betty Uken of Huntsville. She had been trying to call her mother but got no answer. Officer Martin Killion got no answer when he rang the bell, but through the window he could see Mrs. Pack sitting in a chair. He could tell she wasn't breathing and her skin had started to discolor. Other officers and Mr. Hibbs were called and they went in through an unlocked rear door and found the 2 women.

There was no sign of foul play or violence of any kind, and Mr. Hibbs ruled they both died natural deaths.

Mrs. Lavigne was living with her daughter Tonya Slay in Atlanta. Mrs. Pack's daughter Polly Naler also lives in Atlanta. Through a mutual friend they heard that Mrs. Naler was looking for someone to stay with her mother in Guntersville. Mrs. Lavigne was glad of the chance. Both women were deeply religious and they became good friends while they shared the home here.

Their obituaries will be found on another page under "Deaths and Funerals."

TVA has no plans to rethink YMCA land deal

By Anthony Campbell

The Huntsville YMCA has asked TVA to reconsider their proposal for a lakefront subdivision at Camp Barber, but the agency has no plans to reverse its earlier decision.

The YMCA asked TVA to lift deed restrictions so they could sell 50 acres of the 111-acre camp for a lakeside residential development. TVA said no after a public hearing where the majority of the comments were against the proposal. The YMCA countered a few weeks later by asking TVA to rethink its answer.

"Our position remains the same," Tim Gilbert of TVA said this week. "We are going to maintain the existing deed restrictions."

He said if the YMCA had other options they'd like to explore under the existing deed restrictions, TVA would be glad to listen.

"As of yet, they have not scheduled a meeting with us to talk about any other ideas they might have," said Mr. Gilbert, who's over TVA's Guntersville office.

TVA made public its final environmental assessment on the proposal this week. The document contained some interesting details.

In the draft version, TVA stated its

Belva Aargus has her own Atlanta Braves corner, complete with a handy tomahawk.

At 79, Belva's a Braves fan like no other

By Angela Otts

Play ball!

Monday is the season opener for the Atlanta Braves— and Belva Argus will have her stats notebook poised, her tomahawk handy and her TV tuned in for the play-by-play.

She readily admits she's addicted.

"My daughter and son-in-law are visiting this weekend," she said. "I told them I hope I don't have to go to the airport on Monday to see anyone off. The Braves kick off the season that day."

The 79-year-old, petite Mrs. Argus says she likes football, tolerates basketball, and l-o-v-e-s baseball.

Since 1991, she has filled stacks of steno tablets with her notations on balls, strikes and hits for every Braves game. She filled 7 tablets during the championship 1995 season.

She also clips newspaper box scores and stories on each game.

She watches every game on TV, exhibition and regular season. Her schedule is attuned to the Braves schedule. She checks the sports sections of the papers and highlights the dates so she won't miss a game. A second schedule is tacked to her refrigerator— with a Braves magnet.

ALTHOUGH SHE only goes to one Braves game each year, she knows every player, all their stats, how long it's been since they've had a hit and if they're likely to get a hit. She knows the names of the wives and children and just about everything about their high school or college playing days.

"I remember the stats and biographies pretty well," she said. "I may not remember what I had for breakfast, but I sure do know all about the Braves."

She subscribes to the "Tomahawk" and "Chop Talk," 2 seasonal publications put out by the Braves organization. She also gets "Baseball Weekly" which gives her an overview of the leagues every week throughout the year.

One of the rooms in her home has a corner devoted to the Braves team. A giant poster of the championship team dominates her bulletin board. She has a collection of Braves books, their championship video, a special World Series Limited Edition, and an autographed baseball signed by Ryan Klesko.

She has a championship sweatshirt, 5 tee shirts, 2 caps, a Christmas ornament, magnets, pins, posters and a red tomahawk.

HER FRIENDS know she's an avid fan. She'll always get a chop/chop high sign from her friend Kathleen Stribling during church services at the Presbyterian Church. Mrs. Stribling is a Braves fan too.

Her neighbors Dan and Sue Dandridge and their family have taken her to Atlanta to see the Braves. Even when she sees a game in person, she has her neighbor Bob Barrett tape the game so she can watch it again when she gets home. She doesn't want to miss the commentary of her favorite announcer, Don Sutton.

Mrs. Argus' love for baseball started young when she and her father went to Rickwood Stadium in Birmingham to watch the Barons play. He taught her how to keep score during the game.

Her late husband Chris Argus always enjoyed the game. He played softball in a church league. They had been married for 51-1/2 years before his death 6 years ago. He owned Calumet Fiberglass, which used to be located on Signal Point Road.

THE COUPLE met during the World's Fair in Chicago in 1933, when she was 16. Mrs. Argus' mother warned her not to flirt with Yankees but he flirted with her. He visited her 7 times in Alabama and on the 8th visit, they were married.

They lived in Indiana and Illinois and they both liked the Chicago Cubs. When they moved to Guntersville in 1966, the old Milwaukee Braves were moving to Atlanta. Their loyalities changed to the Braves.

Mrs. Argus takes her games seriously. There is no talking during the play-by-play. She lets neighborhood children visit during game time but they have to abide by her rules. One youngster made her a 'Braves Game in Progress' sign for her door.

"If the Braves lose, there's a pall on the following day," she said.

She really gets wrapped up in the game, sometimes yelling at the top of her voice.

"I get my tomahawk out and cheer a bit," she said. "I have even been known to tell them what to do."

Her 3 children are not big baseball fans.

"They keep telling me, one nut in the family is enough," she said.

Bingo operation said to be closing

The bingo parlor at the All-American Trade Day is apparently closing.

Operator Jimmy Cornelius is reported to have been told by Guntersville officials that Alabama law doesn't allow bingo except in 3 counties, where it has been legalized by the legislature, and Marshall County isn't one of them.

Mr. Cornelius' wife, who helped run the Monday and Friday night games, said they would have no comment.

The bingo was recently moved to a different building on the Trade Day property. It had been operating in a large hall in the back of the main Trade Day building. It was moved to a separate building, which originally housed Rush Construction.

The property was recently annexed into Guntersville at Mr. Cornelius' request.

The bingo building was inspected this week by fire marshal David Chandler. He said it failed to meet the safety requirements as a gathering place for large numbers of people.

Fire Chief Buck Brown said the Guntersville Fire Department hadn't received any donations from the bingo parlor. In a story on the bingo in the Wednesday paper, it was reported that the Fire Department was among those the operation had contributed to. Chief Brown said that's not the case.

Book & card store

Anne Armentrout has opened Capricorn Corners at 532 Gunter Avenue, across from the First Alabama Bank. She sells books and greeting cards.

She bought the Bookstore & More business from John and Nancy Hill. The Hills aren't sure of their plans at this point.

Mrs. Armentrout is carrying hardbacks and paperbacks and a variety of greeting cards. She plans to increase the stock of children's books and to add more specialty items such as cookbooks, gardening books, books by Alabama authors and books about Alabama and the South.

The store is open Tuesday through Saturday, 10:00-5:30.

Mrs. Armentrout's family is from here but she grew up mainly in Maryland, as did her husband, Russell Armentrout. He retired 2 years ago and they moved from the D. C. suburbs to Arab. Her mother, Laura Culbert Webb, lives with them.

Mrs. Armentrout is a writer and editor, and she has taught writing classes. She's also into theatre. She directed "MacBeth" last fall at the Von Braun Civic Center in Huntsville.

The phone at the store is 582-4567.

Car-tag computer ready, but give 'em some time

The probate office will have its new computer system up and going next week. But they say it'll take a little while for them to get used to it, and they hope folks will be patient with them.

"If people can avoid coming in for their tags the first 3 or 4 days of April it will be a big help to us," chief clerk Sheila Smith said.

"Our people haven't had a lot of chances to train on the new computer because they've been busy helping people in the office. They came Saturday for training, but we'll be a little slow till we get all the way into it. Once we get familiar with it we think it's going to work out real well."

The office expects to get back into mail-out tags in the early part of April, after sending out notices to people whose tags need to be renewed. People whose last names begin with N, G and F come up in April. They had to stop the mail-out system during January, February and March for lack of a computer.

The new computer will handle licenses for cars, trucks and boats, plus business privilege licenses.

Last week to qualify, here's who has so far

Friday is the deadline for candidates to file for local offices in both the Republican and Democratic primaries, set for June 4.

These are the qualifiers so far:

Democrats

Tax collector — Incumbent Carl Boatwright, Tony Reaves.

Tax assessor — Incumbent Joey Masters, Russell Kilpatrick.

County School Board — Ken Burns. Incumbent A. C. Cole isn't running.

District judge — No qualifiers yet, but incumbent David Evans has his paperwork filled out and plans to send it off this week. They qualify with the Secretary of State.

Constable, Beat 1, Guntersville — L. C. Mitchell (incumbent).

Constable, Beat 4, Albertville — Harry Taft.

Constable, Beat 16, Friendship — James Brown.

Republicans

Tax collector — Mark Mathis.

Tax assessor — Bryan Waldrop.

County School Board — No qualifiers yet.

District judge — No qualifiers yet.

Constables — No qualifiers yet.

Republican chairman Carl Wisener said their candidate recruiting committee is talking to several others about possibly running for office.

He noted that 3 Republicans from Marshall County are running for state office. Barry Guess and Kerry Rich are running for the U. S. House of Representatives and Sid McDonald is running for U. S. Senate.

"We feel like we've made a good start," Mr. Wisener said.

His 31 cases take up 6 pages on court docket

Floyd Arnold may have set a record for the most cases ever appealed from a municipal court to Circuit Court in Marshall County.

Mr. Arnold, 24, of 71 Sunset Circle near Brashiers Chapel, has 31 traffic-related charges on the docket for the term of Criminal Court that will begin April 15.

The charges include resisting arrest, reckless driving, failure to stop at a stop sign, improper passing, speeding, attempting to elude, failure to signal, driving on a revoked license, leaving the side of the road, following too closely, improper turning and not wearing his seat belt.

He faces several counts of some of those charges.

Arab police said he was driving 105 mph in a 50 mph zone on Highway 69 last May.

This 1996 Advertiser-Gleam looked a lot like its predecessors of 50 years earlier, testimony that newspapers could succeed without front-page color, flashy layouts, and computer-driven graphics.

In 1985, a semi-retired newspaperman, Tom Riordan, did a piece on the *Gleam* for *Editor & Publisher*, a national magazine about newspapers. He noted the paper's unusual appearance and the lack of such customary features as an editorial page: "If there happens to be an editorial, it can appear anywhere, set in regular body type and width, like this one on page 15, squeezed over the top of a giant Food World ad . From the beginning in 1941, the paper has followed Porter Harvey's newspaper credo: Make it local. Make it a paper people enjoy reading, with news they're interested in."

Marshall Cook, a journalism instructor at University of Wisconsin-Madison, read the *Editor & Publisher* piece and took out a subscription. He later wrote a textbook on community newspapers and quoted from half a dozen *Gleam* writeups in his chapter on handling deaths.

Another journalism professor, Don Sneed of San Diego State, wrote Porter in 1987 for some copies of the paper. He had once worked for the *Cullman Times* about 35 miles from Guntersville. "Often our graduates want to work for metropolitan newspapers, but I try to encourage them to start at smaller newspapers where I think there are many rewards," he wrote. "I know the *Advertiser-Gleam* is a newspaper that is close to the people and publishes stories that people care about, and that is what I try to convey to my students, since so many newspapers today try to look alike and report alike."

In a playful mood, Auburn journalism instructor Ed Williams in 1988 sent a copy of the *Gleam* to Edmund C. Arnold, perhaps the most renowned newspaper designer in America. Mr. Arnold wrote a "Page of the Week" column in *Publishers' Auxiliary* in which he critiqued the layout of newspapers from all over the U.S. "The *Gleam*," he wrote, "is a damn good paper." But the design left him shaking his head: "The front page is not irresistible . . . Were I visiting in Guntersville or had I just moved into the community, I don't think I'd spend two bits to buy the *A-G* off a counter or out of a coin box." Mr. Arnold ticked off the paper's many violations of accepted design practice and concluded, "Again stressing the excellence of content, I suggest that good content deserves good packaging."

A Kentucky columnist, Don Edwards of the *Lexington Herald-Leader*, somehow got hold of a copy of the *Gleam* in 1989 and read it over the weekend. Despite what Thomas Wolfe said, he wrote, "You can go home to hometowns you never even had. All you have to do is pick up a hometown newspaper." He cited stories in the *Gleam* about kids at the Elementary School putting California Raisin dolls and other things in a time capsule, about a World War II veteran who had turned down a Purple Heart for his wounds because he didn't want the attention, about Kenneth Stover saying Lynn Duke hit him up side the head with a BB air pistol and half a dozen more. "As we kept reading, we gradually found ourselves going home to Guntersville, Alabama," he wrote. "How was it possible to feel that way about a place that, 10 minutes before, we hadn't known existed?"

Porter had reached the standard retirement age of 65 in 1968, but he gave no thought to stopping. He got too much enjoyment out of what he was doing. He worked a five-and-a-half day week till about 1980 when he cut back to five days like others at the paper. Till then his only concession to age had been a long lunch hour to accommodate his nap. He continued to arrive at 7:30 in the morning and stay most days till 6:00 in the evening.

His longevity can be seen in the case of twin girls who were born in 1941, shortly after the *Gleam* started publishing. They were the first twins in the new City Hospital and Porter wrote a story about their birth. They grew up in the Grassy community, and both became nurses and raised families. They retired together in 1989, and Porter wrote that story too.

He began to attract attention in other media because of his age and the fact that he was still going strong. The *Alabama Publisher,* a tabloid put out by the Alabama Press Association for conventions, had a front-page picture of Porter in 1989 at his typewriter under the headline, "Still Rolling With the Presses." The *Huntsville Times* carried a writeup about him in 1990. Laranda Nichols, the *Times*' Marshall County reporter, noted that at 86 he was still covering several of the *Gleam*'s heavy news beats—the sheriff's office, the courts, and the county schools—in addi-

Ninety feet in the air, Porter planted one foot on a girder and held on with one arm to photograph a wedding on the bridge over the Tennessee River at Guntersville. He was 67 at the time.

tion to writing most of the obituaries. Jamie Cooper of Channel 31 in Huntsville did a piece showing Porter gathering news around town and even got him to stand on his head for the camera just as he did at home as part of his daily exercise routine. In 1991, Porter was written up in the *Sand Mountain Reporter* by Brandon Terrell, a young newsman who had gotten to know Porter when they covered the sheriff's office together. "Harvey can often be seen around the Courthouse, walking slowly, cane in hand," he wrote. "When he first came to Guntersville in 1941, the sheriff's department had five employees—a sheriff, two deputies, a jailer who lived at the jail, and a secretary . Now there are more than 40 employees but Harvey is still reporting the news, just like he did when he first came."

Porter had become president of the Alabama Press Association in 1967. Don was elected to that same office in 1982. When Sam was elected president in 1993, it marked the first time in the APA's 122 years that three presidents of the organization were still active on the same newspaper. That prompted writeups about the paper and the family in the *Huntsville Times* and the *Birmingham News*. The *News* writer, Frank Sikora, noted that Porter, Don and Sam were all still hammering away on manual typewriters, in an age when most reporters had long since gone on to computerized keyboards. "Publisher Porter Harvey, who turned 90 this month, growled good-naturedly, 'I guess the day is coming when I'll have to learn to use one of those electric typewriters or word processors or whatever they call them.'"

Over the years the *Gleam* was mentioned from time to time in the *AlaPressa*, the APA newsletter. Auburn's Ed Williams picked up some of those items in compiling a history of the APA in 1996:

> 1964—"Porter Harvey, editor of the *Advertiser-Gleam*, used an 8-by-10 advertisement to proclaim the fact that he once was elected a constable in Dodge City, Kansas, as a gag. Harvey hung his certificate on the wall of his office. 'That was several years ago,' Harvey said. 'Thousands of people have been in the office since then and only two or three of them have ever noticed the certificate hanging on the wall.' The ad would serve two purposes, Harvey said. 'First it will build up the editor's pride by letting people know what a great honor was once bestowed on him. And second, it will demonstrate that although something may go unnoticed even if posted in the most conspicuous place, you can bring it to the people's attention promptly by advertising it in the paper'."
>
> 1969—"Porter Harvey, 66-year-old publisher, skinned his nose while jumping on the trampoline in Civitan Park. The newspaper reported that Harvey 'was doing a belly-down landing and his nose hit the canvas'."
>
> 1988—"The *Advertiser-Gleam* started running a new house ad claiming that 'We're 99.9% Right. We Can Hardly Believe It Ourselves.' Publisher Porter Harvey showed in the ad that a news item in the *Gleam* measuring two square inches contained 16 facts. Harvey then explained that an average issue of the *Gleam* had about 850 square

> inches of news, not counting headlines, art and ads. 'At eight facts per square inch, that's 6,800 facts in the news,' Harvey said. He said the errors found in the paper amount to much less than one-tenth of one percent of that number."

The Associated Press sent out a piece in November 1993 that focused on the *Gleam*'s way of handling obituaries. It was written by Jay Reeves, who knew Sam and Val's daughter Anne and her husband Andy Hails in Montgomery and had seen the paper in their home. "Not many newspapers would begin an obituary by recalling that the dearly departed once shoved a piece of fruit up his nose," the AP story began. "But the *Advertiser-Gleam* isn't like most newspapers." Obituaries, he said, "aren't the only stories that get a folksy touch. The *Advertiser-Gleam* takes a conversational approach to everything." He gave several examples: "A correction: Larry Morris helped John Woodall fire a shotgun into a barrel to simulate a cannon when the high school band played 'The 1812 Overture' back when they were in school. We only told about Mr. Woodall." And "Mary Helen Avery woke up about 2:00 in the morning and heard somebody trying to force his way in the back door of her home. Her brother Adam Avery scared the burglar off by opening and closing the front door several times so the sound would carry to the back."

The AP writeup came to the attention of the people who produce a program called "Whaddya Know" for public radio stations around the country. The host, Michael Feldman, emceed a mixture of talk, music and quiz-shows. They arranged to interview Porter by phone on a Saturday morning, a day when he and Don were the only ones working. Don was out when Mr. Feldman called from Madison, Wisconsin, where the show was being taped in front of a live audience. Mr. Feldman noted that Porter was ninety years old. He had him tell how the paper came to be called the *Gleam* and how it printed only local news. "Do you still write for the paper?" he asked. "Yes," Porter replied, "I'm at the office now." He said he was working on a story about a couple who had gotten married on horseback, only the horses got so fidgety that the maid of honor and the best man had to hold the reins during the ceremony. "One thing my father told me," Mr. Feldman cracked, "was that you have to hold your horses till you get married." It got a big laugh from the audience, and the host said, "Porter, you can use that if you like. I believe you use jokes in the paper." He asked if anybody ever got mad because the paper printed too many personal details. Porter told about the time when a lady came into the office, steaming mad. "A member of her family had committed suicide, and we printed that it was a suicide," he said. The article had told in some detail how the man ran a hose from the exhaust pipe of his car and into the car window. "She said we never should have put that in. The longer we talked the madder she got. She finally grabbed the bookkeeper's desk and actually turned it over with all that stuff on it. It made the biggest mess you ever saw." The woman swept everything off another desk, threw a chair across the room and stormed out.

"Hey," Porter told Mr. Feldman, "I'm by myself and the phone's ringing." The host responded, "That's OK, you get it and we'll wait. We'll have a little musical interlude." Piano music went out over the national hookup. "Probably a late-breaking story," Mr. Feldman said. More music, then some simulated horse sounds in the background. "We'll come back to Porter in just a minute." It turned out that Porter had broken the phone connection in taking the other call, and it was a minute and 55 seconds before they got him back on the air. "Sorry I cut you off," Porter told him. "That's all right," Mr. Feldman said. "Late breaking news story?" Porter replied, "No, a lady wanted to cancel a want ad she'd placed. I told her I was on long distance and I'd call her back." They talked a while about the *Gleam*'s policy on obits, and Mr. Feldman read from several of them. He asked Porter how the *Gleam* got so much information after people died. "We call them up, and people are surprisingly willing to tell you about their folks. Usually you can find something interesting about nearly everybody." Mr. Feldman said that when he died, "they should mention the time I got my foot stuck in a sewer when I was two years old. The firemen came out and they used a foot extractor for the first time anywhere." He asked Porter if he had written his own obituary. "No, I haven't thought about that," Porter said. "I'm not planning to die."

A 1992 family reunion at John Harvey's place at Mentone. From left:
LEFT OF STEPS: Seated—Coley Woodard, Mary Woodward, Porter Harvey, Alice Wells Harvey, Frances Harvey Wood, Ellen Harvey Jervis. Standing—Kenneth Harvey, Don Woodward, Vicki Bailey (Woodward), Steve Woodward, Jo Kirkpatrick Harvey, Joe Harvey, Fred Wood. ON STEPS: Front Row—Anne Harvey Hails, Rebecca Hails, John Hails, Valerie Yencha Harvey. Second Row—Patricia Lacey Harvey, Joe Michael Harvey, Kevin Harvey. Third Row—Taylor Woodward, Annette Woodward, Aubrey Woodward, Bruce Harvey, Mark Harvey. Fourth Row—Craig Woodward, Alec Woodward, Evan Harvey, John Harvey. Fifth Row—Sheila Matthews Harvey, Jane Harvey, Alice Yencha Harvey. RIGHT OF STEPS: Seated—Sam Harvey, Bess Woodward, Ellen Harvey, Coley Harvey, Lisa Harvey, Patrick Harvey, Leith Harvey, Sunny Harvey. Standing—Mary Porter Harvey Grizzle, Jeff Grizzle, Sam Grizzle, Steve Harvey, Gracie Harvey, Barry Hendrixson, Anna Harvey. PRESENT BUT NOT SHOWN: Scott Harvey, Arlo Harvey, and Andy Hails (who took the picture).

CHAPTER 16

At Grandma's House

"Going to Grandma's house was the high point of our whole year," her oldest grandson, Kenneth Harvey, remembered. He lived in Ohio and Kentucky till he was twelve, and a visit to the grandparents "was like a trip to Fantasy Land. It was a special place with special people, and we always cried when we left. It amused Craig and the others who were in Guntersville to see us crying in the car when we drove away."

There were 11 grandchildren. Val and Sam had Kenneth, born 1955; John, 1957; Anne, 1960; and Mary Porter, 1963. Mary and Don had Craig, 1956; Steve, 1959; and Coley, 1971. Jo Kirk and Joe had Bruce, 1958; Scott, 1961; Steve, 1966; and Anna, 1970.

The grandchildren enjoyed Alice and Porter in different ways. Grandma went to extraordinary lengths to figure out things for kids to do while they were at her house, creative things that would challenge their ingenuity or spark their imagination. Grandpa, they quickly learned, still had a lot of the boy in him. He was always good for an adventure or a new experience that he could enjoy along with them.

Both Alice and Porter were always interested in the kids' opinions on the latest crazes in music, dress, hairstyles, etc. They didn't give a lot of advice in return. The grandchildren grew up at a time when young people in general were rebelling against many of the standards and practices their elders had taken for granted. In Alice and Porter they found two grownups who accepted them and enjoyed them without

Alice's house was a magnet for grandchildren, with special projects frequently going on. Craig helps check the cookies.

trying to judge them by the standards of their own younger days.

In 1984, Porter got the grandchildren to write down things they remembered about Alice from when they were small, something Alice had gotten them to do earlier about Porter.

"Most of all," Craig Woodward said, "what I remember about Grandma was her ability to put up with about 10 grandkids at once. Our parents had fits keeping up with two or three at a time, and Grandma could magically handle all of us without a peep of trouble."

"She had arts and crafts, fingerpainting, water colors and her own homemade play dough," John Harvey recalled. "Looking back I realize that even when I was a child, Grandma treated me as an intelligent person, and what was important to me was important to her."

Six grandsons were born before the first granddaughter, so the early get-togethers tended to revolve around male activities. Alice would sometimes pack up the boys in the car for a visit to the lumber store to buy scrap wood. She would turn them loose in the back yard with Porter's saws and hammers, trying to suppress her fear over what they might accidentally do to themselves or to one another. She allowed them to play billy goat's gruff in the front room, using her couch, ottoman, and table leaves to climb over and under. She sometimes joined in the game herself, taking her turn as the troll hiding under the bridge.

"Grandma would paint with me in the back room for hours and hours," said Mary Porter Harvey, who moved to Guntersville when she was three and lived across the street from her grandparents until she was 14. "You could always count on Grandma having at least one or two tins of waterpaint. I was always jealous, though, because no matter how hard I tried, I couldn't paint as patiently as she did."

When out-of-town children came for a visit, Alice would often invite

Porter and Alice invited all their children and grandchildren to Disney World in 1981, and footed the bill. From left, Anna Harvey, Coley Woodward, and Mary Porter Harvey with "Tigger."

their in-town cousins to spend some of the nights as well as days at her house. She was famous for her backrubs. She rubbed her grandchildren's backs to help them get to sleep, just as she had done for her own children. "The most intense anticipation of my childhood was waiting for bedtime backrubs," Steve Woodward said. "Sometimes she had to have count-downs to the finish so we would know when we were supposed to be asleep." Alice would put little trinkets or toys under the beds to surprise the kids when they woke up in the morning, or even from an afternoon nap. The kids didn't stay surprised long, and Kenneth recalled that "before long we were expecting and even demanding presents under the bed." He said it took quite a lady to tolerate that.

"Breakfast always included some form of brown bread, which seemed to be a treat for everyone," Bruce Harvey said. "But I always placed a special order for white bread, lightly toasted, and Grandma always came through. Tea parties were standard ritual in the afternoon with Kool Aid, cookies and marshmallows."

Alice was determined not to play favorites. At Christmas the grand-children got presents plus varying amounts of cash, using the money to equalize the difference in the cost of the gifts. Anna and Steve Harvey recalled that practice as part of the rhyme they contributed: "For Christmas this woman is always in range. She buys you a present and gives you the change."

Anne Harvey, like her sister Mary Porter, spent a lot of time across the street at Grandma's while growing up "Sometimes Mom would send me on an errand and I would stay for hours," she said. "Grandma always had good stories to tell about her family. Sometimes I would stay for supper. When it was time to go home, way after dark, Grandma always watched me walk from her house to mine. When I got home I would wave or flick our lights to let her know I was home safe. I would act brave, but I was glad she was watching me." Mary Porter added, "I still miss that."

Porter discovered Kipling's *The Jungle Book* a couple of generations before Walt Disney made it into a feature-length cartoon movie. He would gather the grandchildren around him and half-read, half-tell the

Porter and Joe (rear) set off on a camping trip with, from left, Scott and Bruce Harvey, Steve Woodward, and John Harvey.

marvelous story of Mowgli growing up as part of the wolf pack. He had read the same stories to Sam, Mary, and Joe, along with *Gulliver's Travels* and other tales. John remembered "sitting all over Grandpa's arms and legs" to listen. Porter liked getting down on other people's level, literally as well as figuratively. He would sit on the floor and help them build houses out of cards or machines out of Tinkertoys. When the *Wizard of Oz* had its annual showing on TV, he and Alice would ask the younger grandchildren to watch with them. Porter would sometimes lead a make-believe version of the story, with Coley Woodward playing Dorothy.

His lifelong fascination with apes and movie monsters held a special appeal for the grandchildren. When Steve Harvey was seven, he wrote this description of Porter: "He had all kinds of monster books. He has a big poster of Frankenstine. He watches Frankenstine movies. He aspeceley watches King Kong movies. One night after super at our house he went to bed so he could see Crecher Fecher it's on at ll oklcok p.m. When he got up crecher fecher wasn't even on." The grandchildren and others took to giving Porter posters and other renditions of apes and monsters

Well into his 80s, Porter liked to plunge into the river at Mentone from a rope swing and from a tree.

which soon filled the walls of the room that served as his office at home It came to be known as the Monster Room. The most spectacular exhibit was a lifesize replica of Frankenstein's monster. Craig helped Porter cut it out from a poster and mount it on cardboard so it would stand erect and greet people as they walked into the room. One night Porter and Craig carried the seven-foot cutout across the street, stood it in front of Earl and Louella Stroud's door, rang the doorbell and hid where they could watch.

Porter took his monsters seriously. In 1976, when the second *King*

Kong movie was coming out, he wrote to the editors of *Time* magazine. "When they made 'King Kong' in 1933," he wrote, "you folks at *Time* gave a vivid description of a 40-foot ape they had built for the movie. Nostrils as big as tennis balls. Animated by electric motors with an intricate control system. I remember thinking what a spectacle Kong would be, stalking across the California countryside. When I saw the picture I had a considerable letdown. And much as I loved the big ape, I was disillusioned with *Time*. You obviously hadn't told it like it was. Years later I read in a monster magazine that they had several Kongs of various sizes, but no 40-footer powered by electric motors. Now here comes 'King Kong' again, and here is *Time* describing a huge ape with 3,100 feet of hydraulic hose and 4,500 feet of electric wiring in his innards. Please, *Time*, don't let me down again. Please tell me that this time it's true."

The grandchildren loved the occasional weekends at the family cabin at Mentone, Alabama, 65 miles away, the one Porter's father built. It was shared by three families—Porter's, Ellen's, and Frances's. Their brother Coley had built next door and lived at Mentone full-time. There was a rope swing on a tree at the edge of the river in Coley's yard. Porter liked to swing out over the river and plunge in, just as he had done on the Oostanaula as a boy. "Grandpa would climb the tree higher than anyone else in order to dive from the swing," Kenneth said. "Everyone else would only jump." Bruce remembered when he, Joe and Porter were attaching a new swing to the tree. "Grandpa was going to test the swing after Dad tied it," he said. "Grandpa took a big leap off the bank and about the time he got right out in the middle of the river, the trunk of the tree broke off about two feet below Dad. There went Dad, falling and grabbing hold of a small branch, while Grandpa went plunging into the river like Tarzan fully dressed." Once Anne lost a tennis shoe in the river. It was just an old shoe, but Porter was determined to show the kids it could be retrieved. He tied a rock to his foot to hold him down while he looked on the bottom, and some of the kids still insist he nearly drowned in the process. He survived but the shoe stayed lost.

When children spent the night at the grandparents' house, Porter would sometimes go to bed, get up, and wake them up to watch the late show on TV with him if an especially good horror film was showing, or if a comet or meteor shower was expected in the sky. (He was able to go back to sleep immediately. From the time he was in his 40s, he had set an alarm clock to awaken him and Alice for trips to the bathroom, rather than waiting for the slow unpleasantness of nature's call. As they grew older he would set the clock for two or even three awakenings.)

When Kenneth was a teenager, he finally talked Sam and Val into letting him buy a motorcycle with his earnings. Right after he got it, he and Grandpa needed to go to the *Gleam* one night to finish up some work. "It was raining hard," Kenneth said. "Grandpa called me up and asked whose car we were going in. I said it didn't matter to me. He said 'Is your wheel running?' I said, 'Sure, but it's raining.' He said, 'Doesn't it run when it rains? Let's go on it.' I said it was dangerous to ride in the rain, and besides, the drops stung when they hit your face. He said 'Well, OK, I guess we'll go in my car'."

Porter required some getting used to on the part of his son-in-law and his two daughters-in-law.

Don said he never knew Porter had a fondness for poetry till the night he and Mary told Porter and Alice they were getting married. A beer or two was consumed in celebration, and before the night was over Porter had recited Poe's "The Raven" from start to finish. He had learned it in Rome, after graduating from Emory. He needed Latin to get into Harvard, so he took it that summer from a tutor. He memorized "The Raven" while walking to and from the tutor's home.

When Sam was driving Val from Washington to Guntersville for the first meeting with his parents, he cautioned her that some of Porter's habits might seem a little unusual, like sprinkling sugar on his tomatoes and eating bread along with his dessert.

Jo Kirk had been around Porter and Alice a lot while she and Joe were dating. But Porter's up-front way about things could still be a little jarring. "There was the time we brought Bruce to Guntersville for the first time, this practically perfect baby," she said. "Grandpa took one look at him and said, 'Don't you think his eyes are a little too close together?'" Jo Kirk called Porter "the happiest person I know, always smiling, the most contented, and interested in other people."

Although Porter and Alice were steady churchgoers the great part of their lives, both had gone through periods of doubt about religion. In a letter to Alice before they married, Porter said he and a friend "got into an argument about religion last night that lasted until about 2:30. I found I had forgotten some of the things that made me decide a few years ago that I was an agnostic. I guess I'm still one. I figure that unless a person has a definite reason to be something else—that is to believe something—that he is an agnostic." Alice replied, "I am glad you defined 'agnostic.' Even though I once thought I was an agnostic, I had forgotten the distinction between that and an atheist. For a while I thought I was the latter because it didn't seem plausible to me that in an orderly universe controlled by a just God, the problem of evil should have entered into it." She said one of her friends convinced her that she was really an agnostic, since she didn't really believe there was no God, only that it was impossible to prove one way or the other. But in a subsequent letter to Porter, she wrote, "I am thankful for you, and your love and our home and the promise of a long life of happiness together. I think I'll pray a little prayer like that now. And I had to add a request that God watch over you and keep you safe for me always."

Religion was never something Porter and Alice talked about much with their children. And specific doctrine wasn't very important to them. Both were brought up as Methodists, and in Dodge City Porter started taking Sam to Sunday school while Alice stayed home with the younger children. They didn't belong to a church the year they lived in Birmingham. In Trussville the family attended the Presbyterian Church all three years because the Presbyterians were the first to invite them and also offered them a ride each Sunday, since they didn't have a car. In Guntersville they became Methodists again, and attending church every Sunday was automatic for the whole family. Porter was a member of the same Sunday school class for over 50 years. Alice went to Sunday school, sang in the choir, and joined a church circle.

At home, the blessing wasn't said at meals except on special occasions, which generally meant when visitors were present. But after the children were grown, Porter and Alice got into the habit of holding hands at the table and saying the blessing before they ate. It was a custom they never stopped.

Although they didn't expound religion to their children, they laid down clear guidelines on the kind of behavior that was expected of them. Joe remembers Alice crying when he told her about the spankings he got in first grade. "I got six of them," he said. "And I could never figure out why she didn't cry when I got the three in fifth grade unless it was because I had decided not to tell her about those. I wasn't supposed to read the comic books in Rayburn's Drug Store unless I bought them. One day Mama caught me there, poring over Superman, Captain Marvel, and Bugs Bunny. I had to take my allowance (10 cents per week) and buy five comic books (at 10 cents apiece) as punishment. As I remember, the ones I had to buy were the ones I'd already read."

"A characteristic that Mama and Daddy both had," Joe said, "one we've talked about more than any other, was refraining from saying anything bad about anybody. They always saw the best in everyone."

In 1980,when Porter was driving near Rome, he knocked down a highway sign. Nobody was around to report it. But when he got home he looked up the address of the Georgia Transportation Department and wrote to the man in charge. "I'd like to pay for the damage," he said. "Please let me know the amount and I'll send you a check."

In the late 1980s Porter and Alice wrote all their children and grandchildren and asked that they stop sending them Christmas presents or birthday presents. They noted that they had made the same request before. "Everybody cooperated fine for a while," they said, but the gifts had started up again little by little, "and we're afraid it has reached the point that some of you feel it's something you ought to do. We know we're hard to buy for and you all are busy people . . . so how about skipping us in the future." They added, "The checks we send you don't count. They don't require any thought and they are no trouble, and the money comes out of what will eventually be yours anyway."

In a remembrance of Alice on her eightieth birthday, Mary said

The 1983 Guntersville Christmas parade spotlighted Porter and Alice.

"Mama was one of the few parents who could always be counted on to chaperone groups of teenagers for church and school trips, and I remember being proud of the way she related to my friends. I remember what a good sport Mama has been through the years, doing so many things she was really afraid of or didn't care about doing, but was talked into by Daddy or us. Most of all I remember her tenderness and her kindness and concern, and I think I better stop here."

CHAPTER 17

BOATS AND BUNGEE JUMPING

From the time he was a boy on the Oostanaula at Rome, Porter had a thing for rivers. He enjoyed paddling a flat-bottom fishing boat on the Little River at Mentone with his children and later with his grandchildren and great-grandchildren. He never had much use for the motor that went on the boat, just as he didn't have much use for the indoor toilet that less hardy members of the family installed in the Mentone cabin around 1950. Porter preferred to make his way through the woods to the little outhouse, even at night when it required a flashlight. What was the use of going to the cabin, he asked, if it was going to be like home?

In 1969 he took his first of four long-distance river trips in Bill Harris's 12-foot fishing boat, "Miss Guntersville Lake." Bill, Porter, and Reynold Lurwig traveled 1,100 miles in six days to and from Nashville along the Tennessee, Ohio, and Cumberland Rivers. In 1970 the same three men went upstream on the Tennessee to Knoxville. They went to St. Louis in 1971 on the Tennessee, Ohio, and Mississippi. And in 1974 at 71, Porter went back to St. Louis with Bill and Billy Dyar. The four trips amounted to 3,900 miles in the little craft.

Bill Harris managed the movie theater in town and had lived two doors down from Porter and Alice's first house in Guntersville. Twelve years younger than Porter, he did all the driving while his passengers rode up front on inflated doughnut seat cushions. Each day was an endurance test. They got up with the sun and hit the river right away. They ate breakfast and lunch in the little boat while Bill drove at full throttle, determined to make all the miles he could before dark. "I had two speeds," Bill said, "wide open and stopped." They ate mostly from cans—vienna sausage, pickled pigs feet and Possum-brand sardines—plus cheese and crackers. Bill, the lifelong movie theater man, carried Cracker Jacks for dessert and snacking.

They stopped only once in the middle of the day to gas up. Other than that they stayed on the move, except when they had to lock through a dam. If they had reached their day's destination when evening came, they might eat supper in a restaurant. Otherwise, they ate out of cans and kept going. They slept in the open, putting air mattresses and sleeping bags on boat docks along the way. With three of them in the small boat, they necessarily traveled light—life jackets, rain suits for bad weather, a minimum of other clothing, and enough food for the trip.

Bill would get to a phone each morning before they shoved off so he could call the Guntersville radio station and give people at home a detailed account of their adventures. They ran into storms and once in

Porter traveled 3,900 miles in this 12-foot fishing boat owned by Bill Harris (left). The third man on this trip was Billy Dyar, the mayor of nearby Boaz, who wore a tie for the picture before shoving off.

September it got so cold they nearly froze, but they kept going. "We didn't stop for wind, waves or lightning," Bill said.

They were generally welcomed at their destination by the mayor or someone from the mayor's office and Bill would be given a key to the city. Sometimes transplanted Guntersvillians also came down to see them pull in. Then, after brief pleasantries, the travelers would climb back into the boat and strike out for home.

Bill realized he was putting his passengers through quite a test. On one trip they ran into a storm on the Mississippi. "There was lightning and thunder and we were dodging logs and trying to stay out of the way of all the tugs and barges going up and down the river," he said. "We were in the boat that day from 6:00 in the morning to 9:30 at night. Porter and Reynold never complained, never said they were scared. The only thing they asked me was when night was coming on they'd say, 'Bill, are you sure you can still see?' and I'd tell them when it got where I couldn't see, I'd stop."

Porter (second from left) organized a family white-water rafting trip on the Ocoee River in 1980. Grandson Scott Harvey is in the front.

Porter, he said, "was as tough as the toughest concrete that was ever poured." Bill tried to talk Porter into going on other trips but Porter begged off, citing age and not wanting to worry Alice. Bill made 24 trips in all, from 1968 to 1992, racking up 53,500 miles in the little boat and earning the nickname "Mississippi Bill" for several ventures on the Father of Waters.

Taking risks appealed to Porter. When he was about 75, he got into a discussion with some of the people at the sheriff's office about marijuana and how it compared to alcohol as a problem for society. One of the deputies told him they could let him have a little marijuana they had seized if he'd like to see first-hand how it affected people. Porter was intrigued, just as he had been intrigued as a teenager to know what it was like to get drunk on alcohol. He told Don and Sam about the offer to see if they'd be interested in joining him in an experiment. Less adventurous by nature than he was, the younger men talked him out of it, just as Harry Powers had persuaded him not to get drunk some 60 years earlier.

Another kind of river adventure beckoned to Porter in 1979. His grandson Scott Harvey told him about white-water rafting on the Ocoee River in southeastern Tennessee. The Ocoee was supposed to have more thrill-producing rapids in a short stretch than almost any other river anywhere. Rafts and guides could be rented from outfitters along the river. Porter set out to talk others in the family into going. Predictably, some of them tried to argue him out of it. He was 76 years old with a bad leg and he knew absolutely nothing about rafting on wild rivers. But he was convinced it was safe or it wouldn't be allowed, and he figured it would be lots of fun. Most of his grandchildren were grown by then and they helped convince Sam and Joe that it would be a great experience for everybody, even for them. A dozen or so from three generations gathered on the Ocoee for the ride. It turned out to be so much fun that most of them (including Porter) went back a year later and did it again.

Porter organized a calmer trip in 1985. He and Harry Powers had talked from time to time about their boyhood adventures on the Oostanaula and how they would like to revisit those days. Joe told Porter that if he and Harry ever got around to actually doing it, he'd like to go

Porter and Harry Powers, at ages 82 and 83, relived some of their boyhood exploits during an all-day canoe trip on the Oostanaula River. At right, grandsons John Harvey and Craig Woodward.

along. The idea grew. Porter and Harry invited all their children and grandchildren and ended up with a party of 10. They put five canoes into the river at Calhoun and paddled 15 miles to downtown Rome, a trip that took most of the day. Porter was 82, Harry 83. The Rome newspaper ran a piece about it on the front page, saying Porter and Harry had found a way to travel back in time. "The world has changed a lot in 50 or 70 years," Porter told the reporter, "but the river is one place where things have pretty much stayed the same." Making the trip were Joe and Sam, Joe's son Steve, Sam's son John and his daughter Anne, Anne's future husband, Andy Hails, Mary's son Craig Woodward and Harry's son Robert Powers.

The last family adventure that Porter organized was the one that made headlines and TV all across the U.S. and even beyond. Porter had read in the *Birmingham Post-Herald* in October 1991 that a bungee jump had been set up in Heflin about 70 miles from Guntersville. The reporter, Cary Estes, had taken the leap himself. "Maybe this is crazy,"

Mr. Estes wrote, "but it's a lot of fun too." Porter, who seldom watched TV, had never seen a bungee jump. But he had always liked carnival rides and roller coasters and this sounded to him like the ultimate thrill. Joe's son Scott, who had missed a family reunion in 1987, was trying to organize another reunion at Mentone in 1992. Porter lobbied for a side trip to Heflin for a bungee jump. "We went white-water rafting on the Ocoee River and had a great time," Scott quoted Porter in the invitations to the reunion. "Now that I have acquired a little more experience and maturity I'd like to tackle something not quite so sedate." Scott said others in the family, "claiming to be concerned only about the many hours such a trip would take, are throwing cold water on the idea."

They didn't go bungee jumping at the 1992 reunion. But Porter was nothing if not persistent. Further research pointed to a bungee jumping place in Chattanooga as a more likely locale—Raccoon Mountain High Adventure Sports. Joe and some of his family went by for a look when they were in Chattanooga for a ball game. Porter scheduled the get-together for August 28, 1993. He started making phone calls and writing letters, and his enthusiasm and early planning paid off. All three of his children and all 11 grandchildren made the trip along with spouses, great-grandchildren, and a friend or two. In all, 39 showed up that morning. Some planned to jump. Some didn't know whether they'd jump or not. Some went for the thrill—and pride—of seeing Porter at age 90 plunge off a 176-foot platform with an elastic cord fastened to his back.

What they hadn't counted on were the reporters, photographers and TV cameramen who were waiting there for them. Laranda Nichols, the *Huntsville Times* reporter in Marshall County, had heard about the gathering and showed up with her husband, her son, and her notepad. The *Times* sent a photographer, Dave Dieter, with telephoto lenses and color film. And the bungee operators had tipped off the Chattanooga newspapers and TV stations that a 90-year-old man was about to become the oldest person in the world to take a bungee plunge.

Laranda's son Jonathan made the first leap. Grandsons Craig Woodward and John Harvey volunteered to go ahead of Porter and flipped a coin to see who would be the first family jumper. John won (or lost, depending on how you look at it) and made the initial leap. Craig went next. Then Porter walked out to the lift, with the TV cameras catching his limp and zeroing in as the attendants strapped on the harness. Porter climbed into the cage and stood there alone while the cage was hoisted 176 feet into the air. "You're at the top, Porter," co-owner Loraine Riche called out over the loudspeaker. "Now very carefully get in your bungee dive position. Get your toes out over the edge just a little. Put your hands outside the bars." Porter edged to the front of the cage. "Keep your head up," Loraine called. She told the crowd. "I want everybody here to help me with this countdown. Here we go. Three . . . two . . . one . . . hiiiiigh adventure."

Porter plunged headfirst as if he were going off a diving board, the thick red cord trailing behind him, stretching, snapping him back up, dropping him again, spinning him around with his legs and arms flopping as if he were a rag doll. "Give us a thumbs up if you're okay," Loraine called out as he stopped bouncing. And again, "Give us a thumbs up." The people craning their necks below couldn't tell if Porter was okay or not. Then he reached one hand down to his left foot and Loraine's relieved voice came over the crowd, "He's worried about losing his shoe!" Someone else called out, "Oldest bungee jumper in the world!" The voice was picked up on half a dozen video cameras that were trained on the man dangling at the end of the long cord. Porter grinned and waved both hands as the winch lowered him to earth. He sat on the ground while his harness was taken off. Reporters and photographers crowded around, popping questions. "Was that your biggest thrill?" one asked. "I guess it was," Porter replied, but then he said no, the biggest thrill of all came nearly 65 years earlier, the time Alice said "Yes." (In a column in the *Scottsboro Sentinel*, publisher Rick Loring commented admiringly, "You old smoothie!")

The Chattanooga TV stations put the bungee jump on their evening news shows. The piece on Channel 3 included an interview in which Porter said he couldn't understand why folks his age should be less willing to take risks than young folks: "It looks to me like it would be the

This bungee jump at age 90 made newspapers and TV around the world. Photo by Dave Dieter of the Huntsville Times.

other way. A young man may be risking 30 or 40 years. I'm not risking much." Alice was asked what she thought about her husband's stunt. "It's wonderful for anybody that's got enough nerve to do it," she said. Anchorman Mike Hooker closed the TV segment by disclosing that Porter tried to talk his family into letting him go again and actually walked back out toward the lift before he was persuaded that one bungee jump a day was enough. "Heck of a guy," the newsman signed off.

Fifteen members of the family had gone bungee jumping before the day was over, and in the process they claimed another world first, jumps by four generations in the same family—Porter, 90; his son Joe, 58; Joe's son Bruce, 34, and Bruce's son Kevin, 11.

The story and color photo of Porter in mid-bounce took about a third of the *Huntsville Times*'s front page the next day. The photo was sent around the world by the Associated Press, along with abbreviated versions of Laranda's story. One Guntersville traveler sent back a three-column photo from the *Hong Kong Standard.*

The Channel 3 video footage was picked up by CNN and broadcast every hour or even more frequently. Loraine Riche of High Adventure Sports said she counted it on CNN 36 times. NBC obtained the same footage to use on the "Today" show. They also sent a remote-broadcast truck to Guntersville with a two-man crew and set up a camera in the *Advertiser-Gleam* office. Katie Couric in New York interviewed Porter and Sam by long distance. She asked Porter how he got his family to let him jump, and he replied, "I finally just wore 'em down." Sam said he and the others felt compelled to jump once Porter did because his example didn't leave them with any excuses.

The jumpers from Sam's family were himself and his four children, Kenneth and John Harvey, Anne Hails, and Mary Porter Grizzle, plus Anne's husband, Andy Hails. From Mary's branch were her three children, Craig, Steve, and Coley Woodward, plus Steve's wife, Vicki Bailey. From Joe's family were himself and two of his children, Bruce and Scott Harvey, son-in-law Barry Hendrixson, and Bruce's son Kevin. Five others took the "bungee launch." The long elastic cord was stretched down to the ground and the rider was attached to it. The cord propelled the person skyward, bouncing him around in mid-air like those making the jump from above. Taking the launch were Mary Woodward, Joe's son Steve Harvey, Joe's grandson Joe Michael Harvey, Mary's daughter-in-law Annette Woodward, and Sam's daughter-in-law Sheila Harvey.

The sudden burst of fame brought Porter and Alice letters from old friends and complete strangers. A teacher in Florida had all of her kids write Porter. He wrote back, "Hi, Dudes: Dudes must be a popular word there. Two or three of you called me dude in your letters." In answering their questions, he described what the jump felt like: "Right after I jumped I felt like I was floating in the air, although of course I was falling. When I got to the end of the cord there wasn't any jerk. The elastic cord slowed me down to a stop, then started me back up slowly at first. But on the way up it started flinging me around and that was really an exciting feeling, better than anything I had on a ride at Six Flags or Disney World."

Porter got calls from several radio show hosts around the country who wanted interviews. Like the TV interviewers, some of them asked the question, "What next?" and Porter said he was thinking about hang-gliding. Actually, he had thought about it for a good while. There was a hang-glide place 30 or 40 miles from Chattanooga, and when he invited his relatives to the bungee jump he suggested they might try to do both in the same day. Some of the others said there might be logistical problems. Besides, they said, it would be better to savor one thrill for a while before rushing off to another. So hang-gliding was dropped from the day's agenda.

Val's sister Rene Chrisman of Greensburg, Pennsylvania, heard a radio talk show with Ann Richards, the feisty governor of Texas and former Democratic Convention keynote speaker. Governor Richards was catching some flak about riding a motorcycle. Shucks, she replied, if a 90-year-old man can go bungee jumping, she didn't see why a lady governor riding a motorcycle would upset anybody.

TV Guide carried a piece about actors Barry Corbin and John Cullum of "Northern Exposure" planning to go bungee jumping. "I saw news stories about some really old guy who went bungee jumping, and I figure if he can do it, I can too," Mr. Corbin said.

Porter's jump inspired columns by, among others, Ray Sons in the *Chicago Sun-Times* and Steve Clark in the *Richmond News-Leader* (who talked to fellow jumpers Bruce and Kevin Harvey of Richmond). And it prompted a column in a small weekly in south Alabama, the *Wilcox Progressive Era*, whose publisher Hollis Curl was reminded of something thirty-one years earlier. "Back in 1962," Hollis wrote, "I was a youngish newspaper publisher attending my very first Alabama Press Association convention. I didn't know a soul. I'm not the most glad-handed, outgoing sort. The initial reception was held at a Montgomery country club. Everybody was dressed up, the free bar was open and everybody seemed to know everybody else. I guess my being a newcomer was pretty obvious as I hung around the hors d'oeuvres table grazing on boiled shrimp and little open-faced sandwiches. Anyhow, an old fellow with a gray crewcut and a slight limp came over and introduced himself. It was Porter Harvey, publisher of the *Advertiser-Gleam* up in Guntersville. Porter took me in tow and introduced me around. I've never forgotten it. And I have tried, over the years, to do the same for young strangers entering the newspaper fraternity. I have always seen Porter Harvey as a senior citizen, a grizzled newspaper icon without peer. But on that night in Montgomery he was really about the same age that I am now. . . . This past Sunday evening I saw a human-interest clip on WAKA-TV's late news. It showed a fellow, they called him Harvey Porter, who had celebrated his 90th birthday by going bungee jumping the day before. The name caught my ear and I looked closer at the gray-headed rag doll-looking figure diving off the platform to bounce up and down, limbs akimbo, from the end of the elastic cord. It was my old friend Porter Harvey. Right there bigger than life and whooping and hollering all the way down! Now I'm in his debt again: For his early friendship and, now for becoming a role model. I'm gonna jump too. When I turn ninety!"

Records are meant to be broken. Two months after Porter became the world's oldest bungee jumper, 100-year-old S. L. Potter leaped from a 210-foot bungee tower in Alpine, California. The TV program "American Journal" set up a camera in Porter's living room and filmed his half of a cross-country conversation between the two elderly daredevils. When Porter was interviewed the next year on the national radio program "Whaddya Know," host Michael Feldman brought up the bungee jump. Porter was quick to point out that Mr. Potter "broke my record by 10 years and 40 feet." And when he and Alice put together a scrapbook of clippings, letters and other items about the bungee jump, Porter used the first page not for his own clippings but for a *Los Angeles*

Times writeup about the new record holder from California.

Like most people who manage to stay youthful while they age, Porter always kept his focus on the future. A few minutes after his bungee jump, one of the reporters asked him if he had any regrets. "Well," he replied wistfully, "I won't have this to look forward to anymore."

His brother Coley and his sisters Ellen and Frances had gotten interested in family history. They rounded up old records and even traveled to England and Scotland, where they visited a castle that was supposedly built by their ancient Hume kin. Porter stayed in Guntersville. It didn't matter a great deal to him what his ancestors had done. It was the same in his newspaper work. He sometimes printed accounts of the early history of Guntersville and Marshall County, but seldom with much enthusiasm. What mattered most to him were the new stories still to be discovered and written, new challenges still to be overcome, and new adventures still to be savored.

Writing up the news at age 77.

CHAPTER 18

'I'VE HAD A WONDERFUL LIFE'

Alice and Porter eased into old age with grace and good humor. Alice worked at the office until she was 68, and Porter never stopped working at all. His letters to Joe and Jo Kirk in McMinnville give a picture of a couple not all that worked up over geriatrics.

"We are really looking forward to our Thanksgiving visit," he wrote in 1986. "You don't need to do anything about helping us get there and back. Any time I get sleepy on a trip I just pull over and take a nap and then I'm wide awake again." The same letter contained a couple of health reports, notably an update on Alice, who had fallen and broken her forearm. "Her arm doesn't hurt, she sleeps well and she is learning to do lots of things with her left hand that she ordinarily does with her right, or with both. As you may have noticed, she is a very remarkable lady. She keeps finding things that she can't do with one hand, like opening a can, or opening a jar, or peeling tomatoes or scraping carrots. Some things she discovered right away, like combing her hair and using dental floss and tying shoe laces. She says velcro is a great invention . . . I have added sit-ups to my morning exercises, putting my feet under the chest of drawers. I can do it only two or three times with my hands behind my head. I do the rest of the 10 with my arms folded." He was 83 at that writing.

Porter kept fending off suggestions that he cut down on his driving. In 1989, before another trip to McMinnville, he wrote, "We're looking forward to being there for Christmas. There isn't any point in anybody coming to get us. Some old people may not be good drivers but I'm one of the world's best. I drive frequently (twice this week) to Sand Mountain. There's a stretch of highway at the foot of the mountain that has the most dangerous traffic around here, with frequent wrecks, and I haven't been in a single one of them. So I know a nice safe drive like to McMinnville is no hazard." He added, "I'm glad my driving hasn't gone bad like my typing has."

Alice came from long-lived stock on both sides of her family, and she enjoyed remarkably good health. She had to have her tonsils out when she was 45. She had two mastectomies, one for a tumor that turned out to be benign, one for cancer. But she came through both without any after-effects. She had corrective bladder surgery twice for what apparently was a genetic defect, since both her mother and her grandmother had experienced similar trouble. She broke her wrist three times. But those episodes aside, she was seldom sick.

Porter, on the other hand, was prone to a variety of persistent physical problems. More often than not he found imaginative ways to deal with them. Joe once joked about Porter telling his doctor how he had consolidated his daily health routine: "I've learned to do my finger-flexes while I rotate my arms and do my trunk twists, my neck rolls and my deep-knee bends at the same time I'm gargling after taking my acid." His exercises lasted half an hour or more. He did them early in the morning before getting dressed. More than one person who shared a motel room with him at conventions was startled to wake up and find Porter, naked, swinging his arms, lifting his legs, or doing pushups in a room that was still almost pitch dark.

He once had to have surgery for a rectal fistula. The painful and awkward recuperation made him a fanatic about keeping his bowels regular to avoid a repeat. He wound up taking larger and larger amounts of Metamucil before breakfast. Eventually he was dosing himself with 16 heaping teaspoons of the fibrous material, followed by 11 glasses of water, with predictable urinary consequences as the morning wore on.

When he was 40 or so, he had begun to have digestive trouble. He remembered that his mother had taken diluted hydrochloric acid because her gastric system didn't produce enough acid of its own. He told his doctor about it and the doctor put a tube down Porter's throat to sample his juices. He found them deficient. Porter started taking hydrochloric acid as a supplement after each meal, a practice he continued for 30 or more years. He kept the acid in his medicine closet, next to a pint fruit jar where he diluted the acid in water. He drank it through a glass straw to keep the acid away from his teeth, but his front teeth suffered acid damage just the same, despite gargling with diluted milk of magnesia to rinse his teeth and mouth. He had acid capsules to take on trips. Once he forgot them and seemed to get along all right. He and his doctor finally came to the conclusion that his gastric problem no longer existed. He wondered how long he had been needlessly taking acid.

He exercised every day for his cardio-vascular system, always mindful of the spell with his heart when he was 56. He couldn't jog or even walk fast because of his bad leg. To give his heart a workout, he would walk in place and flail his arms. Rotating his arms and flexing his fingers also helped his bursitis and arthritis, and so did rotating his head.

He read that standing on your head was good for your brain, so he added that to his ritual. When he was 75 or so, he had to have a hernia operation. Two days after the surgery, a nurse went into his hospital room and was aghast to find Porter standing on his head. He said he felt well enough to resume his exercises, and nobody had told him not to.

After his heart spell in 1959, his doctor had advised a low-cholesterol diet. Porter followed it with a vengeance. The doctor said no more than three egg yolks a week. Porter figured none at all would be even better, so he ate egg whites flavored with ketchup and Alice fed the cooked yolks to the birds at their backyard feeders. He never cared for coffee or tea, and had always drunk milk at every meal. They switched to powdered skim, with extra powder to make it more palatable. Beef and pork just about disappeared from their diet. Porter got interested in soy products as a meat substitute, and he and Alice ate toasted soybeans from a health store they found in Huntsville. He went to the Birmingham Library to read up on amino acids. He got into a lunch routine built around three items which he and Alice ate in rotation—cheese today, peanut butter tomorrow, beans the next day, then cheese again and so on. His cholesterol level dropped into the low 160s and his doctor told him he could ease up. But in 1989 he still posted a 167, a mark most men could only dream about.

He wrote himself notes before his annual checkups so he'd remember everything he wanted to ask the doctor. He filed some of the notes and they reveal an observant nature coupled with an inquisitive mind. The 1978 note lists these things he wanted to bring up: "Fallen arch. Thumb. Tender place by nose. Fungus. Back. Biopsy. Sore place behind left ear. Shin (left). Heartburn. Eat and wipe nose. Slow to heal (thumb, heel). Drugs and alcohol bad? Spot on left cheek. Right knee when sit long. Flash of light. Toilet paper. Cheaper Metamucil. Pushups. Trouble clearing throat." The following year his list included, among other things, "Knee. Thigh muscle. Stand up quick, feel faint. Had to increase Metamucil six to nine heaping teaspoons. Do mealtime drinks count for Metamucil liquid (why need all that water?)" In 1989, his concerns included: "Phlebitis. Gum disease. Metamucil, 16 rounded teaspoons and 10 1/3 cups water. Bladder. Yoga. Fingers."

Alice's eyes began to give her trouble after she retired. She found she had a rare form of glaucoma. Her vision had already been damaged when it was discovered. Worried about the progressive nature of the ailment, Porter argued that they ought to consult the best authority they could find. Her local eye doctor came up with the name of a doctor in Chicago. She and Porter spent two or three days there while she had tests run. A newspaper friend of Sam's from Columbus, Paul Gapp, showed them around Chicago, and gave them a tour of the *Chicago Tribune* where he was then working (and where he had won a Pulitzer Prize the year before). The doctor told them pretty much the same thing the Alabama doctor had told them. Alice continued using eyedrops for glaucoma while the doctors monitored the signs that cataracts were also starting to develop. They were relieved to find out that cataract surgery had become almost routine and highly effective, and she eventually had it.

Porter had problems from time to time with his bad leg. When he was about 45, he stumbled over a child visiting in his home and tore the cartilage in his knee. He had to have surgery in Birmingham and used crutches for nearly a year. He could never get his left leg to completely straighten out after that. It meant he couldn't rest his weight on it the way he'd been able to do before, putting that much more of a burden on his good leg. As his age crept up, he walked slower and sometimes had to stop and rest while climbing stairs. After a couple of spills in his 80s, while walking in town, he took to carrying a cane to help him keep his balance. He had a bout with phlebitis and for a long time kept his left leg elevated at work and at home.

If he ever felt any resentment over his various physical afflictions, he never let on. He seemed to almost relish the challenges they posed, and never more so than with what he called, for want of a better term, his "memory lapses." He had his first one when he was 85. He woke up one morning and couldn't remember what day it was or what he had done the previous days, even though it had been a memorable weekend. After a few minutes his memory came back, and he went on to work. The same thing began happening occasionally when he woke up from his noon nap. His doctor wasn't able to come up with anything conclusive. A year after the first one, he had one in the middle of the night and he decided to put something on paper as a record: "Like the first lapse this one was the morning after an unusually eventful day. The first time, it was the day after we went to McMinnville, Tennessee, for our grandson Steve and Lisa's wedding. This time, it was the morning after Alice fell in the Glover Restaurant and cracked a bone in her wrist. We were up in the night every two hours, taking off a cold pack. The lapse was the fourth or fifth I've had. You wouldn't expect a person with memory trouble to know exactly how many."

After a few more spells, his Guntersville doctor sent him to the Sleep Center at Huntsville Hospital, where he spent the night wired to an array of monitoring devices. The doctor there concluded that sleeping on his back might be triggering a breathing problem that interfered with his heart rhythm and deprived his brain of oxygen. He recommended that Porter sleep with a tennis ball sewed to the back of his pajamas so he would stay turned on his side. Alice fixed up the equipment. But the lapses still occurred from time to time. He had also started having occasional moments at the office when he felt as if he was about to pass out. After a night-time episode early in 1991, he wrote his sleep doctor and in the process he painted a picture of a right active 87-year-old. "I had been busier than usual the three days before it happened. Monday night I covered a meeting of the County School Board. Tuesday night I attended a meeting of the civic club I belong to, the Civitans. Wednesday night I played poker with a bunch that gets together once a month." He had some more heart tests, and his cardiologist prescribed some medicine for heart irregularity. Before long, his memory lapses pretty much stopped.

Alice and some others in the family had been wondering for a while whether Porter ought to be driving as much as he was, or even driving at all. The debates generally found Alice and Mary in favor of restrictions, while Porter and Sam argued for leniency. In a 1993 letter to Joe and Jo Kirk, he said, "Well, Joe, you don't have to cast the deciding vote after all on whether I can keep driving. Mary and I have worked out a compromise. I can drive but not on or across Gunter Avenue [the main drag] or the Arab Road [Highway 69 near his house]. That's not quite as restrictive as it sounds. I can go most places on the east side of Gunter by using an alley and parking in a parking lot on the west side and walking across the street, and go to some places on the south side of the Arab Road by using a parking lot on the north side." He added, "Regarding my driving, do you remember the saying, 'Children, obey your parents?' When you get old it's 'Parents, obey your children'."

In another 1993 letter to Joe and Jo, he asked, "Did I tell you about this typewriter? It's the one we started the *Gleam* with, on an apple box. We've had it in the monster room for the kids to peck on. Recently the one I was using at home began giving me trouble, and I found this one is in better shape than the one many years newer, so I'm using it and letting the kids use the newer one. No matter which one I use, my typing is still getting worse and worse."

In late 1993 or early 1994, he decided to give up driving entirely, afraid he might have some kind of spell that would cause him to hurt somebody else. From then on Sam, whose home was only about a mile away, carried him to and from work. Porter kept his car as a spare for anybody in the family whose own car might be in the shop.

He had started turning his news beats over to Anthony Campbell in 1992, when Anthony went full-time at the paper, first the sheriff's office and then the courts. Porter continued to cover the County School Board. After he stopped driving he would get Sam to carry him to the board's office at the south edge of town for their meetings, which usually started about 6:00. He would call Mary or Sam to come get him when the meeting was over.

It was early November 1994 when Mary and Sam noticed that Porter's skin was looking yellow. Mary carried him to Dr. Neil Christopher on November 9 and the doctor sent him immediately to the Guntersville-Arab Hospital for tests. A CAT scan showed a shadow on his pancreas. A tumor, which the doctors said was almost certain to be malignant, was pressing on a duct and blocking the flow of bile from his liver. That explained the jaundice. An operation November 11 removed his gall bladder and took care of the duct problem. But the cancer was, for all intents and purposes, inoperable. Porter was told he might have as long as a year or even two. Ever the optimist, he assumed two. He went home from the hospital November 19 and started back to work December 1, feeling pretty good for a man 91 years old with a fresh scar across his belly.

In January he started feeling weak and nauseated. It turned out he was losing blood internally from the tumor. He went back into the Guntersville-Arab Hospital on January 25. He was given blood to replenish what had been lost, and he was put on an IV for nourishment because he wasn't able to eat. The bleeding seemed to stop of its own accord (tumors do that, the doctor explained) and after 12 days in the hospital Porter went home. But the bleeding started back a couple of days later. He went to University Hospital in Birmingham and spent two days being examined by specialists. They found that the bleeding had stopped again—but the cancer had spread to his liver. He went home February 11, knowing that his time was going to be a lot shorter than he had thought.

He hadn't gone to the office since January 24, but he had continued to do some work at home, primarily obituaries, calling funeral homes and then contacting the families. His last story, other than an obituary, was a short piece on a woman who had been hired to help out at home while he was sick, Jo Johnson. She mentioned something that had happened to her 40 years earlier, and he was able to write the kind of headline he admired, "They Took Her Heart Out, Then Put It Back In." She was a "blue baby," one whose heart arteries weren't connected right, so at age 23 she had surgery. "At that time she was the oldest person who ever had that operation," he wrote, making the kind of flat statement he loved being able to make. "She was in surgery 13 hours. At one point the doctors had her heart entirely out of her body. Somehow they kept the arteries, veins and nerves working. . . . Afterwards one of the doctors told her she might live long enough to see her son nearly grown. The son now has a son who is 18."

That story came out in the paper of February 18. That was the day Mary heard him typing in his office at home while she talked to Alice. Before she left he handed her two sheets of copy paper, folded up, and asked her to handle it. Typically, his message got right to the point, with no preliminaries: "I'd like to have the funeral at the church if that will work out all right," he wrote. "Rudy [the First Methodist pastor] to conduct, Carr [the funeral home] to direct. No sermon. I hope Val will sing 'Ave Maria.' I have said for years that I wanted our Sunday school class to sing 'Peace Be Still' but we've lost several members and may not have enough left that they'll want to try it. Ask Don. The coffin as inexpensive as it can be without seeming too cheap."

He had previously suggested to Sam a possible lead for his obituary. In this memo he proposed a slight change to say that "he kept working until January in his job of part-time reporter." He asked that his grandsons and grandsons-in-law be pallbearers, with the *Advertiser-Gleam* people, past and present, as honoraries. In later conversations, the honorary pallbearer list was expanded to include his Sunday school class, his Civitan Club, and the members of his once-a-month poker club.

He asked that this part of his memo be passed around: "I'm ready to go. I've had a wonderful life, especially since I found Alice. We've had a great bunch to work with at the paper. We have a great family. As many as there are in it, you'd expect some of them to be morons, or mean, or crooked, or shiftless, but you all aren't any of these. You're every one smart and nice looking and good people. Thanks for being like you are."

The Civitan Club had a tradition. When it came time for a motion to adjourn, Ernie Miller ordinarily did the honors. Porter wrote, "How about getting word to the Civitan Club that I wished the funeral could include a mini-meeting with Ernie Miller saying 'I make it,' but it didn't seem like it would fit in. And get word to the poker bunch that I wish the funeral could have included a part where they all stood and said 'I raise it a dime,' but it didn't seem like that would have been appropriate."

On February 20, two days after he wrote that, he left home for what was to be the last time. Grandson Scott Harvey had flown in from Maryland for a 24-hour visit. Scott and Mary carried him to Dr. Christopher's office, dehydrated, weak and frequently nauseated. The doctor sent him straight to the hospital. His digestive system was past helping. On March 2, seeing no need to stretch things out, Porter had the nurses disconnect the IV that was supplying him with glucose. He never had pain from the cancer, and the only shot he ever got for pain was for his hip after he lay on one side too long.

Members of the family took turns staying with him. Mary and Alice spent long stretches there in the day, and Sam generally went there in the evening. Joe took a week off from work and insisted on sleeping on a cot in the hospital room at night. Alice's sister Helen Kass and her husband, Matthew, had driven in from Texas to stay with Alice. Coley Woodward took four days off from her job in Birmingham and spent two nights in the hospital along with Mary. Sam and Val's son Kenneth and his wife Jane Armstrong flew in from Texas the weekend of March 4, planning to stay through the funeral. That same weekend Porter called his boyhood friend Harry Powers for a long chat, but he was so weak he couldn't talk more than a minute or so. He had reached the point where he was unconscious a good bit of the time.

When the March 8 paper was made up Tuesday morning, Sam sent two versions of the obituary page to the printers in Albertville, one with Porter's death in it, one without. That allowed a couple of extra hours to make the paper if his death should occur on press day. Sam knew Porter wouldn't want to be scooped on his own demise if there was any way around it. But his system was proving to be surprisingly strong, and the deadline came and went. By Friday morning he had been unresponsive for nearly three days, and all the signs said death was imminent. Sam again sent two versions of the March 11 obit page to Albertville, this time with a deadline of 1 p.m. before making the last plate and putting it on the press. Mary took Alice home shortly before noon so she could nap, and Mary went back to the hospital. There she joined Sam, Val, Kenneth and Jane. Don wasn't back yet from taking the pages to the printer. Porter's breath would stop briefly, then start up again. About 12:50 it stopped, and this time it didn't start back. Mary felt his wrist and found no pulse. While they watched, the color suddenly drained from his face. They got a nurse, who checked him and called for a doctor from the emergency room. Porter had left instructions that no special effort was to be made to revive him. The doctor confirmed what everyone in the room knew. Don had arrived by then. It was about 12:58 when Sam called the printers in Albertville and told them to use the page with Porter's death. Then they all drove back to the house and told Alice.

Porter and Alice in 1993 with Sam, Joe, and Mary.

CHAPTER 19

A LEGACY

Porter's obituary ran on page 11 of the March 11, 1995, *Gleam* along with eight other deaths. It ran 27 inches, the longest the paper had run since the death of Mayor T. E. Martin in 1969. Sam hoped the readers would indulge him.

Porter Harvey, 91

• He was a working newspaperman for over 68 years.

• He and his wife Alice started the *Advertiser-Gleam*.

• Although the paper broke a good many newspaper traditions, today it has more readers than any other weekly or twice-weekly in Alabama.

• He got national newspaper and TV attention when he bungee-jumped at 90.

Porter Harvey died Friday in the Guntersville-Arab Medical Center. He had had cancer of the pancreas since November. He worked at the office through January 24 and wrote a few pieces for the paper after that from his home at 1305 Alves Road and from the hospital. He was 91.

His funeral will be Sunday at 2:00 at the First Methodist Church, with Rev. Rudy Guess officiating. Burial will be in Crestview Cemetery, directed by Carr Funeral Home.

Mr. Harvey came to Guntersville in 1941 and started publishing the weekly Guntersville *Gleam.* He rented a one-room office on the second floor of the building where D. Wright's clothing store is now. He had the paper printed in Albertville.

In 1944 the owner of the long-established paper, the *Guntersville Advertiser*, died. Mr. Harvey bought that paper and its printing plant on Worth Street. He began putting out 2 papers a week, and it's been twice-weekly ever since.

He was born Evan Porter Harvey Jr. in Rome, Ga., to E. P. and Fanny Coley Harvey. He had polio when he was 3 and walked with a limp as a result. He graduated from Emory University in Atlanta, where he was campus correspondent for the *Atlanta Constitution.* He spent a year at Harvard University in Boston studying literature and writing. He worked briefly as a newspaper reporter in New York and Nashville.

In 1927 he went to Kansas as a reporter and news editor for the *Daily Globe* in Dodge City, the town that later served as the scene of the TV series "Gunsmoke." In 1929 he married Alice Wells, an English teacher. They and their 3 children moved to Birmingham in 1937. He worked 4 years for the old *Birmingham Post*, editing copy and writing headlines.

During that time he was also the unpaid editor of a free mimeographed paper, the *Cahaba Hub.* It was put out once a month by residents of Trussville, where the family lived. His work there helped him develop an informal style of telling the news, and he continued that when he came to Guntersville.

Gathering and writing news was his specialty. But he also tended to other aspects of the business, especially in the early years. He wrote ads and laid them out, sold subscriptions, managed the mailing and supervised the employees. He built the paper's present building on Taylor Street in 1955.

He never wrote a lot of editorials. He preferred to report the news and let readers make up their own minds. But he wrote a series of editorials in the 1960's during a controversy over closing the old City Hospital, and they won first prize from the state newspaper organization, the Alabama Press Assn. He served as president of the association in 1967-68.

His wife worked nearly 30 years at the paper, full-time and part-time, before she retired in 1970. The couple's 3 children all worked at the paper while they were growing up. In 1960 Mary and her husband Don Woodward moved back from Opelika and he took charge of the advertising. In 1967 Sam Harvey moved back here from Louisville, Kentucky, as editor, and he and his father shared the news duties after that.

He attracted national attention twice after he was in his 90's. He organized a family bungee-jumping trip to Chattanooga in 1993 and wound up with his picture in newspapers and on TV all across the country. Then the Associated Press sent out a story about his style of writing obituaries, using a lot more detail than most papers use.

In 1992 the Chamber of Commerce named him Guntersville Citizen of the Year.

Mr. Harvey was a former president of the Guntersville Civitan Club and had been a member longer than any other current member. He was a member of the Oscar Horton Sunday school class at the First Methodist Church for about 50 years.

One of the last things he wrote for the paper was about the 103rd birthday of the county's oldest resident, Minnie Bishop. When he died, Mrs. Bishop was in the hospital room next to his, being treated for pneumonia.

A couple of days before he slipped into a coma, he made a phone call to the man who had been his best friend since high school, Harry Powers, now 92, of Calhoun, Georgia. They worked together on their school newspaper and had kept in touch all their lives. About 10 years ago they and several of their children and grandchildren took an all-day canoe trip on the Oostanaula River near Rome, a river the 2 men used to boat on and swim in when they were boys.

When he was in Guntersville, Mr. Harvey made 4 long-distance river trips with Bill Harris in Bill's 12-foot fishing boat, Miss Guntersville Lake.

He enjoyed old-time monster movies and the films of early comedians such as Charlie Chaplin, the Marx Brothers and Laurel and Hardy. He belonged to a once-a-month poker club. He liked to work in his vegetable garden. But his favorite pastime always was finding news and writing it up.

He is survived by his wife, Alice Wells Harvey; a daughter, Mary Woodward of Guntersville; 2 sons, Joe Harvey of McMinnville, Tenn., and Sam Harvey of Guntersville; 11 grandchildren; 17 great-grandchildren; a brother, Coley Harvey of Mentone; and 2 sisters, Ellen Jervis of Rome, Ga., and Frances Wood of Charlotte, North Carolina.

Grandsons and grandsons-in-law will be pallbearers at his funeral. They are Kenneth Harvey, Craig Woodward, John Harvey, Bruce Harvey, Steve Woodward, Andy Hails, Scott Harvey, Jeff Grizzle, Steve Harvey, and Barry Hendrixson.

Honorary pallbearers will be past and present employees of the *Advertiser-Gleam* and members of his Sunday school class, his Civitan Club and his poker club.

The family suggests that memorials take the form of contributions to the First Methodist Church Building Fund.

His death prompted writers for several publications to comment on his life:

"He missed nothing and wrote about everything and everybody. The way he dealt with people, the fair and honest way he wrote about them, is why his newspaper has the largest circulation of any weekly or semi-weekly in the state."—Lee Woodward, editor of the *Huntsville News*.

"He was a model of hard work and independent judgment. His legacy is a newspaper like no other."—Sam Hodges, *Mobile Register*.

"For Porter Harvey, the big story was always the little people he served."—Bill Easterling, *Huntsville Times* columnist.

"We will miss Porter Harvey, the gleam in his eye, the turn of his phrase, the clip of his prose."—David Moore, editor of the *Arab Tribune*.

"Most of us likely won't have the light in the eyes he carried into his

90s, or his zest for the 'scoop' or the unique ability to see a story in the most obscure places."—Laranda Nichols, *Huntsville Times.*

"The *Gleam* moved years ahead of most other newspapers in treating its readers the same, whether rich or poor, black or white, male or female. The *Gleam* was one of the first newspapers in the state, probably one of the first in the South, to treat blacks and whites the same in its news stories."—Bill Keller, executive director of the Alabama Press Association, in the APA newsletter.

"He probably would have skinned anyone who tried to give him a paneled, special office separate from the rest of the *Gleam* staff. He preferred to be in the newsroom, accessible to visitors and story tipsters, and banging away on his a manual Royal typewriter."—Tom Gordon, *Birmingham News.*

"He had the courage to record the everyday events in the lives of common people in nearly all the communities that make up this mountain area. Often he was the only historian they had. There will be generations who will thank him for his insight into what was really important."—*Historic Arab*, published by the Arab Historical Society.

Lots of people wrote to Alice and others in the family. Among them were the county's two circuit judges, whom he had come to know well in his years of covering the courts.

"I will remember him with smiles and chuckles," Judge Bill Jetton wrote. "He has been a total part of my life—in my job, in my reading, and in his reporting of the news."

"My very favorite tale of Mr. Harvey involves the Whole Backstage," wrote Judge Bill Gullahorn, who was a leader in that local theater group. "Back when we were replacing the wooden seats, the 'glory job' was to use the big power screwdriver and zip out the screws that held the old seats to the floor. The rotten job was to go ahead of the power screwdriver and, using a small hand screwdriver, to get 60 years of filth out of the screwheads so the power tool could do its thing. He came and volunteered to help that day (when he was well into his 80s). He denied having the strength or skill to use the power screwdriver but insisted on cleaning out screwheads. I will never forget him down on his hands and knees working along, screw by screw. It changed my perception of how much work I was doing and the 'sacrifice' of my time and effort."

The heads of the state's two largest journalism education programs also wrote.

"To ensure its survival, the newspaper business needs more people who are as dedicated to the finer points of good grass-roots journalism as Porter was."—Dean Ed Mullins, journalism chair Paul Delaney, and placement director Jim Oakley, University of Alabama.

"We greatly admired Porter for both his character and his work. Now those two have combined to create a legacy, for which we may all be thankful."—Jerry Brown, professor and department head, Auburn University.

A different kind of note came from Jim Posey, who had grown up in the neighborhood where Alice and Porter lived. "The Harveys built a very nice basketball goal for their son Joe in their backyard," he wrote. "But after his high school graduation, it went unused. For many years they very graciously let all of the young boys in the neighborhood come and play basketball any time they wanted. They never complained about the number of kids, the noise, the hour of the day, balls bouncing in the shrubbery and their grass being trampled down to the dirt for months on end. This memory of kindness is 40 years old, but I have often thought of how much that meant to me."

The funeral was held March 12, a Sunday, in the First Methodist Church. Rev. Rudy Guess asked everybody to join Porter's Sunday school class in singing "Peace Be Still." Porter always enjoyed that song for the way the volume receded and swelled. Val had gone to the church earlier in the week and recorded "Ave Maria" so it could be part of the service, as he asked. She had been singing in public for 50 years but thought it prudent not to try to do it live on this occasion.

Rudy read the familiar passage from the Book of Matthew about serving God by serving the least of His people. He said it was one of Porter's favorites "because it spoke to him . . . his life was one of interest in others. All you had to do was read the *Gleam* and discover this concern he had for people and their lives." But Porter didn't want to be in the news or in the spotlight himself "and he gave me specific instructions as to that, and not only in writing. Tuesday a week ago we were talking in his hospital room and he knew this moment was near at hand. He said there was to be no eulogy. I said, 'But, Porter, you mean I can't even tell where you got some of your jokes?'" Rudy had seen a good many jokes from his sermons show up as fillers in the *Gleam*. "He smiled and said, 'Well, yes,' and we went on and before it was over, I got his permission to share briefly about his life. But preachers aren't good at editing. And how do you share briefly about a man whose life spanned so much living?"

He said Porter often commented after church on his sermons. "My first time in the pulpit here he greeted me afterward and said, 'You didn't read your sermon and I didn't fall asleep.' Other times he'd come out and say, 'Lots of narrative. That's great.' On his last time in church, January 12, I started out with a story and I blew the punchline. The congregation got a good laugh. Porter came out afterward and said 'I've got to remember that story.' I said, 'I hope you get it right.' His words were, 'We don't get them wrong.'"

Rudy said he had visited in the hospital three days before Porter's death. Porter had given no sign for more than a day of being aware of anything. But for a brief moment, "Porter opened his eyes. Alice was standing there. And as soon as he saw her, the biggest smile you ever saw came across his face. The love of his life lit up his life, and that love spread to his family . . . I think the most important part of the final note he wrote to his family was where he said, 'Thanks for being like you are.'" Rudy said the grandchildren and great-grandchildren would have special memories "because how many grandfathers get up a bungee-jumping trip—and then lead the pack?"

He spoke of the newspaper Porter had created and what it had meant to the community over the last half-century. He read three verses from Porter's poem listing the scores of places in the county, "That's Where You'll Find the Readers of the *Advertiser-Gleam*."

"Through his living and his writing we have been introduced to life in a more full way," Rudy said. He added that this was especially true of the people in the groups that made up Porter's honorary pallbearers—those who had worked at the paper, the men in his Sunday school class and the men in his Civitan Club. Porter would have understood perfectly well why Rudy didn't mention the other honorary pallbearers, the men in the poker club, of whom all but one were members of the First Methodist Church. The omission would have given him a good chuckle.

EPILOGUE

At the *Gleam*, Porter had prepared carefully for the time when he would no longer be there. He had long since installed Don and Sam in the managing positions, and while he was alive he insisted that they take charge in fact as well as in name. He had given most of the stock in the business to the three children and their spouses. He had turned over most of his news beats to Anthony Campbell. So the transition at work after he died was a smooth one. A few months later, Angela Otts, a woman whose husband had taken early retirement, was hired as a part-time reporter. She spent two days a week in the office and also worked some from her home. She tended to write longer stories than Porter liked to see—but so did Sam and Anthony. So while the *Gleam*'s news reporting was lacking a certain flair, there was no reduction in the volume of it.

The paper continued to do a healthy business. Larger advertisers were gradually shifting to pre-prints, called "inserts" by newspaper people and "circulars" by most readers. By 1996, the *Gleam* was carrying half a dozen of them most weeks. The shift meant fewer full-page ads in the paper than in earlier years, but there were a lot more small ads. In 1996, the paper was running about 150 display ads in a typical week, twice as many as 30 years earlier. Classified ads were filling about 16 columns a week, almost a three-fold increase over that same period. The annual financial report in October 1995 showed that the gross volume in the final year Porter worked on the paper had crept over the million dollar mark for the first time at $1,003,272.

Don and Sam were often asked about chances for keeping the *Gleam* in the family into still another generation. None of their children or Joe's children were in newspaper work. Sam's daughter Anne had worked as a reporter for the *Birmingham News* and the *Montgomery Advertiser,* but then she became a teacher, pursuing a line that had been in her family even longer than journalism. Don's son Craig worked in advertising, first for the Alabama Press Association and then for a Birmingham ad agency, before taking a public relations/advertising job with Kappler Safety Group, a manufacturing company based in Guntersville. So the long-range prospects for family operation remained up in the air. But although Don and Sam both turned 65 the year Porter died, neither was ready to step down. Each was enjoying what he did.

Alice continued to live in the house at 1305 Alves Road where she and Porter had lived since 1951. A lady came in a few hours most mornings to help with the housework and the cooking. Alice's life was slower-paced than before. She slept till 8:00 or even later when she felt like it. She continued to attend church, gatherings of her church circle, and DAR meetings. As she celebrated her 91st and 92nd birthdays, she was still keeping up with the birthdays of all her children, grandchildren, great-grandchildren and their spouses, carefully selecting a card for each one and folding a check inside. She was a life-long bird lover. Her favorite relaxation was looking out the picture window of her dining room at the birds flocking to the feeders that different members of her family had given her over the years. Porter had lifted her up at that same window in 1951 when they were househunting so she could look inside. She enjoyed good health. She used eye drops for her glaucoma and pills to help her memory. Like most older people, she found that her most vivid recollections tended to be of things that happened many years ago, especially during her early years in Kansas. One day in May 1996 she commented to Mary, "You know, our memory is the most wonderful thing we have. If I have to lose my abilities, I want to lose my memory last."

She knew she had a lot to remember.

Appendix

THAT'S WHERE YOU'LL FIND THE READERS OF THE ADVERTISER-GLEAM

From the point of Preston Island
To the mouth of Parches Cove,
From Swearengin to Horton,
From Mobbs to Cedar Grove;
By Town Creek's quiet waters,
By Shoal Creek's rushing stream—
That's where you'll find the readers
Of the Advertiser-Gleam.

You can ask them in Click Hollow,
Snug Harbor, Rayburn Switch,
On Minkie Creek or Mink Creek,
It makes no difference which;
At the Painted Bluff, at Langston,
High Point, Clear Spring, Fairview,
In Bucksnort Beat, or Ringold Street—
They read It through and through.

Around the dam and Hebron,
Where the cedar thickets grow,
At Alder Springs and Grassy,
At Feemsters Gap, Shiloh;
In Polecat Hollow, Friendship,
On Mayo Mountain's peak,
On Holiness Point, at Guntersville,
At Douglas and Beech Creek;

Where Wyeth Rock rears toward the sky,
Where Short Creek Falls plunge down,
At Pine Grove, Big Spring Valley,
Bonds Chapel, Kirbytown,
Ney-A-Ti, John R. Hollow,
Rockdale and Lattiwood,
Old Union, Rabbits Cross Roads,
At Thompson Falls, Haygood;

Cathedral Caverns, Bethel,
Suck Egg Road from end to end,
At Nixon Chapel, Wakefield,
Hopewell and Horseshoe Bend;
On the slopes above South Sauty,
Where the wildcats used to scream—
Reedbrake, East Lake —
That's where they take
The Advertiser-Gleam.

At all the pleasant places—
Pleasant Hill and Pleasant View,
Mount Pleasant, Pleasant Valley,
Pleasant Grove—they read it too.
And at all the homey places—
Free Home and Happy Home,
At Welcome Home and Sweet Home,
New Home and Honeycomb;

On Simpson Point, on Pea Ridge,
Half Acres, Valley View,
At Claysville, Little New York,
On O'Brig Avenue;
Morrow Acres, Mirror Lake,
New Prospect, Chigger Hill,
Lane Switch and Bakers Chapel,
Oak Grove and Meltonsville;

At Warrenton, at Solitude
On Sunset Drive, Red Hill,
Star Point, Columbus City,
Kings Hollow, Butlers Mill;

On the short steep curve at Lucas Gap,
Where brakes and tires scream—
That's where you'll find the readers
Of the Advertiser-Gleam.

All through Short Creek Canyon,
Where the cliffs are steep and rough
In Sherwood Forest, Corinth,
At Dogant, at Streets Bluff;
At Haneys Chapel, Grove Oak,
Mount Tabor and Mount High,
At Cottonville, at Bakers Gap,
At Browns Creek and the Y;

On all the various mountains—
On Brindlee, Gunter, Sand,
On Georgia, Grassy, Center Point,
On Merrill, Lewis, and
McCorkle, Bishop, Wyeth,
Little Mountain, Taylor too,
On Lang and Long and at Mount Shade,
Grant Mountain, Mountain View;

At Mountain Gap, Mount Olive,
Mount Moriah, Mount Oak,
Rocky Mount, Mount Carmel—
They read it—that's no joke.
At Mount High and Mount Pleasant,
Blacks Mountain, Mountain Crest—
That's where they read our paper—
They say it is the best.

Buck Island and Pine Island,
Where the big boat houses are,
Asbury, Lindsey Hollow,
Browns Valley, DAR;
Anderson Ridge, Rehobeth,
Where the pulpwood barges load,
Long Hollow, Sorters Cross Roads,
Along the Fish Trap Road.

At Poplar Springs, at Five Points
Near the big Monsanto plant,
At Rock Springs, Pisgah, Ebell,
At Meadowwood and Grant;
'Mid the State Park's fabled splendor,
Where it all seems like a dream—
That's where you'll find the readers
Of the Advertiser-Gleam.

Buck's Pocket, where defeated
Politicians used to meet,
Jughandle Hollow, Martling,
Wrights Cove and Henry Street;
At Hyatt and at Liberty Hill,
Which aren't very far apart,
Holiday Shores and Diamond,
Scant City and Boshart;

At Brashiers Chapel (Brindlee),
At Brashers Chapel (Sand),
On Paint Rock, where the river
Sometimes gets out of hand;
Hog Jaw and Hide-Away Acres,
Snow Point and Kennamer Cove,
On Lakeview Hill, at Henryville,
Manchester, Union Grove;

And when the end of earth shall come
And time shall cease to be,
When Carlisle Park and Wesson Branch
Are swallowed by the sea,
When Signal Point and Sims behold
The dying sun's last beam—
They'll believe it when they read it
In the Advertiser-Gleam.

—PORTER HARVEY

Index

C

D

E

F

Y